교원임용시험 전공영어 대비 [제1판]

Build Up

박문각 임용 동영상강의 www.pmg.co.kr

박현수 영어교육론 Ⅱ

Worksheets for Pre-service Teachers
Authentic Data for Classroom Teaching

Preface

내가 가는 길에 대한 확신이 있는 사람이 얼마나 될까요? 내가 걸어가는 이 길이 옳다고 여겨 선택한 이도 있을 것이며, 등 떠밀린 누군가도 있을 것이며, 시작은 했으나 벗어나지 못하고 그 안에 갇힌 이들도 있을 것입니다.

우리가 가고자 하는, 그리고 가고 있는 그 길은 어떤 길입니까? 학생들보다 앞선 걸음으로 사회를 보여주고, 세상을 알려주고, 자신의 가치를 찾아 나가도록 도와주는 스승의 자리입니다. 따라서, 이 길은 누군가에게 등 떠밀려서도, 단지 시작을 했다고 막연히 벗어나지 못해 가고 있는 그런 길도 되어서는 안 됩니다. 누구보다 확신이 있어야 하며, 자신에 대한 믿음이 확고한 사람이 가야 할 길임을 다시금 생각해 봐야 할 것입니다.

저 또한 여러분 앞에서, 선배로서 걸었던 그 길에 대한 확신을 주고 여러분의 존귀함이 앞으로 여러분의 제자들의 존귀함으로 이어질 수 있도록 노력하려고 합니다. 우리 모두가 자신의 제자들 앞에서 더욱더 당당할 수 있도록, 세상 속 가치와 기쁨을 찾아 나가는 여정을 기꺼이 도울 수 있도록, 그렇게 지금 이 순간도 스스로 다짐하며 이 길을 걸어나가야 하겠습니다.

어지러운 세상 속 더 위태로운 학교에서 여러분은 제자들과 마주할 것입니다. 그 순간순간에 여러분이 걷는 그 길에 대한 확신이 없다면 여러분 자신도, 그리고 그 어린 제자들도 어지러운 세상과 위태로운 학교에서 길을 잃을 것이라 생각됩니다. 그러므로 그 길을 선택한 지금 다시 한번 자신을 돌아보십시오. 여러분이 선택한 그 길이 어떤 길인지에 대한 확신을 가지고 있습니까? 누구보다도 그 길을 흔들림 없이 걸어갈 자신이 있습니까?

오늘도 저는 강의를 시작하기 전 여러분이 그 믿음과 확신을 지켜 나갈 수 있도록 다짐합니다. 제가 열어가는 세상 속에 여러분을 담고, 그 세상 속에 여러분의 세상이 열려 여러분의 제자들에게 이어질 수 있길 바라고 또 바라봅니다.

여러분의 믿음이 확신이 될 수 있도록 노력할 것이며, 2025년 여러분과 제가 만들어 갈 세상이 서로에게 따뜻한 위로가 될 수 있길 바랍니다. 또한, 그 위로가 앞으로 여러분이 걷고자 하는 그 길의 든든한 버팀목이 될 수 있길 바랍니다.

이번에 새롭게 개정한 Build-up II는 2024년 진행됐던 12번의 모의고사와 7번의 채점으로 인해 중등 임용 시험에서 여러분이 들인 1년간의 노력과 애쓴 보람을 잃지 않으려면 무엇이 필요한지 고민한 끝에 깨달은 결과의 산물입니다. 교육론 전반적인 지식과 적용에 대한 노련한 이해가 있더라도 시험 중 전략 부재-data processing과 direction analysis-로 인해 필요 정보 파악에 대한 충분한 훈련이 이루어지지 않았을 경우 득점 손실 또는 감점 처리가 되었습니다. 따라서 본래 하반기에 진행됐던 data processing과 direction analysis 및 답안 구성에 대한 연습을 상반기부터 시작하고, Chapter마다 data analysis를 넣어 문제 풀이 접근 전략에 대한 훈련에 중점을 두었습니다.

따라서, Part 1과 Part 2로 구성된 Build-up I를 통해 영어교육론을 전반적으로 이해하고, Build-up Ⅱ에서 해당 Chapter별 학습한 내용을 토대로 심화된 교실 수업자료를 기반으로 한 data processing과 해당 문항 분석을 통한 답안 작성까지 One-stop Strategy를 진행하려고 합니다.

Build-up II은 세 부분으로 구성되어 있습니다. Section 1은 토픽별 Classroom Data와 Data Analysis Worksheet으로, Section 2는 기존 객관식 문항들을 서답형으로 재구성한 문제풀이가 주어져 있습니다. 마지막으로, Section 3은 2024년 기출 동형 평가와 학생 답안 첨삭 및 2022년 개정 교육과정의 주요 쟁점과 중 · 고교 수업 방향을 정리한 내용이 담겨 있습니다.

단연코 여러분의 가치를 증명하는 2025년이 되길 희망하며, 그 앞에 Build-up Series와 박현수가 함께 하겠습니다.

2025년 여러분의 새로운 시작을 응원하며,

박현수

2025학년도 기출분석 및 2026학년도 대비 영어교육론 시험 전략

2025학년도 중등 임용시험의 영어교육론은 총 23문항 중 2024학년 기출 문항수(11문항)보다 한 문항 적은 10문항이 출제되어 총 80점 중 36점을 차지하였다. 여전히 교사 시험답게 영어교육론의 출제 비중이 50%에 달하는 것을 확인할 수 있다. 이것은 중등 임용시험의 정체성에 따라 영어교사의 필수 자질인 how to teach에 대한 자필평가의 중요성을 반영한 것으로 판단된다. 2025학년도 중등 임용시험은 전년도에 비해 비교적 난이도가 중/중하로 구성된 문항들이 출제되었으며, data-based item과 knowledge-based item이 기입형과 서술형에 고르게 출제되었다. 우선, 2025학년도 중등 임용 출제 방향을 살펴보면 첫째, 2022년 개정 교육과정의 주요 학습 개념인 Project-based learning과 digital literacy가 반영된 것을 확인할 수 있다. 둘째, 학생 중심 교실 수업을 계획할 수 있는 교사의 자질에 대한 평가로써 material adaptation, lesson objectives 및 modified lesson의 방식과 특징들이 출제되었다. 셋째, 학생 측면에서는 중간언어 형태의 특징과 reading strategies 등의 유무에 초점을 두어 출제되었으며, 마지막으로 언어학습의 최종 목표가 목표 문화의 수용이라는 측면에서 매년 문화지도가 출제되는 경향이 있는데 이번에도 역시 문화지도에 대한 내용이 출제되었다.

A형 기입형 문항

기입형 3, 4번은 예년보다는 평이한 개념이자 반복적으로 출제된 term인 'modifying'과 'inter-rater reliability'를 묻는 문항이 출제되었다. 이때 3번의 경우, term 도출 방식은 Original Material을 토대로 Adapted Material에 어떤 변화가 있는지 살펴보고, 해당 변화를 설명한 term을 data에서 고르는 방식으로 출제되었다. 4번의 term인 'inter-rater reliability'는 두 선생님의 대화 내용과 Mr. Lee의 Teaching Journal로 유추하여 찾을 수 있으며, comments에 나온 definition으로 해당 term을 확정할 수 있다. 다만, 4번은 data에서 찾아 쓰는 data-matching 방식으로 term을 도출했던 3번과 달리 example이나 situation, definition을 보고 해당 개념을 정확히 도출하는 knowledge-based 방식의 문항이다.

A형 서술형 문항

- 8번(data-based item)은 〈A〉에 학생들의 중간언어 발전 단계에 대한 L2 학생들의 다양한 변이적인 중간언어 형태에 관련된 설명과 예시를 data로 주고, 〈B〉에서 제공한 학생 대화와 matching하는 문항이다.
- 9번(data-based item)은 말하기 평가 원리에 관한 문항으로, 〈A〉에서 4개의 평가 원리를 제시하고 〈B〉에서 Mr. Jeong이 Item 1과 2에서 평가한 사례를 보고 matching하는 문항이다.
- 11번(knowledge-based item)은 〈A〉에서 각각 듣기/읽기와 말하기/쓰기에 대한 수업 목표를 제시하고, 〈B〉의 Teaching Procedure에서 제시되는 활동과의 관계를 파악하는 문항이다.
- 12번(data-based item)은 〈A〉에서 다양한 Reading Strategies에 대한 category를 제시하고 〈B〉에서 학생들의 읽기에 대한 문제점을 제공하여, 이를 해결할 수 있는 Reading Strategies를 고르는 문항이다.

B형 서술형 문항

- 6번(data-based item)은 〈A〉에 2022년 개정 교육과정의 핵심 교수 방법 중 하나인 Project-based learning에 대한 학습 단계가 제시되었고, 〈B〉에 실제 일정 기간(1st Week~6th Week)의 교실 수업 단계가 제시되어 두 단계 간의 mismatching을 묻는 문항이다.
- 7번(knowledge-based item)은 〈A〉에 제시된 초임교사와 주임교사 간 대화로 효율적인 수업을 위한 수업 계획 수정(modified lesson)에 관련된 문항으로, intensive listening을 이해하고 creative writing에 대한 개념을 묻는 문항이다.

• 10번(data-based item)은 다년간 중등 임용시험에서 주요 토픽으로 다루고 있는 문화학습 관련 문항이다. 〈A〉에서 문화학습 과정인 noticing, comparing, reflecting, interacting의 개념들과 두 학생의 문화학습 단계를 보여주는 발화 간 matching을 묻고 있고, 〈B〉에서는 두 학생의 대화로 알 수 있는 문화학습 과정을 규명하는 문항이다.
• 11번 문항(knowledge-based item)은 〈A〉에 how to use digital tools에 대한 원리를 제시하고, 〈B〉에서 8차 시간 수업 중 원리 mismatching에 대한 것을 고르는 문항이다. 이 문항은 discovery learning과 drill 간의 차이와 individualized feedback의 이해 여부를 묻는 문항이다.

2025학년도 대비 중등 임용 영어교육론의 방향

A형과 B형의 문항 유형에서 살펴봤듯이, 2025년 기출의 가장 큰 특징은 실제 교실 수업에서 교사의 자질과 학생들의 주도적 학습을 위한 교실 계획 및 언어학습의 궁극적인 목적인 목표 문화학습으로 꼽을 수 있다. 중등 임용시험에서 영어교육론의 난이도는 문학과 영어학 등 다른 영역에 비하면 중간 정도의 익숙한 문항들이 출제되고 있으나, 다른 내용학의 어려움에 대한 득점 손실을 만회할 수 있도록 영어교육론의 감점을 최소화하는 전략을 2026년 대비 중등 임용의 핵심 전략으로 삼아야 할 것이다. 이 목표를 성취하기 위해서는 영어교육론의 개념을 폭넓게 이해하고, 실전 문항의 data-processing / direction analysis/ correct answer에 대한 연습을 상반기부터 진행해야 한다.

2025학년도 기출 | 전공A 기입형

03. **Read the passage and follow the directions.** [2 points]

Materials can be adapted by using different techniques such as *adding, deleting, modifying,* and *reordering.* For example, we can add materials when a language item is not covered sufficiently in the original materials. Materials that are too easy or difficult for learners can be deleted. Modifying can be used to make them more relevant to students' interests and backgrounds and to restructure classroom management. Reordering the sequence of activities is another technique, which includes separating items and regrouping them.

Consider the original material extracted from a grammar exercise book and its adapted version below. In the adapted version, the original exercise has been adapted by using the ① __________ technique.

Original Material

❶ **[Individual Work]** Describe the man's routine in four sentences.

____

____

❷ **[Individual Work]** Answer the following questions.
What time do you wake up?
What do you usually wear to work?
What do you usually cook for dinner?

Adapted Material

❶ **[Individual Work]** Describe the student's routine in four sentences.

❷ **[Pair Work]** Work in pairs and ask each other the following questions.
What time do you wake up?
What do you usually wear on school days?
What do you usually eat for dinner?

Fill in the blank ① with the ONE most appropriate word from the passage.

모범답안 modifying

2025학년도 기출 | 전공A 기입형

04. Read the conversation in <A> and the passage in <B>, and follow the directions. [2 points]

A

(Two teachers, Mr. Lee and Ms. Kim, recently scored students' speaking assessments. They later discussed the scoring process and Mr. Lee reflected on his scoring experiences in his journals.)

Mr. Lee : As I was reviewing my ratings, I noticed that they were staying consistent throughout the scoring process.

Ms. Kim : Good, it's actually hard to keep the same perspective when grading multiple students. But you mean you found actual similarities in your scores for the same students over time?

Mr. Lee : Yes, exactly. I think I might have benefitted from reviewing my previous scores before re-evaluating anyone's performance to see if I'm staying consistent.

Ms. Kim : That makes sense. You know, I've noticed that we have some scoring differences between us on certain criteria.

Mr. Lee : Right. I normally give a score of 10 if students have natural flow even though they may demonstrate some errors in grammar or vocabulary. How about you?

Ms. Kim : Oh, I've constantly made efforts to adhere to our scoring criteria, and I give a perfect score only when they speak without any errors or hesitation.
Mr. Lee : All right. Now I can see why we have different scoring results and it makes me think—these different results could send mixed messages to students.
Ms. Kim : I agree. Let's review our criteria and stick to following our rubric.
Mr. Lee : Sure. That would be fairer for the students.

B

Mr. Lee's Reflective Journal

After today's grading session, I reviewed my scores and luckily noticed consistency in my ratings for the same students across different sessions. However, after talking with Ms. Kim, I realized that we provided different scores for the same students. I'm concerned this could lead to some confusion if they receive different scores based on which teacher assesses them. I think it would be helpful if Ms. Kim and I could go over the rubric together to ensure a more unified scoring approach.

Fill in the blanks with the TWO most appropriate words.

Based on <A> and <B>, Mr. Lee is concerned about the lack of ____________ ____________ in the scoring process. His concern is not about the consistency of rating by a single rater but about the consistency of rating by different raters.

모범답안 inter-rater reliability

Guide

2025학년도 기출 | 전공A 서술형

08. **Read the passage in <A> and the conversation in <B>, and follow the directions.** [4 points]

A

Understanding second language (L2) learners' interlanguage is an important step for teaching L2 learners. In analyzing interlanguage, it has been found that deviations from characteristics of the target language exist in learners' utterances. For example, deviations in early L2 learners' utterances can be categorized into several types.

<Deviations in Early L2 Learners' Utterances>

Type	Description	Example (The intended meaning is in parentheses.)
Mismatched lexical class	The lexical class does not match.	*It's a pink.* (It's pink.)
Semantic deviation	Utterances are semantically ill-formed.	*What's the spaghetti?* (Do you like spaghetti?)
Number of arguments	Utterances contain more or fewer arguments than required.	*I wore.* (I wore a shirt.)
Word order	Word order is violated.	*I this book read.* (I read this book.)
…	…	…

B

(Two students are carrying out a two-way spot-the-difference task in their English class.)

S1 : Now, let's get started. In your picture, are there chairs?
S2 : Yes.
S1 : How many chairs are there?
S2 : Two chairs.
S1 : There are also two chairs in my picture. Now, please ask me about my picture.
S2 : What's the pen?
S1 : I'm sorry? Do you mean, "Do you have a pen?"
S2 : Yes.
S1 : Okay. Then, yes, I do. Do you have a pen?
S2 : No, I do not have a pen.
S1 : Okay. Then we've found one difference. Next, your turn.
S2 : Is there a girl?
S1 : Yes, there is. What is she doing?
S2 : She is giving Mary.
S1 : Um, what is she giving Mary?
S2 : Ah, she is giving Mary a book.
S1 : Oh, in my picture, she is giving Mary an eraser.
S2 : Yeah! Finally, we got them all.

Note: S=student

Based on <A>, identify the TWO types of deviations found in the students' utterances in <B>. Then, explain your answers, respectively, with evidence from <B>.

모범답안 In the conversation, S2 demonstrates 'Semantic deviation' and a deviation in the 'Number of arguments'. First, S2 produces the ill-formed utterance. 'What's the pen?' instead of the intended meaning. "Do you have a pen?". Additionally, S2 says "She is giving Mary," Where the necessary arguments. 'a book' is omitted.

2025학년도 기출 | 전공A 서술형

09. **Read the passage in <A> and the teacher's reflection log in <B>, and follow the directions.** [4 points]

A

Mr. Jeong, an English teacher, was tasked with evaluating speaking assessment items in his students' final exam. Reviewing key principles of speaking assessment, he noted the following:

- ✔ Clarity: Prompts should be straightforward to avoid confusion.
- ✔ Authenticity: Speaking tasks should mirror real-life communication, enabling students to demonstrate natural language use.
- ✔ Integrated Skills Assessment: Tasks should assess speaking alongside other skills, such as listening comprehension, to reflect communicative performance.
- ✔ Practicality: Test items should be feasible and manageable in terms of the time spent in assessment.

B

Teacher's Reflection Log

After reviewing the items, I felt that the two items had some good and bad points. Item 1 asked students to describe a memorable experience that they had with a friend, including details such as when it happened, what they did, and why it was memorable. After observing students' responses, I realized that this item resembled a conversation topic in real-life contexts. However, I regret that I didn't set time limits for the item and it took too much time to score it, which made the assessment difficult to manage.

For Item 2, after looking at a picture of a busy street, students were asked to describe what they saw. Most of the students did very well on this task because the item clearly described what sort of response was desired. I think this item was effective in assessing pronunciation, one of the criteria for assessing speaking skills. However, next time I want to add some more items such as asking students to listen to a short audio and discuss their opinions. It might be more challenging but I believe I can assess multiple skills in the test.

Based on <A>, identify the speaking assessment principles applied in Item 1 and Item 2 in <B>, respectively. Then, explain how each principle was applied in each item with evidence from <B>.

모범답안 Authenticity is applied to Item 1 because the conversation topic about memorable experience with friends reflects real-life contexts. On the other hand, Clarity is applied to Item 2, because the use of a prompt. 'a picture of a busy street', enables students to clearly describe what they observed.

2025학년도 기출 | 전공A 서술형

11. **Read the passage in <A> and the teaching procedure in <B>, and follow the directions.** [4 points]

A

Ms. Kim, an English teacher, is selecting lesson objectives to implement into a new lesson. The following are the lesson objectives for reception and production.

Lesson Objectives

Reception

R1. Students can recognize reduced sounds of words.
R2. Students can identify specific details from a text or discourse.
R3. Students can distinguish between literal and implied meanings.

Production

P1. Students can explain the sequence of an event in the right order.
P2. Students can write a simple journal, letter, or email.
P3. Students can argue for and against a topic in a respectful manner.

B

Step	Teaching Procedure
Step 1	In groups, students brainstorm the pros and cons of using AI in education and create a mind map. AI — Pros: convenient, immediate feedback, no constraints (place, time) AI — Cons: distracting, cheating, less human interaction
Step 2	Students listen to an audio clip on AI and digital tools in class and complete a worksheet. ▶ Listen to the conversation carefully and follow the directions below. A. Mark the sentences True or False. 1. Sora says that the use of AI should be prohibited in the classroom. [True/False] 2. Inho asks an AI chatbot to do his assignment. [True/False] 3. Minji compares the outputs on a topic from three different AI chatbots. [True/False] B. Match the person with his or her concern. Inho · · Excessive screen time Minji · · False information Sora · · Theft of personal data

Step 3	Students work together and write rules for the use of digital tools in class. **Class Rules for the Use of Digital Tools** 1. *e.g., Never download software to a school device without permission.* 2. ____________________ 3. ____________________ ◆ Useful expressions for polite agreement or disagreement - I agree. That's a good idea. That's right. - I don't think/believe so. I don't agree/disagree (with you). - What do you think? Would you agree with me? Don't you agree?

Identify ONE lesson objective for reception and ONE lesson objective for production from <A> that the teaching procedure in <B> targets. Then, explain your answers, respectively, with evidence from <B>.

모범답안 One objective for reception is for students to identify specific details from an audio clip by marking statements as True or False and matching a person with their specific concern. Additionally, one objective for production is for students to argue for and against a topic in a respectful manner while discussing class rules for the use of digital tools, using useful expressions for polite agreement or disagreement.

Guide

2025학년도 기출 전공A 서술형

12. **Read the passages in <A> and <B>, and follow the directions.** [4 points]

A

Metacognitive awareness of reading strategies is considered a conscious procedure utilized by readers to enhance text comprehension and encourage active reading.

Understanding its importance, Ms. Yu, a high school English teacher, used the Metacognitive Awareness of Reading Strategy Questionnaire to measure students' awareness on three categories of reading strategies. These include Global Reading Strategies (GLOB), Support Reading Strategies (SUP), and Problem-Solving Strategies (PROB). She also interviewed her students after the survey.

The Metacognitive Awareness of Reading Strategy Questionnaire

Category	Item	1	2	3	4	5
GLOB	G1. I have a purpose in mind when I read.					
	G2. I think about what I know to help me understand what I read.					
	G3. While reading, I decide what to read and what to ignore.					
	G4. I take an overall view of the text to see what it is about before reading it.					
	...	...				
SUP	S1. I paraphrase what I read to better understand it.					
	S2. I take notes while reading to help me understand what I read.					
	S3. While reading, I translate from English into my native language.					
	S4. I use reference materials (e.g., a dictionary) to help me understand what I read.					
		...				
PROB	P1. When the text is unclear, I re-read it to increase my understanding.					
	P2. I try to guess the meaning of unknown words or phrases.					
	P3. I adjust my reading speed according to what I am reading.					
	P4. I try to visualize information to help understand what I read.					
	...	...				

Note: 1=never, 2=occasionally, 3=sometimes, 4=usually, 5=always

B

Based on the survey results, Ms. Yu conducted interviews with the students who reported low ratings in the survey. Parts of the interview excerpts are below. One of the interview questions was "Do you feel challenged while reading?" After the interview, Ms. Yu identified reading strategies that students need to promote their active reading skills.

Interview Excerpts

S1 : "I thought reading was just about understanding the words. When I don't understand something, I tend to skip over it. I think if I try to draw a picture in my mind when I'm not sure, I'll understand texts much better."

S2 : "I usually analyze texts sentence-by-sentence until I fully understand them. After checking my low ratings on the questionnaire, I found that reading selectively may help me become a more efficient reader."

Note: S=student

Identify the TWO items of reading strategies in <A> that Ms. Yu may apply to her reading instruction in relation to <B>. Then, explain your answers, respectively, with evidence from <B>.

모범답안 Ms. Yu may instruct S2s to "decide what to read and what to ignore" from G3, encouraging them to avoid analyzing texts sentence-by-sentence and instead focus on reading selectively. Additionally, she can guide S1s to "visualize information" from P4, helping them picture what they read to enhance comprehension.

Guide

2025학년도 기출 | 전공B 서술형

06. Read the passages in <A> and <B>, and follow the directions. [4 points]

A

Project-based learning (PBL) is a teaching method that facilitates students to use an inquiry process with an integrated goal and interrelated subsidiary tasks. One possible procedure for implementing PBL is provided below.

Students collaboratively set the goal and scope of the project. This makes students feel in control of their own projects from the beginning. Once the goal is set, students as a group actively discuss and decide upon what to include in their project. When collecting information for the project, students develop integrated language skills in meaningful ways. Students then create their projects collaboratively with their group members. Finally, students present their projects in class. When assessing student projects, the teacher evaluates students' learning progress, focusing on the process as well as the product.

B

Referring to the procedure as described in <A>, Ms. Park, a middle school English teacher, implemented PBL into her class over six weeks. Each week, one class session was allocated for the PBL project. When each session was over, Ms. Park briefly wrote a teacher's log to record events and observations. Some entries of her logs are provided below.

Week 1

I decided on a specific goal for the project and announced it to students. The goal was to make tourist brochures and distribute them to the local communities. I assigned students to groups of four. I also provided guidelines on the project.

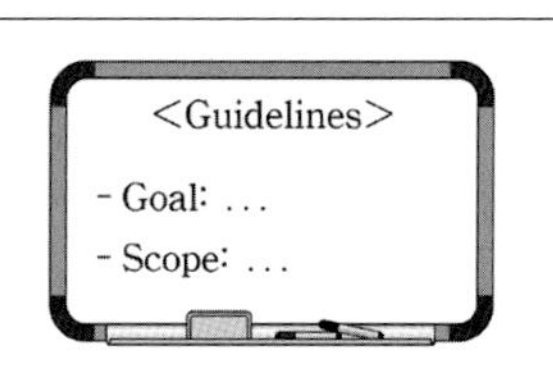

Week 2

The groups explored possible destinations to include in their brochures. Students also searched the Internet for various brochures and analyzed the sections within. They found details including attractions, activities, and food.

Week 3

The groups conducted a survey on their classmates' recommendations for the destination their group decided upon. They did so by asking and responding to each other. Then they summarized the survey results.

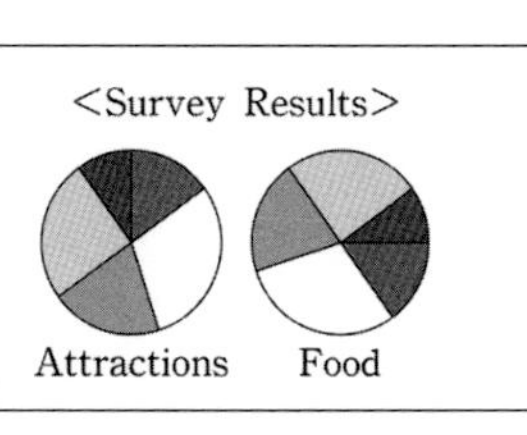

Week 4

The students worked closely in a group to make their brochures. Upon completion, they prepared for a group presentation.

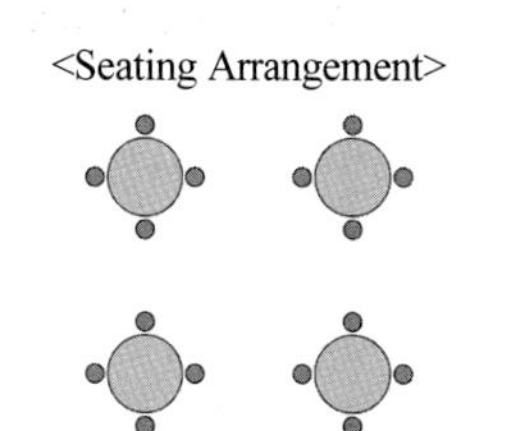

Week 5

Each group gave a ten-minute presentation. Students also prepared for distributing the brochures to the local communities.

Week 6

As the final step, I evaluated students' brochures based on a rubric, which consisted of vocabulary, grammar, and layout.

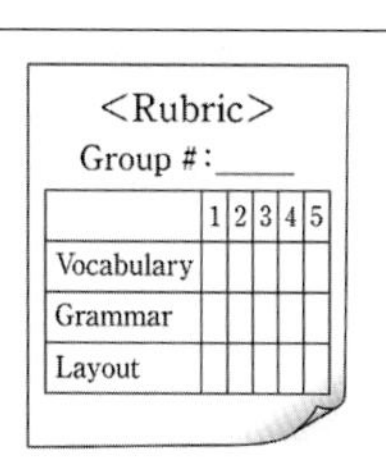
<Rubric>

Group # : _____

	1	2	3	4	5
Vocabulary					
Grammar					
Layout					

Identify the TWO weeks in <B> that do NOT follow the procedure provided in <A>. Then, explain how the identified weeks deviate from the procedure in <A>.

모범답안 Week 1 and Week 6 do not align with the PBL procedure. In Week 1, Ms. Park directly sets and announces the project goal to the students, instead of allowing them to collaboratively determine the goal and scope of the project. In Week 6, she evaluates students' learning progress based solely on the final products—brochures—without assessing both the learning process and the product.

Guide

2025학년도 기출 전공B 서술형

07. Read the conversation in <A> and the lesson plans in <B>, and follow the directions. [4 points]

A

(Mr. Choi, a supervising teacher, is talking with his student teacher, Ms. Han, about her lesson plan.)

SupT: Ms. Han, I checked your lesson plan and found a couple of things that may help improve it.
ST : Oh, did I miss anything?
SupT: As you know, before you get to the main listening stage, we want students to recognize the purpose of listening, right?
ST : Yeah, and it sounds quite challenging. How can I do that?
SupT: You can try activating schemata. Making connections between personal experiences and learning can facilitate students' comprehension.
ST : Oh, I see.
SupT: And I recommend intensive listening. You know, authentic conversations have a lot of contractions. So, how about playing parts of a radio show focusing on particular language features?
ST : Good idea. Thank you. Is there anything else I missed?
SupT: Hmm, why don't you also try making some creative activities? Students can sing a song or chant, or they can record their own voice.
ST : Got it. I'll try to find some that are exciting.
SupT: Great. That's all I wanted to point out.
ST : Your suggestions are extremely helpful. I'll make some changes following your advice.
SupT: If you have any questions, don't hesitate to ask.
ST : I really appreciate your advice.

Note: SupT=supervising teacher, ST=student teacher

B

After the conversation, Ms. Han revised her lesson plan based on Mr. Choi's suggestions. Below are the original and modified lesson plans.

Original Lesson Plan

Stage	Teaching & Learning Activities
Pre-listening	• T shows the aim of the listening activity. • T asks about what will happen to a person in a picture. • T engages Ss in small talk.
While-listening	• T asks Ss to listen to a story. • T asks Ss to make inferences about the main topic of the story. • T asks Ss to retell the story.
Post-listening	• T asks Ss to write a summary on the story. • T asks Ss to present on their summaries. • T provides comments on Ss' presentations.

Modified Lesson Plan

Stage	Teaching & Learning Activities
Pre-listening	• T presents the purpose of the listening activity. • T asks Ss to predict what will happen to a person in a picture. • T engages Ss in small talk.
While-listening	• T asks Ss to listen to a story. • T asks Ss to guess what the main topic of the story is. • T asks Ss to do a gap-filling activity.
Post-listening	• T asks Ss to summarize the story. • T asks Ss to act out assigned scenes from the story. • T provides feedback on Ss' performances.

Note: T=teacher, Ss=students

Identify the supervising teacher's TWO suggestions from <A> that are reflected in the modified lesson plan in <B>. Then, explain your answers, respectively, with evidence from <B>.

모범답안 The supervising teacher provides two suggestions: intensive listening and creative activities. The student teacher incorporates these suggestions into the modified lesson plan. First, during the listening activity, the original story-retelling task is replaced with a gap-filling activity. Additionally, after listening, the student teacher plans for students to act out assigned scenes instead of merely presenting their summaries.

Guide

2025학년도 기출 | 전공B 서술형

10. Read the passages in <A> and <B>, and follow the directions. [4 points]

A

Intercultural language learning in the classroom can be conceptualized as a series of four interrelated processes: *noticing, comparing, reflecting,* and *interacting*. First, noticing is for learners to experience new input about culture and attempt to understand it. Teachers may use various exemplifications of the target culture as input, such as videos, written texts, and cartoons. Second, comparing occurs when learners are engaged in identifying similarities and differences between learners' culture and the target culture. Third, reflecting implies that learners make personal interpretations of experiences and react to linguistic and cultural diversity. Finally, interacting involves learners communicating personal meanings about their experiences, exploring those meanings, and reshaping them in response to others.

The two excerpts below are parts of students' speeches in class.

Excerpt from Seoyeon's Speech

"I imagined what I would and wouldn't like about attending a U.S. high school. I'd be excited about having many options for extracurricular activities, but I wouldn't want to join any sport teams because I don't like playing sports."

Excerpt from Taesoo's Speech

"I think the level of engagement in extracurricular activities seems different between Korean and U.S. high school students. For example, many U.S. high school students tend to spend much more time doing community service than Korean students."

As seen above, Seoyeon is most likely involved in the process of ① ____________, and Taesoo is most likely involved in the process of ② __________.

B

(Seoyeon and Taesoo are talking about their speeches.)

Seoyeon: I really liked your speech. There are a lot of things we can do for the community when it comes to extracurricular activities.

Taesoo : Thank you. That was the exact point I wanted to make.

Seoyeon: I'd like to hear more about the ways in which we can serve our communities.

Fill in the blanks ① and ② each with the ONE most appropriate word from <A>, in the correct order. Then, explain one of the four processes in <A> that Seoyeon in <B> is most likely involved in with evidence from <B>.

모범답안 ① reflecting ② comparing

Seoyeon in <B> engages in the process of interacting as she shares her personal meanings after learning about extracurricular activities in the U.S. and reshapes her understanding of extracurricular activities to include diverse ways to provide community services through her interaction with Taesoo.

2025학년도 기출 | 전공B 서술형

11. Read the passage in <A> and the master plan in <B>, and follow the directions. [4 points]

A

Ms. Kim, a high school English teacher, attended an ICT workshop for English teachers. There she learned how to select digital tools that best fit her students' needs and use them appropriately. Below is the list of principles she took note of during the workshop.

<Guiding principles for using digital tools>

① Encourage students to independently explore and discover language rules.
② Support learners with diverse learning styles (e.g., auditory styles, visual styles).
③ Teach digital ethics (e.g., citing properly).
④ Assess student achievement and provide individualized feedback.

B

Draft of the Master Plan

Unit	Save the Earth	
Objectives	Students will be able to: • identify the main idea and details of a text or discourse • write an opinion using textual and non-textual elements • use digital tools responsibly and ethically	
Objectives	Contents	Technology
1st	• Introduce the topic, 'Save the Earth' • Watch a video on environmental problems • Teach how to use the Internet properly (e.g., locating information, sourcing, netiquette)	- Online videos - Internet search engines
2nd	• Make predictions about a text using titles and pictures • Read the passage, 'Plastic Pollution' • Identify key words and main ideas	Word cloud generator to visualize key concepts
3rd	• Provide definitions of new words • Teach grammar points explicitly using drills	PPT slides
...	...	...
7th	• Brainstorm ideas to solve environmental problems and share in groups • In groups, create a 'Save the Earth' poster	Online collaborative writing platform
8th	• Exhibit groups' posters on the walls • Conduct a team-based quiz and provide comments to groups	Online quiz platform

Based on <A>, identify the TWO guiding principles that Ms. Kim does NOT conform to in her lessons in <B>. Then, explain your answers, respectively, with evidence from <B>.

모범답안 Ms. Kim does not conform to guiding principles ① and ④. First, she explicitly teaches grammar points through drills instead of encouraging students to independently explore and discover language rules. Additionally, she conducts a team-based quiz and provides comments to groups rather than assessing individual performance and offering personalized feedback.

Contents

PART 01

Theoretical Consideration for Language Learning

Chapter 01 Theoretical Background in Language Learning and Teaching
- 언어 습득 유형 및 학습 모델 중심으로

Chapter 02 Pedagogical Key Concepts
- 현 교실 수업의 주요 개념 및 원리 중심으로

Chapter 03 Classroom Context
-syllabus, materials, activities, learner variables 중심으로

PART 02

Practical Classroom Teaching and Learning

NEW
Build Up

Part 01

Theoretical Consideration for Language Learning

Chapter 01

Theoretical Background in Language Learning and Teaching

– 언어 습득 유형 및 학습 모델 중심으로

01 Behaviorism / Audiolingual Method - 행동주의의 구두 청각 교수법적 관점

기계적인 반복 학습으로 인한 언어 습관 형성이 목적이다. (good habit formation)

1 Structural Syllabus

각각의 개별적 항목(discrete points)에 초점을 둔 교수요목이다.

• Example Structural Syllabus for 2nd Grade Language Classroom •

	Objective	Grammar Focus	Activities
Unit 1. Basic Sentence Structure	Students will learn subject-verb-object (SVO) structure.	Simple sentences (e.g., "She eats an apple.")	Sentence building games, matching subjects with verbs and objects, creating sentences from prompts
Unit 2. Present Simple Tense	Students will learn to describe daily routines and facts.	Present simple (e.g., "I go to school every day.")	Fill-in-the-blank exercises, talking about daily routines, writing short paragraphs about family members' routines
Unit 3. Present Continuous Tense	Students will learn to describe ongoing actions.	Present continuous (e.g., "They are playing soccer.")	Role-playing current actions, drawing and describing pictures of people in action, creating dialogues

2 Classroom Activities

Drilling, repetitive oral practice of a language item, such as a sound, a word, phrase or a sentence structure. Drills that are targeted at sentence structures are sometimes called pattern practice drills.

Classroom context: An English classroom where students are practicing pattern drills to reinforce the use of present continuous tense.

Teacher : Okay, class! Let's practice using the present continuous tense. Remember, the structure is 'I am [verb]ing [object].' Let's go around the room and take turns making sentences using this pattern. Start with 'I am reading a book.' Ready?
Student 1 : I am reading a book.
Teacher : Good, Jungsoo! Now, let's switch it up a bit. Jenny, can you change 'reading' to another verb?
Student 2 : Okay. I am drawing a picture.
Teacher : Nice work, Jimin! Sumin, your turn. Use the same structure but change both the verb and the object.
Student 3 : Hmm... I am eating an apple.
Teacher : Perfect, Sumin! Now let's add a question. How would you ask someone else what they are doing? For example, 'What are you doing?' or "What is the girl(boy) doing?". Let's try it. Look at the picture and then, ask each other what people are doing in the picture?
Student 1 : Jimin, what is the girl doing?
Student 2 : She is taking a walk in the park. Jungsoo, what is the boy doing?
Student 1 : He is reading a book.

T=teacher, S=student

3 Contrastive Analysis Hypothesis

제2언어 습득을 방해하는 요인을 모국어의 **간섭현상(interference)**으로 간주하고, 모국어와 L2의 차이점을 파악해 제2언어 학습에서의 어려움을 덜고자 하는 언어 분석 방법이다.

Example

한국어를 모국어로 갖는 영어 학습자는 한국어 발음 /ㄹ/sound의 간섭(interference)으로 인해 영어의 /r/sound를 /l/sound로 발음하는 오류를 범하게 된다. 또한, 한국어 meaning system의 간섭(interference)으로 인해 영어 'pork'는 pig meat(돼지고기) 문자 그대로 번역(literal translation)하는 오류를 범하게 된다.

NS(T) : Hey, Min-soo, are you going to school?
Min-soo : Yeah, I'm on classroom duty today. That's why I go to school earlier than usual.
NS : Do you? So, have you eaten breakfast?
Min-soo : I ate r(/l/)ice with pig meat.
NS : Sorry?

- **Key Concepts**: interference, strong version, weak version, cross linguistic influence
- **Criticism**: All of the errors learners make in L2 cannot be traced to the differences between L1 and L2.

02 Innatism - 선천주의적 Natural Approach 관점

선천적으로 언어 습득 장치(language acquisition device)를 갖고 태어나 신체적 발달이 이뤄지듯이 언어 발달도 LAD에 의해 자연스럽게 이뤄진다는 관점이다.

1 Input Hypothesis

Comprehension-based activities 중심의 언어 습득을 강조함으로써, 교사가 교실에서 이해 가능한 언어적 입력(comprehensible input, *i+1*)을 되도록 많이 제공(exposure)해야 하기 때문에 교실에서는 원어 수업(English only principles)을 원칙으로 삼아야 한다.

Krashen's Input Hypothesis

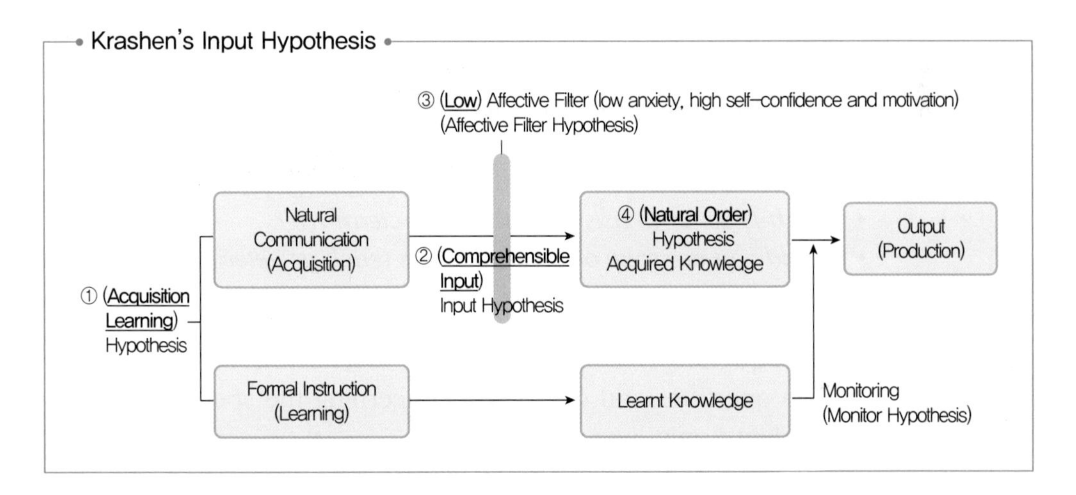

2 Natural Approach

Lesson theme: Washing a Car
Task type: problem solving
Student level: intermediate level

Teaching Procedure

Step 1: The teacher will guide the students in developing the vocabulary necessary to talk about the activity:
- *-rag, water, park, bucket, sponge, driveway*

Step 2: Then together the class and instructor create utterances to describe the sequence of events to complete the activity. The class might say:
- *First I look for a bucket and a sponge or some rags.*
- *Then I park the car in the driveway.*
- *I use the hose to wash the car first with water only.*

These utterances are developed slowly with interspersed discussion.
- *Which is better to use, a sponge or a clean rag?*
- *Should you use soap or other cleaners (such as detergents) to wash a car?*

Step 3: After sequence is constructed, the discussion will broaden to include questions and discussion concerning the specific activity in the students' own lives.
- *How often do you wash your car? when? / where? / Do you enjoy it? / Why? / Why not?*

Lesson Analysis

Step 1: When going through a silent period, students receive comprehensible input usually from the teacher. (comprehension-based activity)

Step 2: Based on the sentence-completion response and personalized questions, students gradually answer to teacher's questions. (Early speech production)

Step 3: Students produce the utterance which are longer and complex. Many errors are still made but, if enough comprehensible input has been internalized, they should gradually decrease as the students move toward full production. (Speech emergence)

03 Cognitivism - 언어 형태에 초점(FFI)을 두는 관점

지식(rules / language systems)을 습득할 때 인지적 역할 및 과정에 초점을 두고 학습 과정을 설명하고자 하는 관점이다.

1 중간언어(Interlanguage / Learner Language)

목표 언어를 학습하는 과정 중에 생긴 불완전한 학습자 언어 체계로서 나름의 일정한 체계(systematic)를 가지고 있으나, 불완전한 특성으로 인해 어떠한 의미를 나타내기 위한 맥락에 따라 이형적인 형태(variable)가 나타나기도 한다. 또한, 중간언어 (또는 학습자 언어) 체계는 끊임없이 수정되고, 변화·발전(dynamic)한다.

Data Analysis

Read the passage in <A> and the conversation in <B>, and follow the directions.

A

Second language learners pass through a predictable sequence of development. Since the early 1990's, some research has investigated the acquisition of pragmatic abilities in the L2. 'Requesting' is one of the pragmatic features that has received attention. In a review of studies on the acquisition of requests in English, six stages of development were suggested.

Stage	Characteristics	Example
1	Using body language or gestures	*Sir (pointing to the pencil).* *Teacher (holding the paper).*
2	Using verbless expressions	*A paper. / More time.*
3	Using imperative verbs	*Give me. / Give me a paper.*
4	Using 'Can I have ___________?' as a formulaic expression	*Can I have some candy?*
5	Using 'can' with a range of verbs, not just with 'have'	*Can you pass me the book?*
6	Using indirect requests	*I want more cookies.*

B

Students are doing a problem-solving task in groups. S1 plays the role of moderator in the activity.

S1: We have to find some ways to make the environment more sustainable. Suhee, what's your opinion?
S2: I'm sorry, but nothing comes to mind now. I need more time to think.
S1: Okay. Tell us if you're ready. Minho, how about you? Can you share your ideas with us?
S3: We should use one-time products as less as possible.
S1: Hold on, Minho. What does 'one-time products' mean? Can I have some examples?
S3: Well, paper cups, plastic bags...
S2: Ah, I see. You mean 'disposable products', right?
S3: Yes.
S1: Minho, I like your idea.
S2: I'm ready. Driving electronic cars reduces air pollution.
S3: Sounds great.

S1: Now I think we have enough opinions for the presentation. Suhee, can you speak for us in the presentation session?
S2: I'm afraid not. Minho can do better than me.
S3: Umm. Okay. I'll take the speaker role. I'll do my best.
S2: Thanks, Minho. I'll write the presentation script for you.
S1: Wow, thank you.

S=student

Q1 Based on <A>, identify the developmental stages when S1 and S2 are, respectively.

Q2 Then, explain your answers with evidence from <B>.

>> Possible Answers p.043

(1) **U-shaped Learning**: a behavior in which the learner first learns the correct behavior, then, abandons the correct behavior, and finally returns to the correct behavior once again

(2) **Overgeneralization**: the phenomenon when one overextends one rule to cover instances to which that rule does not apply. For example, a young child may say "foots" instead of "feet," overgeneralizing the morphological rule for making plural nouns.

(3) **Backsliding**: temporary regression to a previous interlanguage. This occurs when the second-language learner's monitor is down due to either stress or relaxation and usually lasts for very brief periods of time.

Ms. Kim, a new teacher, and Mr. Song, a head teacher, are discussing Ms. Kim's concerns about her student's writing performance.

T1: Ms. Kim, did the process-oriented evaluation in your writing class go well this semester?
T2: I'm still making comments to students, but there is something I'm worried about.
T1: What is it?
T2: I'm afraid that one of my students is making more errors now than he was at the beginning of the semester.
T1: He got worse as the semester went on?
T2: Yes. He turned in the writing assignment. However, there were so many errors in his writing.
T1: What kinds of errors?
T2: Unlike the beginning of the semester, now he has problems with irregular verbs.
T1: Can you give me an example?
T2: When the semester began, he wrote words like "drank," "wore," and "heard" without errors. Now I am seeing errors like "drinked," "weared," and "heared." He is suddenly treating irregular verbs like regular verbs.
T1: Hmm. Now that I think about it, he is probably progressing!
T2: What are you talking about?
T1: Well, according to U-shaped course of development, he is starting to understand the rules of the past tense.
T2: Oh, I see.

T1=Mr. Song, T2=Ms. Kim

➡ In the above conversation, Ms. Kim's student seems to regress, making errors with irregular verbs that he used to use correctly, due to overgeneralization. This phenomenon is commonly called backsliding, in which the learner seems to have grasped a rule or principle but then moves from a correct form to an incorrect form.

(4) **Fossilization**: the state in which a learners does not seem to progress in development of the target language; the learner appears "stuck" at a certain level

2 Information Processing Model

제2언어 학습은 형식적인 수업(formal instruction)을 통해 처음 학습 자료가 제시됐을 때, 일시적으로 한정적인 정보처리 능력(controlled processing)을 갖게 되고, 지속적인 교실 수업의 유의미한 연습 활동(practice)을 통해 점차 일상적인 언어 능력(automatic processing)으로 전환된다.

Rule-governed instruction(controlled processing → automatic processing)

Example

An English teacher developed the following procedure for teaching pronunciation. (Prominent syllables are marked by large-size capital letters.)

Step 1

a. The teacher writes the following three versions of the sentence *I'm listening* on the board.

– I'm **LIS**tening. – **I'M** listening. – I **AM** listening!

b. Students practice producing all three versions.

Teacher asks:	Student should respond:
What are you doing?	I'm **LIS**tening.
Who's listening?	**I'M** listening.
Why aren't you listening?	I **AM** listening!

Step 2

With an explanation on how to chunk, the teacher asks students to listen and circle the prominent words.

A: I'm starved. / Let's go grab a bite to eat.
B: Good idea. / Where do you want to go?
A: Well, / there's a nice restaurant. / It's a

Step 3

a. Students write down words for the items that they want to bring for a picnic.

apple, pasta, napkin, pear, pepper, popcorn, pizza, spoon, soup...

b. The teacher asks students to play a game called "The perfect picnic" with the whole class, using the words that they chose.

Example: Student A says, "We're having a picnic, and I'm bringing pears." Student B says, "We're having a picnic. A is bringing pears, and I'm bringing popcorn." Student C says, ...

3 Form-focused Instruction

(1) **Focus on Form**: It consists of primarily meaning-focused interaction and sometimes spontaneous attention to linguistic forms.

(2) **Focus on Forms**: It involves a primary, emphasis on linguistic structures, often presented as discrete grammar rules or other metalinguistic information.

There are students who can tell us that we have to put an *s* on the end of the verb when making third person singular declarative statements. When making such statements themselves, however, more often than not, they leave off the *s*. These students have **declarative** knowledge (they can state or declare the rule), but not **procedural** knowledge (they can't or don't use the rule when using the language to communicate).

- ▶ Noticing Hypothesis: Nothing is learned unless it has been noticed. Noticing refers to becoming aware of a language feature in the input.
- ▶ Salience: They can't learn what they don't notice—on the role of salience in language learning. This term refers to the property of a stimulus to stand out from the rest.

Example 1

For Third Person Singular Possessive Determiner

Once upon a time there was a king. He had a beautiful young daughter. For her birthday, the king gave her a golden ball that she played with everyday. The king and his daughter lived near a dark forest...

Example 2

1. Read the following about your country.

> In this country, you **have to** start school at the age of 7. You can drive when you are 17, but you can't buy alcohol until you are 18. You also **have to** wait until you turn 18 before you can vote. Men **have to** serve in the military, but women **don't have to**.

2. Listen to a similar conversation about England.
3. Mark the differences between your country and England on the worksheet.

➡ *The activity helps students notice the target structure through input enhancement.*

4 Error Analysis

언어 학습 과정 중 나타나는 오류는 필연적인 것으로 인식하며, 성공적인 목표 언어 체계를 갖기 위해 오류를 관찰·분석·수정하는 언어 분석 방법이다.

(1) **오류의 원인**: interference, overgeneralization, context of learning, communication strategies

> *The teacher asks her student, Dongho, what he did over the weekend?*
>
> T: Hi, Dongho, how was your weekend?
> S: Hello, uh, have, had fun.
> T: You had fun, oh, good. Did you go anywhere?
> S: Yeah, uh, I go, go, went to uncle, uncle's home.
> T: What did you do there? Did you do something interesting?
> S: I play, played with *childs*, Uncle have *childs*, three *childs*.
> T: Your uncle has three *children*?
> S: Yeah uh, one boy and two girls. So three *childs*.

(2) **표면적 특성의 오류 범주**: addition, omission, substitution, misordering

> *The following is Sumi's written feedback about today's English lesson on the online bulletin board.*
>
> I can loved today's lesson! When the teacher asked questions about the words and expressions related to cook using the recipe from cooking magazine. I was clearly able to figure out the meaning of what we supposed to learn. It was really motivating to use the recipe for learning about the words and expressions used practically for cooking.

(3) **의사소통에 따른 범주**: global error, local error

> Local errors do not hinder communication and understanding the meaning of an utterance. Global errors, on the other hand, are more serious than previously mentioned errors because these errors interfere the communication and disrupt the meaning of an utterance.
>
> When the focus is on meaning(fluency), it is inappropriate to interrupt the flow of interaction. In these situations, the teacher can make a note of errors for follow-up treatment later. When the focus is on form(accuracy), the teacher might well interrupt before the students have finished their turn.

(4) **교사의 피드백**: explicit correction, recast, clarification request, elicitation, metalinguistic feedback, repetition

> S: I am very worried.
> T: Really? What are you worried about, Minjae?
> S: Math exam for tomorrow. I don't studied yesterday.
> T: You didn't study yesterday?
> S: No, I didn't studied.
> T: Please tell me why. What happened?
> S: I did volunteering all day long, So I don't had time to study.
> T: Well, Minjae, "don't had" is not the right past tense form.
> S: Uh, I didn't had time, time to study.

> *Ms. Park is talking with the students about what they did last Saturday.*
>
> T: What did you do last Saturday?
> S: Movie.
> T: Excuse me?
> S: I see a movie.
> T: You saw a movie?
> S: Yes, I see a movie.
> T: But you saw a movie LAST Saturday, and last Saturday is in the past, right?
> S: Oh, yes, right.
> T: The correct verb is SAW, not SEE.

(1) Excuse me?	clarification request
(2) You didn't study yesterday? / You saw a movie?	recast
(3) "don't had" is not the right past tense form / But you saw a movie LAST Saturday, and last Saturday is in the past, right?	metalinguistic feedback
(4) The correct verb is SAW, not SEE.	explicit correction

04 Constructivism - 의사소통 교수(CLT) 관점

학습자 중심의 교수(learner-centered instruction)를 강조하며, 학습자들은 자신이 갖고 있는 선험지식(schemata / schematic knowledge)을 토대로 새로운 지식을 재구조화해 받아들인다는 학습 관점이다. 즉, 학습자들이 동일한 지식을 제공받더라도 학습자 개인이 갖고 있는 선험지식에 따라 주어진 지식이 다른 양으로 이해되고 습득될 수 있다는 관점이다.

1 Functions

각 기능은 sentence level에서 파악하기 불가능하며, suprasentential (discourse) level에서 파악이 가능하다. 또한, 각 function들은 사용된 상황에 따라 숨은 의도(intended meaning)가 다르므로, social context에 따른 이해가 필요하다.

▶ **Functional Syllabus** contains a collection of the functions that are performed when language is used.

2 Discourse Analysis(담화 분석)

기능(function)은 suprasentential or discourse level에 존재하므로 담화상에서 언어가 사용되는 상황과 의미를 분석해야 한다. 따라서, 글(말)의 연속체인 담화를 분석함으로써, 문장(발화) 간의 관계에 따른 cohesion과 coherence를 파악하고자 한다.

(1) **Cohesion**: grammatical linkers, lexical linkers, cohesive device

Example

One day, Kyung-min noticed that one of her classmates did not bring his lunch box. So, she wanted to share her lunch box with him. However, he did not want to. All day she wondered why he didn't want to.

(2) **Coherence**: functionally sequenced

Example ①

Mom: This is a call for you. (Request)
Son : I'm in the bath. (Excuse)
Mom: OK. (Accept)
Request → Excuse → Accept

Example ②

Mom: Can you get the phone? (Request)
Son : Sorry, I can't. I'm in the bath. (Excuse)
Mom: OK. I'll get the phone. (Accept)

3 Conversation Analysis(대화 분석)

대화 분석은 대표적인 담화 분석으로, 교실 수업에서 말하기 지도 시 학생들에게 어떻게 대화가 시작되고 진행되는지에 대한 분석 및 지도가 이뤄질 수 있다.

(1) Attention-getting → Topic Nomination → Topic Development → Topic Termination

▶ **Gambit Strategies**
A gambit is a remark which you make to someone in order to start or continue a conversation: "*In my point of view...*" to express opinion or "*Sorry for interrupting...*" to interrupt someone's speaking.

▶ **Adjacency Pairs**
One of the most common structures to be defined through conversation analysis is the adjacency pair, which is a call and response type of sequential utterances spoken by two different people.

Ex *Offer/Refusal*
Sales clerk: Do you need someone to carry your packages out?
Customers: No thanks. I've got it

(2) **Question Types**: display question, referential question

Display questions are those where the information is already known by the teacher. On the other hand, **referential** questions are genuine questions to which the teacher does not know the answer and hence trigger authentic output from the students.

4 Classroom Discourse

(1) **IRE**: Initiation → Response → Evaluation

> *The teacher asks a learner for rules about use of the present perfect, the learner gives an answer, and the teacher says whether that is correct or not.*
>
> T: Hey, guys! Did you remember the form of the present perfect?
> S: Have + PP.
> T: That's right! Good job!

(2) **IRF**: Initiation → Response → Follow-up (Feedback)

> *In the classroom it can provide a useful framework for developing meaningful communication in a controlled form. For example, there is room for authentic input in an IRF dialogue such as:*
>
> T: How many brothers and sisters have you got?
> S: Two younger brothers and one elder sister.
> T: Wow, you have a big family. what good points are there if you have a big family?

5 Teaching Principles

(1) Learner-centered Instruction

It means methods of teaching that shift the focus of instruction from the teacher to the student. Also, it aims to develop learner autonomy and independence. Finally, it includes techniques that focus on or account for learners' needs, style, and goals.

(2) Schematic Knowledge

It plays a crucial role in the process of teaching and learning language skills (especially, listening and reading). For instance, Ms. Park wants to arrange pre-listening / reading activities that aims to facilitate students' comprehension of a text concerning *global warming* as follows: *T shows a video clip about global warming or T asks Ss to brainstorm about global warming.*

(3) Individual Difference

Students in class respond differently to the same stimuli. So, the same learning task may not be appropriate for all of our students because they have different proficiency levels. That is, higher-level students can do well without any problems but lower-level students can have a hard time completing the task.

(4) Whole Language Approach

It is an approach to, or attitude toward learning that sees language as a whole entity, and writing, speaking, reading, and listening should be integrated when learned.

(5) Personalization

It happens when activities allow students to use language to express their own ideas, feelings, preferences and opinions. Thus, it involves true communication, since learners communicate real information about themselves. For example, *the learners have read a text about sports. In pairs they talk about what their favourite sports are and whether they prefer to play or watch.*

6 Communicative Language Teaching & Task-based Instruction

Communicative language teaching sees meaningful communication as the goal whereas task-based learning takes it a bit further, so students need to communicate in order to achieve or do a meaningful task. Both acknowledge the importance of real authentic meaningful communication as a way to learn a language.

Possible Answers

p.029

Q1 While S1 is in Stage 5 of development, S2 has reached Stage 6.

Q2 S1 uses 'can' with various verbs, such as 'share' or 'speak,' to make requests. In contrast, S2 employs indirect requests, like 'I need more time to think' or 'Minho can do better than me'.

Chapter 02

Pedagogical Key Concepts

– 현 교실 수업의 주요 개념 및 원리 중심으로

01 Pedagogical Options

The three interface positions have their own pedagogical realisations: the non-interface position advocated the focus-on-meaning approach to teaching grammar, the strong interface position favoured the traditional focus-on-forms approach (a term coined by Long, 1991), and the weak interface position posited the focus-on-form approach (Long, 1991). The weak interface position and its pedagogical manifestation, namely the focus-on-form instruction, are currently supported as optimal integrative solutions to the interface debate and form-meaning interaction.

1 The Non-interface Position (Focus-on-meaning Approach)
– explicit knowledge can't convert to implicit knowledge

(1) Krashen's Monitor Model or Input Hypothesis

- The structure of language is acquired only through a large amount of exposure to sufficient amount of comprehensible input (*i+1*) which focuses on meaning rather than form.
- The central part of instruction should address developing implicit, meaning-based knowledge of language and no essential role is assigned to explicit knowledge of language forms. (zero option for grammar instruction)

(2) Giving Priority to Fluency over Accuracy

Instruction should, therefore, enable learners to fluently use language without any attention to the accuracy of forms. (the natural approach, the content-based instruction and the immersion programme)

(3) Criticism

Learners need something more than comprehensible input, and they should also produce comprehensible output.

2 The Strong Interface Position (Focus–on–forms Approach)
– explicit knowledge can convert to implicit knowledge

Learners should pay attention to language form and understand of the significance of the noticed input to be.

(1) Focus-on-forms Approach

The strong interface position intended to promote Learned Linguistic Knowledge which required learners to explicitly learn L2 forms. Simply put, L2 learning takes place with explicit focus-on-forms.

(2) Giving Prominence to Accuracy

Drawing upon the widely held belief that 'practice makes perfect', most advocates of this position argued that learning L2 forms is best achieved through a PPP procedure in which linguistic items were taught as part of a structural syllabus.

3 The Weak Interface Position (Focus–on–form Approach)

– explicit knowledge can actually convert to implicit knowledge, but, there are some constraints on how and when this can occur (integrative view)

(1) Focus-on-form Instruction

- This approach to teaching grammar aims at drawing learners' attention to some specific linguistic form through saliency or frequency of that form during meaning-based instruction or when form-based problems incidentally arise in lessons whose overriding focus is on meaning or communication.
- Both form and meaning / both explicit and implicit knowledge and both accuracy and fluency are all simultaneously taken into account.

(2) Noticing and Noticing the Gap

Explicit knowledge converts to implicit knowledge both directly and indirectly. Explicit knowledge directly changes to implicit knowledge through explicit rule presentation; besides, it is indirectly transformed to implicit knowledge through noticing (i.e. attention to some specific features in the input) and noticing the gap (i.e. comparing the targeted features in the input with existing mental grammar).

02 Interaction Hypothesis

1 Negotiation of Meaning (1) – 초기 입장에서 Comprehensible Input 강조

Through negotiation of meaning speakers go through to reach a clear understanding of each other by making input more comprehensible and modifying output more accurately.

(1) **Comprehension Check**: to determine whether the other speaker has understood a preceding message

> NNS: ...... can't speak girl. and why? because this this girl very angry also. *you know what I mean?*
> NS : yes.

(2) **Confirmation Check**: to seek confirmation of the other's preceding utterance through repetition, with rising intonation

> NS : did you get high marks?
> NNS: *Good grades?*
> NS : Yeah, did you get A in English?
> NNS: Oh no, in English, yes em B.

(3) **Clarification Request**: to seek assistance in understanding the other speaker's preceding utterance through questions, statements such as "I don't understand," or imperatives such as "Please repeat."

> NS : so you came here by yourself or did you come with friends?
> NNS: no no I - *what? what you say?*
> NS : did you come to the states with friends or did you come alone?
> NNS: no, alone - from Toronto.

Plus

Text Modification

Spoken language can be negotiated between the speaker and receiver as the language is generated, and the speaker can adapt the message according to their perception of the receiver's understanding and proficiency. However, for readers in a second language, the written input cannot be negotiated in the same way that oral input can be. In short, for negotiation to occur, the material must be adapted before it is received by the language learner (Hatch, 1983). This idea of adaptation or modification often conflicts with the notion of "authentic" input. However, because interaction between writer and reader is largely one-sided, with negotiation of the message depending on the reader's ability to correctly interpret and process the writer's message, pre-reading modifications are crucial in aiding comprehension.

1. Low frequent words are changed into high frequent words or added with linguistic information.

   ① **Original sentence**: The Just Society seems to have sprouted among other founding principles.

   ② **Simplified treatment**: The Just Society seems to have grown among other founding principles.

   ③ **Elaborated treatment**: The Just Society seems to have sprouted (started to grow) among other founding principles.

2. Complex sentences were shortened.

   ① **Original sentence**: Bills of rights, which were very popular in the eighteenth century, had been **affixed** to several state constitutions and promulgated elsewhere as well.

   ② **Modified sentence**: Bills of rights had been attached to several state constitutions.

In the Classroom

The original text is for 2nd year high school students.

Original

No sooner had my plane landed than I was charmed by Korea. I particularly like the outdoor street markets and the strength and openness of the people who work there.

(A)

When my plane landed I was charmed by Korea. I particularly like the outdoor street markets and the strength and openness of the people there.

(B)

No sooner had my plane landed than I was enthralled by Korea. I particularly like the outdoor street markets and the integrity and receptiveness of the people who work there.

The original text has been adapted to suit the students' English proficiency levels. (A) shows how input is simplified through syntactic modification to make the original text easier for the lower level students. (B) shows how input is adapted through lexical modification to make the original text more challenging for the upper level students.

2 Negotiation of Meaning (2)
– 후기 입장에서 Corrective Feedback (Comprehesible Output) 강조

When communication is difficult, interlocutors must "negotiate for meaning" and this negotiation is seen as the opportunity for language development. Merrill Swain (1985) extended this thinking when she proposed "the comprehensible output hypothesis." She observed that it is when learners must produce language that their interlocutor can understand that they are most likely to see the limits of their second language ability and the need to find better ways to express their meaning. The demands of producing comprehensible output, she hypothesized, "push" learners ahead in their development.

Ex L: What do you spend with your wife?
T: *What?*
L: What do you spend your extra time with your wife?
T: *Ah, you should say, 'how do you spend?'*
L: How do you spend.

(1) Repair

Repairs are variously classified as 'self-repair' (corrections, etc. made by speakers themselves responsible), vs. 'other-repair' (made by their interlocutors); as 'self-initiated' (made by a speaker without querying or prompting) vs. 'other-initiated' (made in response to querying or prompting).

Ex Min-su : I just don't see why everyone's always picking on Marie-Antoinette. I can so relate to her. She worked really hard to look that good, and people just don't appreciate that kind of effort. And I know the peasants were all *depressed*.
Min-ji : I think you mean *oppressed*.
Min-su : Whatever. They were cranky.

① **Self-initiated self-repair**: Repair is both initiated and carried out by the speaker of the trouble source.

② **Other-initiated self-repair**: Repair is carried out by the speaker of the trouble source but initiated by the recipient.

③ **Self-initiated other-repair**: The speaker of a trouble source may try and get the recipient to repair the trouble.

④ **Other-initiated other-repair**: The recipient of a trouble source turn both initiates and carries out the repair. This is closest to what is conventionally called 'correction.'

Plus

1. Discourse Model

The following shows an example of one of the routines used by two nonnative speakers to negotiate a nonunderstanding.

Table 1

Utterance Function	Example Utterance
Trigger	NNS1: My father now is retire.
Indicator	NNS2: retire?
Response	NNS1: Yes.
Reaction to Response	NNS1: Yes.

Table 2

Trigger	NNS: We didn't intend to bully him, because he looked so duty.
Signal (recast)	NS: dirty?
Response (uptake)	NNS: Yes, dirty.

2. Positive vs. Negative Evidence

① Positive Evidence: 학습자에게 제공되는 목표 언어의 정확하고 올바른 입력(well-formed sentences to which learners are exposed)

- The most obviously necessary requirement for learning
- It can be authentic or modified. If modified, it can be simplified or elaborated.
- 학습자들은 이와 같은 언어적 입력을 구어(spoken language), 문어(written language), 제스처와 같은 시각적 언어(visual language in the case of sign language) 등을 통해 받을 수 있다.

② Negative Evidence: 학습자의 발화의 부정확성에 대해 언급하는 정보 유형(information that is provided to learners concerning the incorrectness of an utterance)

- Pre-emptive: occurring before an actual error-as in a classroom context. 오류가 실제로 발생하기 이전에 제공되는 오류에 대한 정보를 가리킨다.
- Reactive: 실제 일어난 오류에 대한 교정적 정보로서, 명시적인 형태와 묵시적인 형태가 있다.

A

Options		Description
Reactive	A1. Implicit feedback	The teacher or another student responds to a student's error without directly indicating an error has been made, e.g., by means of a recast or a clarification request.
	A2. Explicit feedback	The teacher or another student responds to a student's error by directly indicating that an error has been made, e.g., by formally correcting the error or by using metalanguage.
Pre-emptive	B1. Student-initiated focus on form	A student asks a question about a linguistic form.
	B2. Teacher-initiated focus on form	The teacher gives advice about a linguistic form he/she thinks might be problematic or asks the students a question about the form.

B

Example 1

It is Monday morning and a group of students have just arrived for their English class. The teacher starts the class by asking the students about their weekend.

T : So what did you do this weekend?

S1 : I ran my first marathon!

T : Wow! Did you finish?

S1 : Yes, eventually.... It was actually a half-course marathon, but really challenging.

T : Way to go! *(turning to S2)* How about you?

S2 : I had gone to the park...

T : *You need to use the past simple when you say the things you did over the weekend.*

S2 : I has b..., I had?

T : Past simple. For example, I saw, I did, or I played...

S2 : Ah! I went to the park with my family last weekend.

T : Great! How was it? Did you and your family enjoy it?

S2 : Very much.

Example 2

Students are doing a communicative task with their conversation partner in their English class. The students are asked to set a date when they can do a project together. While students are checking the date, the teacher shuttles back and forth among the groups.

S1 : Teacher, *is it okay to just say December eighteen?*

T : December eighteen?

S1 : Yeah, like December eighteen or January seventeen.

S2 : You know, we need to fix the date we meet together, and we want to make sure the right way of saying dates.

T : Mmm. It's okay but it sounds a little casual. Usually December THE eighteenth or THE eighteenth of December.

S1 : Aha! December THE eighteenth.

T : Yeah, good.

T=teacher, S=student

(2) Criticism – Pushed Output and Modified Output

The interaction hypothesis suggests a number of ways in which interactions can contribute to language acquisition. More specifically, it suggests that when interactional modifications lead to comprehensible input via the decomposition and segmenting of input, acquisition is facilitated; that when learners receive feedback, acquisition is facilitated; and that when learners are pushed to reformulate their own utterances, acquisition is promoted.

Ex | NNS: I *go* cinema.
NS : *Uh?*
NNS: I *go* cinema *last night.*
NS : Oh, last night.

The above dialogue shows that the interaction has lead to successful communication, but that it does not contribute to the acquisition of the past tense, a morphological feature. Thus, successful communication takes place without the learner needing to modify his or her output by incorporating the past tense marker, showing that *not all pushed output is in fact modified.*

03 Scaffolding Hypothesis

1 Zone of the Proximal Development

It is defined as the space between what a learner can do without assistance and what a learner can do with adult guidance or in collaboration with more capable peers.

2 Scaffolding in the Classroom

One way in which others help the learner in language development within the ZPD is through scaffolding. It refers to verbal guidance which an expert provides to help a learner perform any specific task, or the verbal collaboration of peers to perform a task which would be too difficult for any one of them individually.

Scaffolded assistance can be provided by not only a teacher or more competent peer but also a peer of equal linguistic level, because even equal peers will have different strengths and weaknesses in their abilities, play different interactional roles, and employ working memory and selective attention in achieving communicative tasks. Peer interaction allows learners to learn vocabulary by helping each other in the search for appropriate words or suggesting alternative words. In phonology, learners improve their pronunciation by self-correction or by other correction by peers who notice their pronunciation problems. As for grammar, learners co-construct grammatical forms which they are not yet able to produce independently and notice not only their peer's errors but also, their own grammatical errors, thus benefiting from the syntactic reformulation process. Moreover, collective scaffolding suggests that more than two learners engaging in group work can provide assistance to peer learners and collaboratively construct target linguistic forms. Thus, learners can synthesize each other's partial knowledge and arrive at the correct syntactic construction in group work.

Example

Collaborative Dialogue (T ⇄ L Interaction)

S: I throw it-box. (*He points to a box on the floor.*)
T: You threw the box.
S: No, I threw in the box.
T: What did you throw in the box?
S: My... I... paint...
T: Your painting?
S: Painting?
T: You know... painting. (*The teacher makes painting movements on an imaginary paper.*)
S: Yes, painting.
T: You threw your painting in the box.
S: Yes, I threw my painting in box.

Collective Scaffolding (L ⇄ L Interaction)

Students are discussing classroom disciplines as a speaking task.

S1: We should do attention to what the teacher says.
S2: *do attention to?*
S3: We need to change the verb form. I think it's *pay*.
S4: Oh, yes, *pay attention to* sounds correct.
S1: So, we should **pay attention to** what the teacher says.

Memo

Chapter 03

Classroom Context

– syllabus, materials, activities, learner variables 중심으로

01 Syllabus

1 Structural Syllabus & Functional Syllabus

(1) Structural Syllabus

This type of syllabus contains a collection of the forms and structures, usually grammatical of the language. It covers nouns, verbs, adjectives, statements, questions, complex sentences, subordinate clauses, past tense and other aspects of language form such as pronunciation or morphology.

(2) Functional Syllabus

This type of syllabus contains a collection of the functions that are performed when language is used. It includes: *informing, agreeing, apologizing, requesting, promising, and so on.*

2 Situational Syllabus & Skill-based Syllabus

(1) Situational Syllabus

A situational syllabus contains a collection of real or imaginary situations in which language occurs or is used. It usually involves several participants who are engaged in some activities in a specific setting. The primary purpose is to teach the language that occurs in the situations. For examples: *seeing the dentist, buying a book at the book store, meeting a new student, asking directions in a new town, etc.*

(2) Skill-based Syllabus

The content of the language teaching is a collection of specific abilities that may play a part in using language. Skills are things that people must be able to do to be competent in a language, relatively independently of the situation or setting in which the language use can occur.

Point 1

While situational syllabi group functions together into specific settings of language use, skill-based syllabi group linguistic competencies (pronunciation, vocabulary, grammar, and discourse) together into generalized types of behavior, such as listening to spoken language for the main idea, writing well-formed paragraphs, giving effective oral presentations, and so on.

3 Task-based Syllabus & Content-based Syllabus

(1) Task-based Syllabus

Task-based syllabus contains a series of complex and purposeful tasks that the students want or need to perform with the language they are learning. Examples include: *applying for a job, talking with a social worker, getting housing information over the telephone*, and so on.

Task-based language teaching(TBLT) holds a central place in current second language acquisition research and also in language pedagogy. Some suggest there are six main steps in designing, implementing, and evaluating a TBLT program.

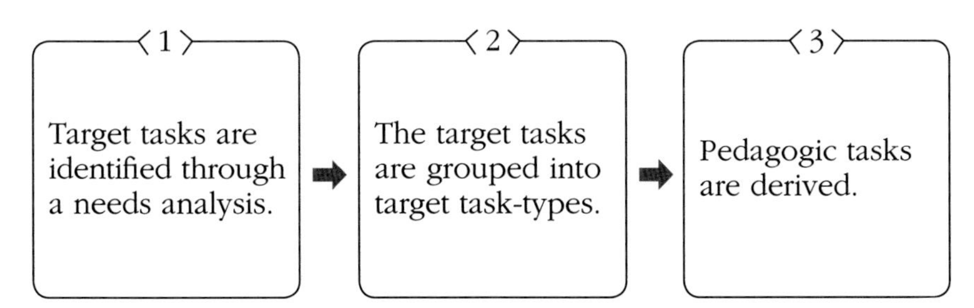

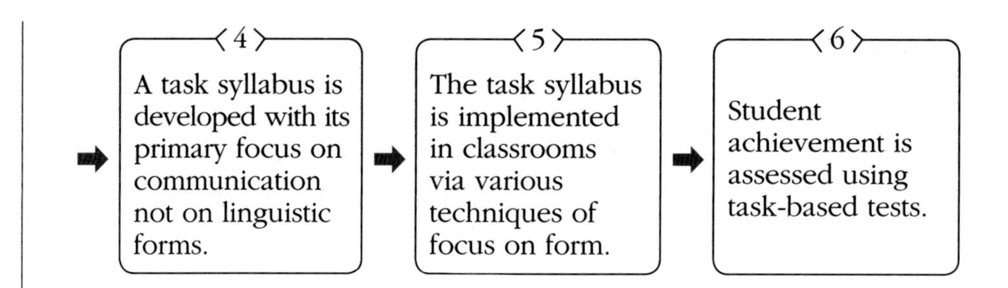

〈4〉
A task syllabus is developed with its primary focus on communication not on linguistic forms.
〈5〉
The task syllabus is implemented in classrooms via various techniques of focus on form.
〈6〉
Student achievement is assessed using task-based tests.

Point 2

Tasks integrate language (and other) skills in specific settings of language use. Task-based teaching differs from situation-based teaching in that while situational teaching has the goal of teaching the specific language content that occurs in the situation (a predefined product), task-based teaching has the goal of teaching students to draw on resources to complete some piece of work (a process). The students draw on a variety of language forms, functions, and skills, often in an individual and unpredictable way, in completing the tasks.

(2) Content-based Syllabus

The primary purpose of content-based syllabus is to teach some extent content or information using the language that the students are learning. The students are simultaneously language students and students of whatever content is being taught. The subject matter is primary, and language learning occurs incidentally to the content learning.

Point 3

A content-based language teaching is concerned with information, while task-based language teaching is concerned with communicative and cognitive process.

02 Teaching Materials

1 Interesting Text for the Learner

A teacher needs to skillfully exploit texts which offer high-interest content to help students acquire new language skills or become fluent in using the skills. That is, he or she selects texts that are inherently motivating—something about the content that makes learners interested to listen or read. (e.g. narratives that can stimulate readers or listeners' schema)

Activity

Which opening lines might be of the greatest general interest to secondary level students?

Text 1

Joanne works for the Lincoln Company. There are two shifts in the Lincoln Company, a day shift and a night shift. Joanne works the day shift. Her schedule is Tuesday through Saturday from 8 am to 5 pm. Her lunch time is 12 noon to 1 pm.

Text 2

Many, many years ago there was a very rich landlord who owned a lot of land and houses.

Discussion

Both texts are linguistically simple. However, something about the content in T2 make students more in more interested in reading;
Why? T2 begins with a recognizable kind of narrative and students engage with the text by activating a relevant schema. On the other hand, T1 is not what we perceive as a "story", because events are unexceptional.

2 Authentic & Simplified Text

Authentic text is assumed to provide more natural language and more naturally occurring cohesion than the simplified text which excludes unnecessary & distracting, idiosyncratic styles to help learners easily comprehend the text. However, simplified text is thought to benefit low level learners because it contains increased redundancy & amplified explanation as well as it is lexically, syntactically, and rhetorically less difficult than authentic text.

Scene: Teacher's office. Ms. Park and Mr. Choi sit at a table with textbooks and lesson plans.

T1 : Hi, Mr. Choi. I wanted to discuss the use of authentic versus simplified texts for our 3rd graders. Authentic texts expose students to real-world language, but many struggle with them. Simplified texts are easier, but they often feel unnatural. What do you think?

T2 : I agree. Authentic texts are engaging, but if students feel lost, they lose motivation. Simplified texts help build skills, but they don't always sound real. We need a balance.

T1 : What if we combine both? We could introduce authentic texts in stages. Start with vocabulary prep and guiding questions, then let them try the authentic text.

T2 : That's smart. We could offer simpler versions for students who need it and link simplified texts to authentic texts on similar topics. For example, start with a story on recycling, then move to a real article on environmental issues.

T1 : Exactly! We can also use graded readers early in the semester to build confidence, then transition to more challenging texts later. Short, naturally accessible texts like blog posts or social media entries could be great starters too.

T2 : I love that. They're authentic but not overwhelming. We can add follow-up activities like summaries or discussions to check comprehension.

T1 : Great! Let's split the work. I'll collect blog entries and social media samples. You can find short articles and scripts. Let's review next week.

T2 : Sounds like a plan. This approach will boost their confidence and prepare them for real-world English. See you next week, Ms. Park!

T1=Ms. Park, T2=Mr. Choi

3 Material Adaptation

Materials can be adapted by using different techniques such as *adding*, *deleting*, *modifying*, and *reordering*. For example, we can add materials when a language item is not covered sufficiently in the original materials. Materials that are too easy or difficult for learners can be deleted. Modifying can be used to make them more relevant to students' interests and backgrounds and to restructure classroom management. Reordering the sequence of activities is another technique, which includes separating items and regrouping them.

Consider the original material extracted from a grammar exercise book and its adapted version below. In the adapted version, the original exercise has been adapted by using the *modifying* technique.

Original Material

❶ Individual Work Describe the man's routine in four sentences.

____

____

❷ Individual Work Answer the following questions.

What time do you wake up?

What do you usually wear to work?

What do you usually cook for dinner?

Adapted Material

❶ Individual Work Describe the student's routine in four sentences.

____

____

❷ Pair Work Work in pairs and ask each other the following questions.

What time do you wake up?

What do you usually wear on school days?

What do you usually eat for dinner?

03 Classroom Activities: Accuracy vs. Fluency in the EFL Classroom

Our learners want to learn to speak English in order to communicate. And if we boil it down to one thing, communication is about being understood. To get all fancy and technical, communicative competence is being able to make use of vocabulary and grammar and their rules appropriately in order to convey a message. So while of course there is a need for a certain amount of accuracy, fluency can be seen to play a bigger role in effective communication.

In your EFL lessons, try not to focus on accuracy to the detriment of fluency. Allow sufficient time for fluency activities, and this includes time for adequate preparation on the part of your students. You still need to scaffold the activity but you don't need to give them step-by-step instructions for what they should say. If your activity is appropriate and relevant for your students, this should actually come naturally to your students, as they will have a purpose for communicating.

In the Classroom

Case 1

(a) Write or say statements about John, modelled on the following example:

John drinks tea, but he doesn't drink coffee.

① like: ice cream / cake
② speak: English / Italian
③ enjoy: playing football / playing chess

(b) The class is given a dilemma situation ('You have seen a good friend cheating in an important test') and asked to recommend a solution.

(c) Choose someone you know very well, and write down their name. Now compose true statements about them according to the following model:

He/She likes ice cream; or He/She doesn't like ice cream.
① enjoy: playing tennis ② drink: wine ③ speak: Polish

(d) Practising conditional clauses, learners are given the cue *If I had a million dollars*, and are asked to suggest, in speech or writing, what they *would do*.

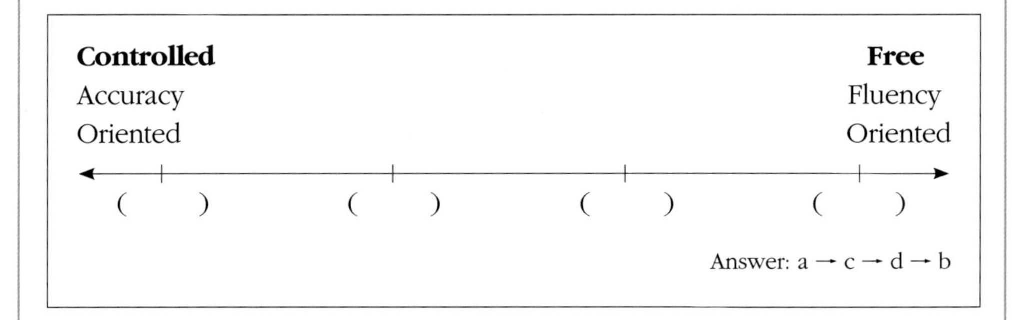

Case 2

An information-gap task is a technique in which learners are missing the needed information to complete a task or solve a problem, and they have to communicate with their classmates to fill in the gaps. For example, learners share their information to complete a class timetable, or learners need to share information about their families and then draw each other's family trees. An opinion-gap task requires the learners to give their own personal preference, feeling, or attitude to complete a task. For example, a social problem such as "divorce" can be given to the learners and be asked to give their ideas on how to tackle it. A reasoning-gap task refers to the new information that are derived by the students through inference, deduction, practical reasoning, or perception of relationships or patterns. For example, someone has to think of an object, a thing, or an animal, for "Twenty Questions." And then, everyone else has to guess what it is.

Activity Procedure

Step 1	• T places various information on a different job in each of the four corners in the classroom. (Each corner is labelled with a different letter, A, B, C, or D.) • T assigns individual Ss a letter (A, B, C, or D) in order to create four groups of four Ss, each of which is a base group composed of A to D.
Step 2	• T provides Ss in each base group with handouts. (Each handout has a set of questions about four different jobs.) • T helps Ss understand that they should be interdependent upon one another not only for their own learning but also for the learning of others throughout the activity. • T informs Ss which corner to go to based on their letter in order to form four different expert groups.
Step 3	• Ss move to their expert groups and find out information about different jobs through discussions and answer the questions on the handouts. • T circulates within the groups and makes sure each of the Ss has all the answers.
Step 4	• Ss return to their initial base groups and exchange the information through discussing what they learned in the expert groups. • All the base groups present their findings to the whole class and decide which job they would like most.

T=teacher, S=student

Why use jigsaw?

- It helps build comprehension.
- It encourages cooperative learning among students.
- It helps improve listening, communication, and problem-solving skills.

04 Classroom Tools

Instructional Modes

- In–person: Students will meet face to face in the classroom on a set schedule.
- Remote Synchronous: Students will meet face to face online on a set schedule.
- Remote Asynchronous: Students will not meet face to face but will interact online.
- Combination: any combination of the above modes

1 Class Content and Lecture Delivery Tools

Class and lecture content can be delivered synchronously or asynchronously—choosing which tool is right for your course will depend on your course goals and instructional mode. Asynchronous delivery of content can be used in courses that primarily meet face-to-face as a way of providing content to students before class and reserving in-class time for students to discuss what they learned.

(1) Synchronous Tools – Zoom

Synchronous audio/video conferencing tool with ability to share screens, chat, etc... Integration with Canvas make Zoom easy to schedule and use with your academic courses.

(2) Asynchronous Tools – Canvas Modules / Canvas Pages

Modules is a Canvas-native tool that allows content to be organized in a linear progression with "Next" and "Previous" button navigation to allow students to quickly navigate material and activities in the order the instructor intended. Canvas Pages are static content pages where instructors can add/embed content for students and link out to other content both within Canvas and beyond.

2 Instructional Tools

(1) Concordancing

Computers are expert at storing and sorting large amounts of information. Concordancing programs are increasingly being used in the language classroom. A concordance is a type of index that searches for occurrences of a word or combinations of words, affixes, phrases, or structures within a corpus, and can show the immediate context. The output from a concordance search can be used in the preparation of teaching materials, such as grammar and vocabulary activities.

(2) MUDs & MOOs

Multi-user domains, MUDs, or multi-user domains object-oriented, MOOs, are both synchronous and asynchronous in form. They are typically text-based virtual spaces that rely on the ability of the user to describe environments, and interact with those environments. By navigating through space, students create stories in an impromptu fashion. They hold dialogs, open boxes, find secret messages, and move through cyberspace. Aside from provoking learners to use language in both planned ways (i.e., writing) and unplanned ways, it also satisfies the psychological correlate of searching for information, critical in the learning process.

(3) Voice Recognition & Production

Voice recognition refers to the capability of an automatic-speech recognition (ASR) software to accept spoken dictation. The current state-of-the-art ASR technology sheds light on the possibility of incorporating CALL for the pseudooral communication in class. In addition, the current text-to-speech(TTS) technology has made it possible to develop speech production programs that read text aloud. ASR and TTS have great potential for English teaching and performance testing.

(4) Learning Apps

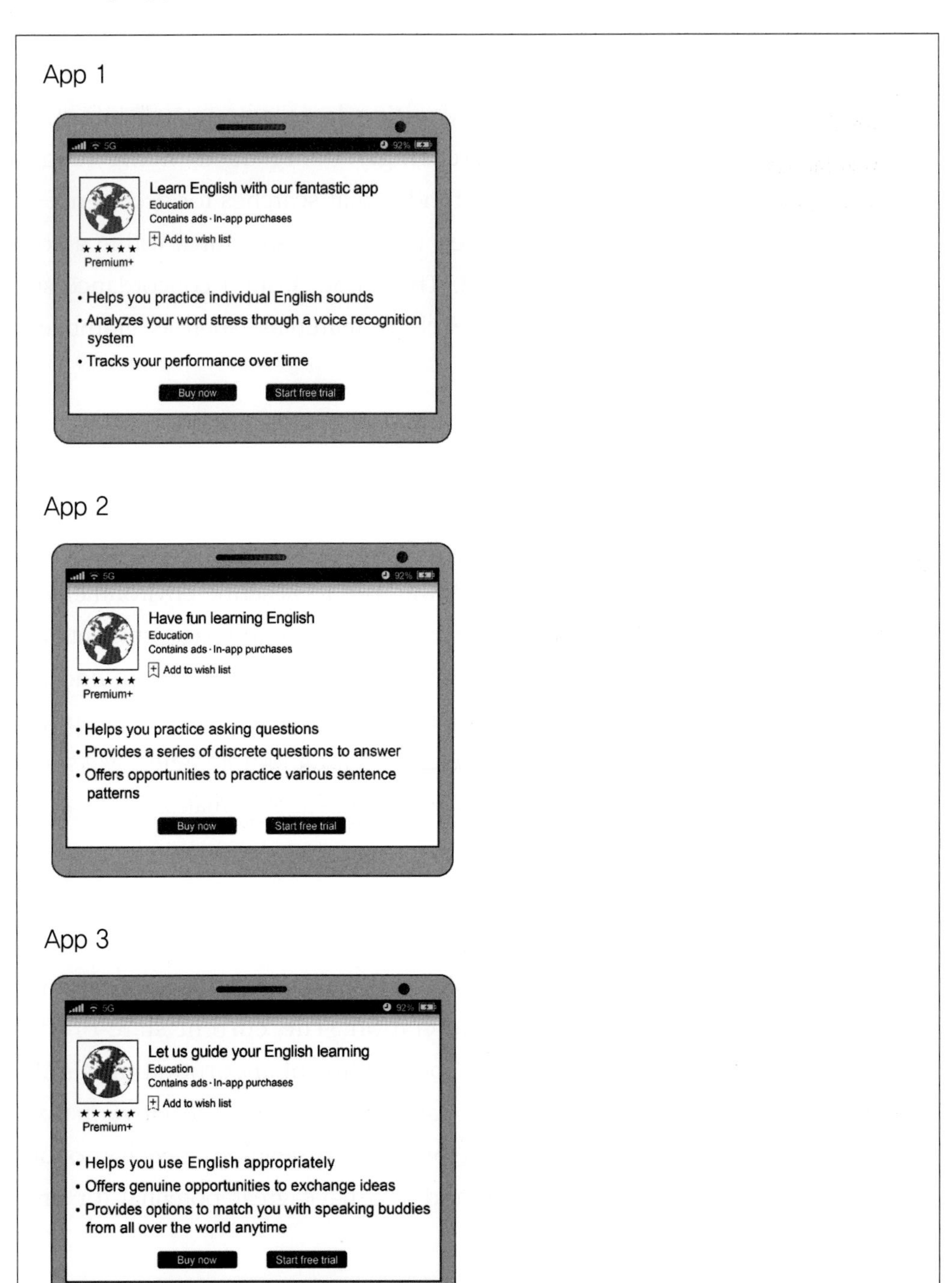

App 1
Learn English with our fantastic app
Education
Contains ads · In-app purchases
Add to wish list
Premium+
• Helps you practice individual English sounds
• Analyzes your word stress through a voice recognition system
• Tracks your performance over time
Buy now
Start free trial
App 2
Have fun learning English
Education
Contains ads · In-app purchases
Add to wish list
Premium+
• Helps you practice asking questions
• Provides a series of discrete questions to answer
• Offers opportunities to practice various sentence patterns
Buy now
Start free trial
App 3
Let us guide your English learning
Education
Contains ads · In-app purchases
Add to wish list
Premium+
• Helps you use English appropriately
• Offers genuine opportunities to exchange ideas
• Provides options to match you with speaking buddies from all over the world anytime
Buy now
Start free trial

(5) CAT(Computer Adaptive Testing)

A test taker is sitting in front of a computer, examining some sample items, and quickly learns how to take computer-based tests. Meanwhile, a computer program begins to 'guess' his ability level, and keeps trying to 'match' the test with his current language ability. This is how this technique works.

The computer program usually begins by showing an item of moderate difficulty, for example, an item that the test taker has a fifty percent chance of getting right. If he gets this item right, the computer program reestimates his ability level in real time and shows either an item of equal difficulty or a slightly more challenging item. If the test taker gets his first item wrong, however, the computer program will show either an item of equal or slightly lesser difficulty. The test taker keeps taking the test until, for instance, he gets several items wrong in a row. To put it another way, the computer program repeats its matching work until it collects enough information to determine the test taker's current English ability level.

➡ The testing procedure described above enables us to make more individualized and educationally useful tests. It can also provide test takers with a better test-taking experience with fewer items, and with increased precision. This testing procedure is commonly referred to as computer adaptive testing / computerized adaptive testing.

3 Realia – Why use realia in class?

The main advantage of using real objects in the classroom is to make the learning experience more memorable for the learner. To give a couple of simple examples, if you are going to teach vocabulary of fruit and vegetables it can be much more affective for students if they can touch, smell and see the objects at the same time as hearing the new word. This would appeal to a wider range of learner styles than a simple flashcard picture of the fruit or vegetable.

Example

Tourist Information

- Gather some *city/town maps* from the tourist information bureau wherever you are. Use them to create role plays that could happen with English-speaking visitors to the town or city. Give students a scenario for them to build a role play out of.
- Collect *brochures* of places of interest (in English if possible but not vital) and ask students to use them to plan a trip for a group of students who are coming to their town for a week. They can plan the itinerary, work out the budget, etc.

T : Today, we are going to read a text about cooking. Are you interested in cooking?
Ss: Yeah.
T : Great. Let's study today's key words first. (*The teacher brings out kitchen utensils from a box.*) I brought some cooking utensils.
S1 : Wow! Are those yours?
T : Yes, they are. I use them when I cook. (*showing a saucepan*) You've seen this before, right?
S2: Yes. My mom uses that when she makes jam.
T : Good. Do you know what it's called in English?
S3: It's a saucepan.
T : Excellent, it's a saucepan. Everyone, repeat after me. Saucepan.
Ss: Saucepan.
T : And, (*showing a cutting board*) what's this in English?
S4: A board?

T : Right, it's a cutting board. Good job. I also brought a couple of things from my refrigerator. This is one of my favorite vegetables. (*The teacher holds up an eggplant.*)
S5: Umm.... It's an egg...
T : Nice try! It's an eggplant.

T=teacher, S=student

4 Languge Teaching Principles

A

In designing activities for cultural instruction, it is important to consider the purpose of the activity, as well as its usefulness for teaching language and culture in an integrative fashion. The most basic issue in cross-cultural education is increasing the degree to which language and culture are integrated. Several suggestions for dealing with this issue are as follows:

1. Use cultural information when teaching vocabulary. Teach students about the cultural connotations of new words.
2. Present cultural topics in conjunction with closely related grammatical features whenever possible. Use cultural contexts for language-practice activities, including those that focus on particular grammatical forms.
3. Make good use of textbook illustrations or photos. Use probing questions to help students describe the cultural features of the illustrations or photos.
4. In group activities, use communication techniques for cultural instruction, such as discussions and role-plays.
5. Teach culture while involving the integration of the four language skills. Do not limit cultural instruction to lecture or anecdotal formats.

B

Lesson 4. World-famous Holidays

Objectives	Students will be able to 1. introduce world-famous holidays using *–er than* and 2. perform activities related to the holidays to deepen their understanding of diverse cultures.

Development	Step 1	• T asks Ss to speak out about anything related to the pictures in the textbook on p. 78. • T asks Ss some questions to elicit their ideas about what cultural features they see in the pictures of world-famous holidays. • Ss tell each other about the cultural differences among the holidays based on the pictures.
	Step 2	• T tells Ss about the origins of the world-famous holidays in detail. • T explains the cultural characteristics of those holidays. • T shares his experiences related to the holidays, and Ss listen to T's stories.
	Step 3	• T has Ss listen to a story about the world-famous holidays, and underline the expressions of comparative forms in the story on p. 79. • T talks with Ss about the meanings and functions of the expressions based on the cultural characteristics of the holidays. • T asks Ss, in pairs, to search the Internet for more information about cultural differences among the holidays and to describe the differences using comparative forms.

	Step 4	• T introduces new words in the story on the screen. • T explains the meanings of the words (*traditional, adapting, polite, etc.*), comparing them with their synonyms and/or antonyms. • Ss note the words and memorize them using mnemonic devices.
	Step 5	• T has Ss sit in groups of four, and choose one distinct aspect of the world-famous holidays, such as costume, food, and festivals. • Ss write a culture capsule in groups about the differences. • T gives preparation time, and each group performs a role-play based on the culture capsule in front of their classmates.

T=teacher, Ss=students

5 Action Research

Teacher Log

Skill-integration is considered more and more important in modern language learning, but I found that at any one time I was almost always teaching just one skill in isolation. As part of my development as a teacher, I wanted to integrate multiple language skills and pursue a more real-life style of communication. To do this, I first investigated my own class practices. I video-recorded eight lessons. After reviewing the video files, I found that in six lessons I taught only one skill. In the other two, I was only able to integrate listening and speaking but never reading or writing. I drew up a plan to integrate language skills more often. What I did was implement the project-based learning approach so that students could collaborate in groups to advance their projects. I conducted the experiments over the second half of the semester and gathered the data. Then, I video-recorded another eight lessons toward the end of the semester to test the effectiveness of the measure I had implemented. After I analyzed the videos and the data, the results were as follows: two of the lessons showed the integration of speaking and reading skills, two other lessons integrated reading and writing skills, and one lesson integrated all four skills! Based on these results, I feel the approach really improved my teaching practice and my ability to teach students with the four skills in an integrated fashion.

➡ The log above describes how the teacher addresses a problem in the classroom and resolves it through a systematic process of inquiry. Sometimes referred to as teacher research or classroom research, action research is considered an important part of self-reflective teacher development. It usually involves four steps: planning, acting, observing, and reflecting. Its major goal is to improve both student learning and teaching effectiveness.

05 Learner Strategies

Data Analysis

Read the passages in <A> and <B> and follow the directions.

A

Metacognitive awareness of reading strategies is considered a conscious procedure utilized by readers to enhance text comprehension and encourage active reading.

Understanding its importance, Ms. Yu, a high school English teacher, used the Metacognitive Awareness of Reading Strategy Questionnaire to measure students' awareness on three categories of reading strategies. These include Global Reading Strategies (GLOB), Support Reading Strategies (SUP), and Problem-Solving Strategies (PROB). She also interviewed her students after the survey.

The Metacognitive Awareness of Reading Strategy Questionnaire

Category	Item	1	2	3	4	5
GLOB	G1. I have a purpose in mind when I read.					
	G2. I think about what I know to help me understand what I read.					
	G3. While reading, I decide what to read and what to ignore.					
	G4. I take an overall view of the text to see what it is about before reading it.					
	…					

SUP	S1. I paraphrase what I read to better understand it.					
	S2. I take notes while reading to help me understand what I read.					
	S3. While reading, I translate from English into my native language.					
	S4. I use reference materials (e.g., a dictionary) to help me understand what I read.					
	…					
PROB	P1. When the text is unclear, I re-read it to increase my understanding.					
	P2. I try to guess the meaning of unknown words or phrases.					
	P3. I adjust my reading speed according to what I am reading.					
	P4. I try to visualize information to help understand what I read.					
	…					

Note: 1=never, 2=occasionally, 3=sometimes, 4=usually, 5=always

B

Based on the survey results, Ms. Yu conducted interviews with the students who reported low ratings in the survey. Parts of the interview excerpts are below. One of the interview questions was "Do you feel challenged while reading?" After the interview, Ms. Yu identified reading strategies that students need to promote their active reading skills.

Interview Excerpts

S1 : "I thought reading was just about understanding the words. When I don't understand something, I tend to skip over it. I think if I try to draw a picture in my mind when I'm not sure, I'll understand texts much better."

S2 : "I usually analyze texts sentence-by-sentence until I fully understand them. After checking my low ratings on the questionnaire, I found that reading selectively may help me become a more efficient reader."

Note: S=student

Q1 Identify the TWO items of reading strategies in <A> that Ms. Yu may apply to her reading instruction in relation to <B>.

Q2 Explain your answers, respectively, with evidence from <B>.

>> Possible Answers p.085

06 Mixed-ability Class

Every teacher has struggled with a mixed-ability class. That is, a class that is comprised of students of different levels of skill and competence. Some students learn fast, others learn slowly. Some students have a lot of knowledge, others seem to ignore the basic concepts. Teaching to the "average" leaves everybody unsatisfied: some will feel anxious because you are going too fast, some will get bored because you are going too slowly!

1 Same Ability Grouping (Like-ability Grouping)

Putting students of similar ability into small groups.

Task Type

Tiered task의 보다 간단한 형태로 학생들의 수준을 두 단계로 나눠 동일한 과업을 진행하되, 교사가 과업의 support를 다르게 제공한다. Dual-choice gapfill이 이에 속한다.

The Dead Sad Animal Rap	MISSING WORDS
Listen to the rap. What are the missing words? Humans... ⓐ ... the dear old dodo, It was... ⓑ ... It couldn' fly Humans... ⓒ ... all the passenger pigeons From the... ⓓ ... American sky.	killed / shot easy / simple hunted / shot south / north

As they listen, weaker students circle one of the words in the box to fill each gap. Stronger students get the same task sheet, but with the missing words box cut off. The task is therefore more challenging for them.

2 Mixed Level Grouping (Cross-ability Grouping)

Students with various levels of academic ability may be paired or placed in the same group.

Task Type

보다 간단한 형태의 bias task의 유형은 jigsawed gapfill의 형태이다. 주로 노래(song)나 이야기(short episode)를 들려주고 학생들에게 요약된 복사본을 주되, 학생들의 수준에 따라 higher-level students(Task sheet A)에게는 보다 많은 빈칸으로 된 복사본을 주고 weaker students(Task sheet B)에게는 빈칸이 상대적으로 적은 복사본을 제공하도록 한다. 이때 각 복사본 A, B의 빈칸은 서로 다른 장소가 지워져 있어야 한다.

The simplicity or complexity of the words you gap can also make the task easier or more difficult. A positive feature of this kind of bias activity is that because the jigsawed gaps are in different places, students are not necessarily aware of who has more gaps and who has fewer.

Plus

There are both positive and negative sides to grouping students. One positive side is that the lesson can be easier to plan and manage in some ways since the teacher does not have such a wide range of abilities to deal with. On the other hand to separate the slow learners can do harm to their social and emotional difficulties because by being placed in a "slow class" they can think of themselves as different, difficult, inferior or other negative terms.

3 Classroom Data

Advanced Level	Intermediate-Low Level
T : Last class, we learned how to make passive forms. Today, we'll learn when it's better to use the passive form instead of the active one. Suppose that someone broke into your apartment and you found your laptop was missing. What would you say about your laptop?	T : Last class, we talked about the way to say that something was done. Today, we'll see why people say, "Something was done," rather than say, "Someone did something." Imagine this. Someone broke into your apartment. You couldn't find your computer. It was gone! What would you say about your computer?
S1 : I would say, "My laptop was stolen."	S1 : I would say, "My computer was stolen."
T : That's right. Do you know who stole it?	T : That's right. Do you know who stole it?
S2 : No, I don't.	S2 : No, I don't.
T : Correct. Let's do another example. People constructed the Pyramids in ancient times, but you don't know exactly who constructed them. What would you say about the Pyramids?	T : Correct. Let's do another example. People built the Pyramids long ago. But you do not know exactly who built them. What would you say about the Pyramids?
S3 : The Pyramids were constructed in ancient times.	S3 : The Pyramids were built long ago.
T : Great. Can anyone tell us when passive sentences are preferred to their corresponding active sentences?	T : Great. So we can say the same idea two ways. We can say, "People built the Pyramids long ago." Or, "The Pyramids were built long ago." Now, when is it better to say, "The Pyramids were built long ago"?
Ss : When we don't know who did something.	Ss : When we don't know who built them.

T : Good. Let's go through a passage together. Try to understand the passage, while also paying attention to the passive forms used in the passage.

Task

Step 1

T : I'm going to read you the passage twice. First, I'll read it at normal speed and then I'll read it again as slowly as possible. As you listen, write down as many words and phrases as possible.

> Have you ever seen the Pyramids of Egypt? Have you ever wondered why they were built and how they were built? The Pyramids were built because the kings wanted to live after they died. They thought why they would live after they died. The Pyramids were constructed on the west side of Nile River. They were built there because the sun rises in the east and sets in the west. They believed why the king and the sun god would be born and born again, just like the sun. The Pyramids were very difficult to build, but the whole world can enjoy them.

T : Good. Let's go through a passage together. Try to understand the passage. Let's see if you can find any sentences like "The Pyramids were built long ago."

Task

Step 1

T : I am going to read you the passage twice. Both times, I will read it very slowly and clearly. As you listen, write down any words you hear.

> Have you ever seen the Pyramids of Egypt? Have you ever wondered why they were built and how they were built? The Pyramids were built because the kings wanted to live after they died. They thought why they would live after they died. The Pyramids were constructed on the west side of Nile River. They were built there because the sun rises in the east and sets in the west. They believed why the king and the sun god would be born and born again, just like the sun. The Pyramids were very difficult to build, but the whole world can enjoy them.

Step 2 T : Now, in groups of three, share your notes and see whether your group can come up with its own version of the text. Once your group has reconstructed the text, check it to make sure the meaning is similar to the text you heard. Also check it carefully for grammatical mistakes.	Step 2 T : Now, let's rewrite the text. First, in groups of three, put together all the words that each member heard. Then, working in your group, try to make sentences with those words. And then compare your group's sentences with other groups' sentences. Using all the sentences available, rewrite the text. And check it to make sure the meaning is similar to the text I read.
Step 3 T : Now, I'll pass out the original text that I read to you. Compare your group's text with the original one. How is the original different from yours? Look at both content and passive forms. And then make a presentation about the differences you've found between the two texts.	Step 3 T : Now, I will give you the original text. On the text, I've already underlined some parts. [Only the passive forms in the text are underlined.] Mark the parts in your group's text that you think match those underlined parts. Make your group's text as similar as possible to the original text.

Possible Answers

p.077

Q1 Ms. Yu may instruct S2s to "decide what to read and what to ignore" from G3 and guide S1s to "visualize information" from P4.

Q2 Ms. Yu can encourage S2s to focus on reading selectively rather than analyzing texts sentence by sentence. Additionally, she may help S1s visualize(picture) what they read to enhance comprehension.

Part 02

Practical Classroom Teaching and Learning

Chapter 01

How to Teach the Receptive Skills

01 Spoken Language & Written Language

1 Main Difference

Spoken Language	Written Language
involves speaking and listening skills	involves reading and writing skills
more informal and simple	more formal and complex
contains repetitions, incomplete sentences, interruptions, and corrections	more grammatically correct and contains long sentences in complex tenses

With the exception of scripted speeches, spoken language tends to be full of incomplete sentences, repetitions, interruptions, and corrections. Speakers also use gestures, tone, pitch, volume, etc. to create additional meaning in spoken language. Some forms and informal grammatical structures are also specific to spoken language. For example, words and phrases like 'my bad', 'y'know', 'busted', 'ain't' etc. which are sometimes used in spoken language, are rarely used in written language.

Written language is typically more formal, complex and intricate than spoken language. It may contain longer sentences in complex tenses. However, some forms of written language like instant messages and informal letters are closer to spoken language. Written language can make use of features like punctuation, headings, layouts, colors, etc. to make a message clearer. Since written language does not receive immediate feedback, it should be very clear and unambiguous.

Coherence	Cohesion
• logical organization of ideas • appropriate paragraphing • clear progression	• range of cohesive devices(=transition signals) • cohesive devices used appropriately (not too many / few) • referencing is clear • substitution is used as needed

2 Classroom Text Examples

(1) Spoken Text

① Interpersonal / Interactional language function

Minhee : Hey, how's it going?
Jungnam : I'm good, thanks! How about you?
Minhee : Doing well, just a bit tired from work. Wanna grab a coffee later?
Jungnam : Sounds great! Let's do it.

This exchange illustrates the interpersonal function of language as it involves maintaining social relationships, expressing feelings, and coordinating plans. The primary purpose here is not just to exchange information but to engage socially and show interest in each other's well-being.

② Transactional language function

Customer : I'd like to buy a ticket to New York, please.
Ticket Agent : Sure, one-way or round-trip?
Customer : Round-trip.
Ticket Agent : Okay, that'll be $250. Would you like to pay by card or cash?
Customer : Card, please.

In this exchange, the language is focused on the transaction—the exchange of goods or services (in this case, purchasing a ticket). The purpose is to convey specific information and achieve a particular outcome, rather than to build a social relationship.

(2) Written Text

Recently, I engaged in a conversation with a friend who expressed **his** distress over receiving offensive messages online. **This situation** is a stark reminder of the pervasive issue of cyberbullying that affects many individuals. The impact on victims can be profound, leading to feelings of heartbreak and helplessness. **Thus**, we should address this issue head-on. One immediate step we can take to prevent the spread of cyberbullying is to refrain from posting or spreading rumors about others. **This simple yet effective action** can significantly reduce the number of cyberbullying incidents and foster a more positive online environment.

Cohesion:

1. Pronouns: The use of "his" in "expressed his distress" and "This situation" refers back to the friend and the described situation, maintaining subject continuity.
2. Conjunctions: "Thus"
3. Linking Phrases: "This situation is a stark reminder" and "One immediate step we can take" use linking phrases to connect ideas smoothly.
4. Repetition: The concept of "cyberbullying" is repeated, reinforcing the central theme and linking different parts of the text through a common topic.

Coherence:

1. Logical Progression: The text starts with a personal anecdote, moves to the broader issue of cyberbullying, discusses its impact, and concludes with a suggested action. This logical flow of information from specific to general and then to solutions helps the reader easily follow the argument.
2. Thematic Unity: The entire passage maintains focus on the theme of cyberbullying and its mitigation, ensuring that all sentences contribute to this overarching topic.
3. Cause and Effect: The text outlines a cause(receiving offensive messages) and its effect(feelings of heartbreak and helplessness), followed by a proposed solution(refraining from posting/spreading rumors). This cause-and-effect relationship enhances the coherence by showing how different parts of the text are related in terms of content and logic.

Together, these cohesive devices and coherent structure ensure that the text is unified, logically organized, and easy to understand, demonstrating how individual sentences and ideas are connected to present a clear and compelling argument against cyberbullying.

3 Cohesive Devices, Transitional Markers, and Discourse Markers

In teaching writing, the terms cohesive devices, transitional markers, and discourse markers are often used to describe various linguistic tools that help structure and connect ideas in a text. While they are related, they serve distinct functions within writing.

(1) Cohesive Devices

Cohesive devices are elements of language that link different parts of a text together, creating a sense of unity and coherence. They include a broad range of tools that ensure a text flows smoothly and that ideas are connected logically.

Example

- Reference: Using pronouns or determiners to refer back to something previously mentioned (e.g., "John went to the store. He bought some milk.").
- Substitution: Replacing a word or phrase with another to avoid repetition (e.g., "I need a pen. Do you have one?").
- Ellipsis: Omitting parts of a sentence when they are understood from the context (e.g., "She can play the piano, and he can too [play the piano].").
- Conjunctions: Words that join clauses or sentences (e.g., and, but, because, although).
- Lexical Cohesion: Repetition of words, use of synonyms, or related terms to connect ideas (e.g., "The car was fast. The vehicle sped down the road.").

(2) Transitional Markers

Transitional markers (or transitional words/phrases) are specific types of cohesive devices that signal relationships between sentences or paragraphs. They guide the reader through the logical progression of ideas, indicating shifts, contrasts, additions, or conclusions.

Example

- Addition: Moreover, Furthermore, Additionally (e.g., "She loves painting. Additionally, she enjoys sculpting.").
- Contrast: However, On the other hand, Nevertheless (e.g., "He studied hard. However, he didn't pass the exam.").
- Cause and Effect: Therefore, Consequently, As a result (e.g., "It was raining. Therefore, we stayed indoors.").
- Sequence: First, Next, Finally (e.g., "First, we will review the assignment. Next, we will begin writing.").

(3) Discourse Markers

Discourse markers are words or phrases used to organize spoken or written language, particularly in conversation or extended discourse. They help manage the flow of communication, indicating boundaries, emphasizing points, or signaling the speaker's attitude. While they do overlap with transitional markers, discourse markers are broader in function and often found in spoken language.

Example

- Organizing: Now, Well, So, Anyway (e.g., "So, as I was saying, we need to start the project.").
- Emphasizing: Actually, In fact, Certainly (e.g., "Actually, I think we should reconsider our plan.").
- Hesitation or Pausing: Um, Uh, You know (e.g., "Um, I'm not sure about that.").
- Changing the Topic: By the way, Incidentally (e.g., "By the way, did you hear about the new policy?").

Distinguishing the Concepts in a Classroom Context

- **Cohesive devices** are taught to help students understand how to create unity in their writing by connecting ideas at the sentence and paragraph level. They are foundational for writing coherent texts.
- **Transitional markers** are emphasized when teaching students to structure essays, arguments, or narratives, helping them signal the logical progression and relationships between different sections of their writing.
- **Discourse markers** are often introduced when focusing on spoken language or when teaching more informal writing styles, such as personal reflections, dialogues, or speeches. They are crucial for making communication more natural and organized, especially in conversation.

In summary, while all three concepts contribute to the clarity and flow of language, cohesive devices are the broadest category, encompassing tools for linking ideas throughout a text. Transitional markers are specific connectors used to guide the reader through the logic of an argument or narrative. Discourse markers are more about managing the flow and structure of spoken or written discourse, often signaling shifts in conversation or emphasis.

4 Extensive & Intensive Listening and Reading

(1) Extensive Listening & Reading (for pleasure): T encourages Ss to choose for themselves what they listen (read) to and to do so for pleasure. (*outside the classroom*)

Two teachers are talking about an after school English reading club.

Ms. Song: You led a reading club at school last year, didn't you?
Ms. Park : Yeah, I did.
Ms. Song: How did you lead the club?
Ms. Park : Well, I tried to help students learn to read by reading. First, I let them **select what they wanted to read** so that they could read as much as possible, and I encouraged them to read for **overall meaning**, and for **pleasure and enjoyment**.

(2) Intensive Listening & Reading (for information): T helps Ss to develop effective listening (reading) strategies and build bottom-up and top-down skills. (*inside the classroom*)

Activity Procedure

1. Ask Ss to **listen** to a five-minute lecture while *jotting down* the main points. Then, give Ss four minutes to summarize the lecture using their notes.
2. Ask Ss to **listen** to the lecture again while they *write down* as many additional main points of the lecture as possible. Then, give Ss three minutes to revise their summary using all of their notes.
3. Ask Ss to **listen** to the lecture one last time while they *write down* as many other main points of the lecture as possible. Then, give Ss two minutes to make a final revision of their summary.
4. Ask Ss to **check** their grammar before submitting their summary.

The following is part of a lesson procedure that aims to facilitate students' comprehension of a text concerning global warming.

Steps

1. Before reading the text, T activates Ss' background knowledge concerning global warming and provides other relevant information to help Ss to have a better comprehension of the text.
2. T instructs Ss **to read** text quickly in order to grasp the main ideas. In doing so, T tells them not to read every word.
3. T asks Ss **to reread** it quickly for specific information, such as the type of disasters caused by global warming.
4. T instructs Ss **to read** the text again at their own pace.
5. T checks Ss' overall comprehension by having them write a brief summary of the text.
6. T then **checks** Ss' understanding of details by using a cloze activity.

5 The Importance of Schematic Knowledge

(1) Content Schemata (Background Knowledge)

This refers to students' knowledge about the subject or topic of the text they will be reading or listening to. Activating content schemata helps students connect new information with what they already know. For example:

Example

- Before reading / listening activity: The teacher can ask students questions related to the topic (e.g., "What do you know about climate change?" if the lesson is about environmental issues).
- Purpose: This helps students to anticipate the topic, making it easier for them to understand the material by relating it to their prior knowledge.

(2) Formal Schemata (Text Structure)

Formal schemata refer to the understanding of how different types of texts are organized and structured. Different text genres (e.g., narratives, reports, news articles) have specific structures, and understanding these patterns can aid comprehension.

Example

- Before reading / listening activity: The teacher can discuss the structure of the text, for example, highlighting that news articles typically follow a "who, what, when, where, why" format or that stories have a beginning, middle, and end.
- Purpose: Activating formal schemata helps students recognize organizational patterns, improving their ability to predict and follow the flow of the text.

(3) Linguistic Schemata (Language Knowledge)

Linguistic schemata refer to students' knowledge of the vocabulary, grammar, and language conventions used in the text. Activating this schemata can be crucial for comprehension, especially if the text contains unfamiliar or complex language.

Example

- Before reading / listening activity: The teacher can pre-teach key vocabulary, explain idiomatic expressions, or review grammar points that will appear in the text.
- Purpose: This prepares students for the language they will encounter, reducing the risk of comprehension breakdowns due to unfamiliar words or phrases.

Plus

Activation Techniques

1. **Prediction Tasks:** Asking students to predict the content based on the title, pictures, or key words.
2. **Brainstorming:** Encouraging students to share what they know about the topic.
3. **Pre-teaching Vocabulary:** Introducing key terms that might be new or challenging in the lesson.

By activating these schemata before listening or reading lessons, teachers can help students engage more effectively with the material and improve their overall comprehension.

In the Classroom

In Subin's class, the teacher plays a dialogue in four segments. After each segment, she stops the recording and asks students to complete a meaning-construction map as in the example below.

Listening Script

A: What do you think?
B: Not bad. I like the menu. It's quite attractive.
A: You should get quite a few visitors once it's up and running.
B: I hope so. I've spent a lot of time on the graphics.
A: I've also set up the payment system, as you requested.
B: Good. Make sure it works on different browsers.
A: I'll work on the server today, and we should be able to get everything online in a day or two.
B: Excellent. I'm looking forward to getting a lot of hits.

Subin's Map

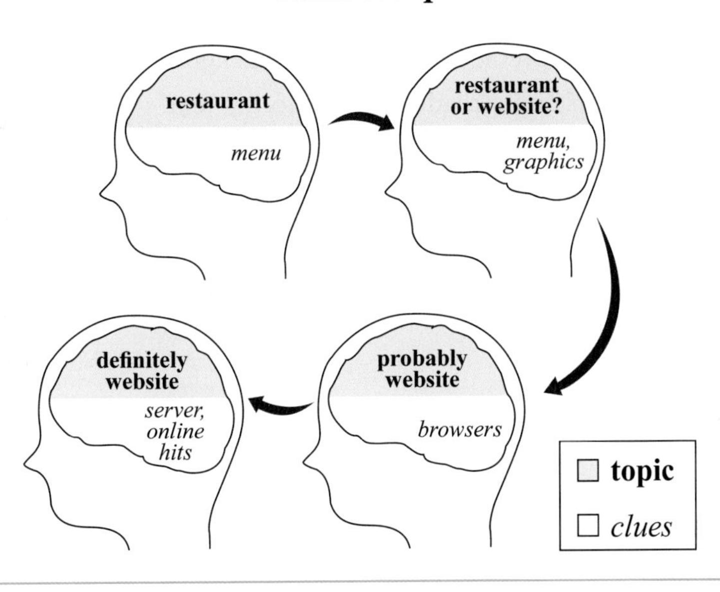

6 Comprehending Process

Mr. Park is an English teacher at a local middle school. According to his school curriculum, students should be able to use a combination of top-down and bottom-up processing when they practice the receptive skills of English, that is, listening and reading. Bottom-up processing is the processing of individual elements of the target language for the decoding of language input, while top-down processing refers to the use of background knowledge in understanding the meaning of a message. Now, he is developing a master plan for one of the units he will teach next semester. To help his students achieve this curriculum goal, he makes efforts to ensure that both bottom-up and top-down processing are practiced during each lesson period.

- Bottom-up: building textual meaning from the individual linguistic units (text-based), from sounds(letters) to words, to grammatical relationships, to lexical meanings, etc., to final "message."
- Top-down: making predictions based on background knowledge(knowledge-based) that the listeners(readers) bring to the text

(1) Practical Lesson Plan A

Lesson 1

Objectives
Students will be able to
- listen selectively for morphological endings
- apply bottom-up skills

The teacher says to students, "Okay, listen, everybody. I'm going to read five sentences. Show me the 'Yes' sign if the verb has an –ed ending, and show me the 'No' sign if it doesn't. Okay? Does everybody understand what to do? Okay, I'm going to read the first sentence." The teacher reads five sentences. All sentences have the structure of 'subject + verb.' Students show their signs after listening to each sentence.

Lesson 2

Objectives

Students will be able to
- make inference
- apply bottom-up and top-down skills

The teacher distributes handouts to students. In the handouts is a telephone message with some missing words. The teacher tells the students to read the message and decide what kinds of information are missing. Then he has the students listen to the recorded message and fill in the blanks.

(2) Practical Lesson Plan B

Mr. Park's Unit 1 Master Plan

1. Lesson: Challenge & Courage
2. Objectives

   Students will be able to
   - listen to a dialogue and explain the content
   - ask for reasons and make decisions
   - read a text and retell the story
3. Study points
   - Functions: asking for and giving reasons
   - Forms: passive, subject-verb agreement
4. Time allotment: 8 periods, 45 minutes each

Period	Section	Learning Activities
1st	Listen 1	• Listen to a series of phrases for consonant / vowel linking between words • Listen to short sentences to discriminate between rising and falling intonation
2nd	Listen 2	• Listen to a dialogue and find the main idea • Do a sentence dictation activity with the active and passive voice
5th	Read 1	• Read the introductory paragraph and predict what will come next • Distinguish sentences containing subject-verb agreement errors
6th	Read 2	• Recognize whether a sentence is in the active or passive voice • Change base forms of verbs into the past participle by adding '-ed / -en'

7 Comprehension Level

(1) Literal Comprehension

Literal comprehension involves understanding the explicit meaning of the text—what is directly stated. At this level, students focus on factual information and details without interpreting or inferring beyond what is clearly mentioned.

Example

- Skills involved: Identifying facts, recognizing main ideas, understanding vocabulary, answering "who," "what," "where," "when" questions.
- Example activity: Asking students to recall specific details or events from a story (e.g., "What did the character do?" or "Where did the event take place?").

(2) Inferential Comprehension

Inferential comprehension goes beyond the literal meaning and requires students to "read between the lines" by making inferences based on context, clues, and background knowledge. Students must derive meaning that is not explicitly stated in the text.

Example

- Skills involved: Making predictions, drawing conclusions, interpreting characters' feelings, and answering "why" and "how" questions.
- Example activity: After listening to a conversation, students might be asked, "Why do you think the speaker was upset?" or "What do you think will happen next?"

(3) Critical Comprehension

Critical comprehension requires students to evaluate and analyze the text, assess the credibility of information, detect bias, and form their own judgments or opinions about the material. This level engages students' higher-order thinking skills.

Example

- Skills involved: Evaluating the author's intent, detecting bias, distinguishing fact from opinion, and forming personal opinions.
- Example activity: After reading a persuasive article, students might be asked, "Do you agree with the author's argument? Why or why not?" or "What evidence does the author use to support their point of view?"

(4) Appreciative Comprehension

Appreciative comprehension involves an emotional or aesthetic response to a text. At this level, students interpret and value the language, style, tone, and the author's creative use of language. This often occurs when engaging with literature, poetry, or narratives.

Example

- Skills involved: Recognizing the beauty of language, appreciating literary techniques like metaphors or symbolism, and connecting emotionally with the text.
- Example activity: After reading a poem, students might be asked, "How did the poem make you feel?" or "What imagery stood out to you and why?"

(5) Applied Comprehension

Applied comprehension requires students to take what they have learned from a text and apply it to real-world situations or new contexts. This level of comprehension connects the text with practical experiences, encouraging students to synthesize information and use it in different scenarios.

Example

- Skills involved: Applying knowledge, making connections between the text and real life, solving problems using information from the text.
- Example activity: After reading an instructional article on saving energy, students might be asked, "How can you apply the energy-saving tips from the text in your daily life?"

Summary of Comprehension Levels

- Literal: Understanding the direct meaning.
- Inferential: Reading between the lines.
- Critical: Evaluating and analyzing the text.
- Appreciative: Connecting emotionally and aesthetically with the text.
- Applied: Using the knowledge gained in practical situations.

In the Classroom

Reading Text

Billy stacked the blocks one by one. They were almost as tall as he was! He couldn't wait to show them to his grandfather. He knew Grandpa would say the real Eiffel Tower was taller, but he would like Billy's smaller version too. Billy's neighbor Akira reminded him he was supposed to come over to her house to swim. It was a hot summer day, and Akira's family's pool was the only way to cool down. But Billy said he had changed his mind. Akira begged him to come, so Billy finally told her she was ruining his concentration and annoying him. Akira ran off. Billy was almost finished with his tower when suddenly... crack! Bang! Pop! Billy's tower fell over! Akira stood behind Billy's tower. Her eyes were still red from crying. She had kicked the tower over! Billy burst into tears too. When she saw her friend crying, Akira felt bad for destroying his hard work. She said that she was sorry. Billy ignored her and started to rebuild the tower. Akira decided not to swim herself that day and stayed in the hot driveway to help Billy. By the time Grandpa arrived, Billy and Akira were friends again.

① Literal Meaning

Q1. What was Billy intending to build?

Q2. What happened to Billy's tower?

② Inferential Meaning

Q1. Why do you think Akira did what she did to Billy's tower?

Q2. What might happen next for Billy and Akira?

③ Evaluative Meaning

Q1. What do you think the author is saying about Billy's and Akira's relationship?

Q2. How do you feel about the way Billy and Akira handled the conflict? Is that how you would handle it?

Sample Answers

① Literal Meaning

A1) The Eiffel Tower.

A2) Akira knocked it over.

② Inferential Meaning

A1) She was disappointed he broke his promise.

A2) Multiple answers are possible, such as "Billy and Akira will swim tomorrow; Billy and Akira will fight and make up again", and more.

③ Evaluative Meaning

A1) Multiple answers are possible, such as "They can fight and make up; They are close and like siblings; It is good to apologize when you hurt someone," and more.

A2) Answers will vary based on your opinion!

Key-concepts check-up : Listening

ACROSS ➡

❷ To choose for themselves what they listen to and to do the listening for pleasure and general language improvement.

❹ A communicative activity in which two or more interlocutors have different pieces of information that must be combined in order to complete successfully the activity.

❽ Learners reproduce the message they hear in a new form, and focus on listening without the extra burden. (2 words)

❾ It allows students the opportunity to focus on discrete points of the language and to develop listening skills, usually takes place in the classroom with teachers' preparation.

⓫ Unnecessary repetition.

DOWN ⬇

❶ Type of listening, which is business-type talk, focusing on content and conveying factual or propositional information.

❸ Integrative task which provides a useful bridge between bottom-up and top-down listening. Aim to provide an opportunity for learners to use their productive grammar in the task of text creation.

❺ Prior knowledge and expectations which are based on our background, education, and life experiences.

❻ Type of listening, which is person oriented to establish and maintain cordial social relationship.

❼ Comprehension processes the listener uses to assemble the message piece-by-piece from the speech stream, going from the parts to the whole.

❽ A higher level listening skill. Beginner learners lack the large vocabulary and grammatical knowledge, so they need to "listen between lines".

❿ Comprehension processes involve the listener in going from the whole to the parts.

Answer

ACROSS ➡ **2.** extensive **4.** jigsaw **8.** information transfer **9.** intensive **11.** redundancy

DOWN ⬇ **1.** transactional **3.** dictogloss **5.** schemata **6.** interactional **7.** bottom-up **8.** inferencing **10.** top-down

02 How to Improve Students' Listening Skills

1 Classroom Lesson

(1) Lesson Procedure A

Context

Below is an excerpt of a listening lesson developed by a middle school English teacher. The listening text is from a talk given by a famous plant expert.

Listening Script

Imagine you are living in the place surrounded by many plants. How do you feel? Yes, That's right! You will feel more healthy and comfortable. That's why most of you want to grow plants. So, let me ask you a question! Say one of the huge advantages of growing plants indoors! As you know, it is the improvement of air quality and the removal of toxins from the environment. At school we have learned that plants convert carbon dioxide into the air we breathe (oxygen). Thus, we are sure that having some space in the home for them can promote good health. For years I have researched air pollutants further and found many of the poisonous toxins that plants help eradicate are produced by furniture, carpets and building materials used indoors. The removal of toxins from the air and renewed oxygen is not the only health benefit of growing house plants. According to significant studies and research, a person's health during an illness is improved quicker.

① Pre-listening Activity

- Have Ss think about the following questions.
  - *Do you like plants? Why or why not?*
  - *Have you ever grown a plant?*
- Introduce the talk and its topics.
  - *Amazing qualities of plants*
  - *The benefits of growing plants*
- Have Ss guess about the content of the talk.

· *to activate Ss' schematic knowledge with personal questions*
· *to introduce today's topic and provide the background knowledge if necessary*
· *to make Ss predict what they are going to listen to*

② While-listening Activity

- Have Ss listen to the talk and check whether their predictions are correct.
- Have Ss listen again to find out key information, jotting down important words.

· *to let Ss confirm their predictions*
· *to have Ss listen for global understanding*
· *to ask Ss to use their note-taking strategy*

③ Post-listening Activity

- Have Ss read the listening script where several words and phrases are blanked out, and then reconstruct it in pairs.
- Have Ss discuss in groups whether they agree or disagree with the speaker of the talk and why.

· *focusing on the integrated approach*
· *completing the cloze task in pairs (collaborative learning)*
· *requiring the evaluative comprehension level*

(2) Lesson Procedure B

Context

The following is the procedure of a lesson that Ms. Park has tried to design based on her beliefs for listening.

Ms. Park's Beliefs

When I teach listening, I want my students to focus more on trying to infer meaning from contextual clues rather than the recognition of sounds, words, or sentences. I believe that the process of listening is more heavily influenced by world knowledge that a listener brings to a text, called schematic knowledge, as opposed to the language items that are available within the text itself. I advise students to rely on content and formal schemata when unsure about the speaker's message.

① Pre-listening Activity

- Before listening, Ms. Park shows students the title 'Kyle's Shopping Trip' of a DVD clip to be viewed, and asks students to discuss in their mother tongue the last time they were out shopping.
  - *When did you go shopping recently?*
  - *What did you buy? / Who is your shopping mate?*
  - *Do you have your own shopping strategies or tips?*

· *activating the schematic knowledge*
· *using referential questions*

- Ms. Park plays the clip once without the sound, and asks students some questions. To guess what the purpose of the conversation is, what the relationship between speakers is and so on.
  - *What is the purpose of the conversation?*
  - *What is the relationship between speakers?*

· *predicting*
· *using display questions*
· *activating Ss' schematic knowledge*

② While-listening Activity

- Ms. Park plays the clip and asks students to confirm or reject the prediction that they have made.
- Ms. Park illustrates how certain words may be linked in natural speech. Then, the teacher plays the clip with the sound on and asks students to find words that are linked in the speech stream.
- Ms. Park plays the clip again and students listen attentively for some phrasal verbs to identify specific details of the conversation and complete the table.

· *top-down skills*
· *bottom-up skills*

Plus

Ⅰ. While Listening (1)

Listening for Gist, Specific Information and Inferencing

Try it again. Two friends are talking on the telephone. Each time you listen, think about the information you need.

1. Listening for the *main idea*

Listen. What is the most important idea? Check (✓) your answer.

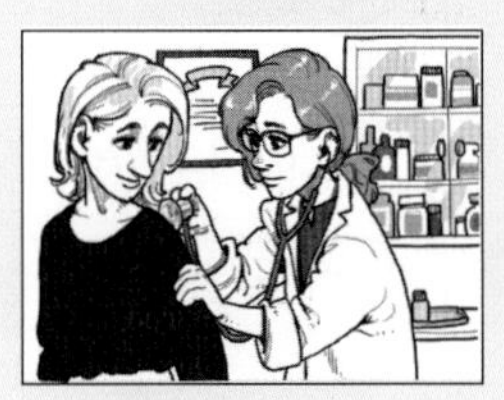

☐ going to the doctor

☐ school

2. Listening for *specific information*

Listen. Which page numbers should she read?
Write the page numbers.

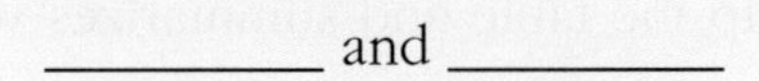

__________ and __________

3. Listening *"between the lines"*

Listen again. Did both students go to school today?
Check (✓) your answer.

☐ Yes ☐ No

You heard the same conversation three times. Each time, you listened for different reasons. Always think about why you are listening.

Ⅱ. While Listening (2)

This Tastes Great!

Listen. People are eating different foods. They don't say the names of the foods. What are they talking about?

Number the pictures (1-4). There are two extra pictures.

☐ Kebab ☐ Fried eggs ☐ Fried chicken

☐ Beef steak ☐ Sausage ☐ Bacon

③ Post-listening Activity

- Ms. Park asks Ss in pairs to check up the table and summarizes what happened in the conversation.
- Ms. Park divides Ss into a group of 4 and asks each group to share their shopping tips (ex. how can we get items much cheaper?).

· *top-down skills*
· *integrated skills*
· *collaborative learning*
· *information exchange activity*

Plus

Ⅰ. Post Listening (1)

Listening Clinic One: Strong or Weak?

Words are stressed when they are important. Words are not stressed when they are not important.

A: ~~A~~ cup ~~of~~ coffee ~~and~~ ~~a~~ donut.
B: ~~A~~ cup ~~of~~ coffee. Anything else?
C: And ~~a~~ donut.

Listen to the dialogue. Draw a slash (/) through the words: *and*, *a* and *of* where they are spoken weakly.

A: Can I help you?
B: Yes, I'd like a piece of cheesecake.
A: Large, or small?
B: Small please. And a cup of coffee.
A: A piece of cheesecake and a cup of coffee.
B: That's right.

Check your answers with your partner. Now say the dialogue together.

Ⅱ. Post Listening (2)

Make you in groups and ask them to talk about their dream job based on listening to *new jobs for a new world*.

2 Listening Techniques

(1) Dictogloss

Steps	Description
Preparation	The teacher introduces the topic, activates prior knowledge, and pre-teaches key vocabulary.
Dictation	The teacher reads the text (usually twice or more). Students take notes but are not expected to write the entire text.
Reconstruction	Students collaborate to reconstruct the text from their notes.
Analysis and Correction	Students compare their version with the original text, discussing grammar, vocabulary, and accuracy with the teacher's guidance.

① **Collaborative learning**: After listening to the text, students work in pairs or small groups to reconstruct it. They pool their knowledge, focusing on grammar, vocabulary, and structure to recreate a version that is as close as possible to the original.

② **Grammar in context**: Unlike traditional dictation, dictogloss encourages students to focus on the meaning and structure of the language, helping them notice how grammar works in context rather than isolating grammar rules.

③ **Student-centered**: The technique shifts the focus from teacher-centered delivery to a more student-centered activity. Students are responsible for reconstructing the text and discussing their choices in small groups, which fosters autonomy.

Data Analysis

A novice high school teacher, Ms. Kim, uses dictogloss as a classroom task for the first time. She plans to use News Script to have students practice passive voice. The teacher's task description is below.

Task Description

- Inform Ss that the class will work on the integrative listening task with specific focus on passive voice.
- Have students watch 7-minute-long news clip and get some gist.
- Ask Ss to write down key words while they are watching the clip the second time.
- Ask Ss to work in groups of 8 for 20 minutes to reconstruct the story.
- Have Ss watch the clip one more time.
- Distribute the transcript and ask them to compare it with their versions.

After the class, Ms. Kim wants to find out what students think about the dictogloss task. She asks the leader of each group to give comments. Their written comments are presented below.

Activity Review

1st group leader

The story seemed interesting but it went on and on. After watching it, we could barely remember anything we heard, except a few words like boy, locked, shivering, and scared. The teacher asked us to listen carefully for examples of passive voice, but we couldn't notice many. There were too many new and confusing expressions.

remedial action
: pre-teaching vocabulary before watching the clip

2nd group leader

It was our first time to do this activity, so it was very, very difficult. Also, we didn't know anything about the story before watching the clip, so we were lost.

remedial action
: activating Ss' schematic knowledge relating to the topic in advance

3rd group leader

When we worked in groups, some students hardly had any chance to talk. So we could not share our idea well.

remedial action
: setting in groups of 4 or 5 instead of 8 so that they can have enough chance to talk

Q1 Based on the student's comments on the task, explain the THREE most notable problems in the way the task was done.

① ______________________________

② ______________________________

③ ______________________________

Q2 Propose an instructional suggestion for each problem to make this dictogloss task more effective and engaging.

① ______________________________

② ______________________________

③ ______________________________

>> Possible Answers p.143

(2) Information Transfer & Partial Dictation

A

Ms. Kang, a new high school English teacher, was assigned to create questions for the listening section of the semester's final exam. In order to make the most effective test items, she goes over her notes from her college assessment class and finds the following:

Item Techniques

- information transfer: transferring aural information to a visual representation
- partial dictation: writing down parts of what you hear while listening to a passage
- sentence paraphrase: choosing the correct paraphrase from 3-5 distractors
- sentence repetition: reproducing a stretch of aural language with oral repetition
- short answer: answering a question with a word or a short phrase without given choices

Looking at her notes, she remembers that each of these techniques has its own strengths. For example, the sentence paraphrase technique has high practicality because it is easy to grade. Other techniques, such as information transfer, partial dictation, and sentence repetition, work well for assessing students' listening ability in a more integrative way. Ms. Kang thinks that she will utilize some of these techniques because she wants to test her students' listening and other language skills simultaneously. Ms. Kang also thinks her students should be able to understand specific details, which is one of her main goals for the class this semester. So, she wants to test this particular ability in the final exam. While all the techniques in her notes are good for assessing the ability to find specific information, Ms. Kang thinks the sentence repetition technique may not be appropriate since it may only require students to simply repeat what they hear.

B

Below are two sample items made by Ms. Kang.

Sample Item 1

Listen to the information about Minsu's daily schedule and fill in his schedule with the correct information. The information will be given twice.

Minsu's Schedule

	Monday	Tuesday	Wednesday	Thursday	Friday
9-10 am					
10-11 am					
11-12 pm					
12-1 pm			Lunch		
1-2 pm					
2-3 pm					
3-4 pm					

Audio Script

Minsu's classes start at nine in the morning and he eats lunch at noon every day. He has math on Monday, Tuesday, and Friday at nine o' clock. English is scheduled on...

Sample Item 2

Fill in the blanks with the words you hear. You will hear the passage three times.

We can find many geographic regions in Korea. The ____________ and ____________ parts of the country have huge plains. The main rivers flow westward because the mountainous region is mostly in the ____________ part of the country.

Audio Script

We can find many geographic regions in Korea. The southern and western parts of the country have huge plains. The main rivers flow westward because the mountainous region is mostly in the eastern part of the country.

Data Analysis

Read the passages and follow the directions.

A

Listening performances in a language classroom vary in purpose and complexity, each type focusing on specific aspects of language comprehension. Below are descriptions of five common listening performances: reactive listening, intensive listening, selective listening, extensive listening, and interactive listening.

1. Reactive Listening

   Reactive listening refers to the process where students listen to short pieces of language (words, phrases, or sentences) and repeat or respond to them. This is a very basic form of listening and is often used to help learners focus on the sound and pronunciation of words or phrases.

2. Intensive Listening

   Intensive listening involves carefully listening to a passage or piece of audio in order to focus on specific language elements such as vocabulary, grammar, pronunciation, or specific details.

3. Selective Listening

   In selective listening, students listen for specific information or key points within a longer piece of spoken language. The goal is to extract particular details while ignoring irrelevant parts.

4. Extensive Listening
   Extensive listening involves listening to longer passages or materials for general understanding or for pleasure. The focus is on the overall meaning rather than specific details.
5. Interactive Listening
   Interactive listening occurs in real-time conversations, where listeners engage by responding, asking questions, or clarifying points. It's a dynamic form of listening that involves comprehension, interaction, and collaboration.

In summary, each type of listening performance emphasizes different skills, ranging from passive repetition (reactive) to active engagement in conversation (interactive), helping students develop comprehensive listening abilities in a language learning context.

B

Example 1: Listening Cloze

Fill in the blanks with appropriate words while listening to an announcement from an airline agent.

Airline agent: Ladies and gentlemen, I now have some connecting gate information for those of you making connections to other flights out of San Francisco. Flight ________ to Portland will depart from gate ________ at ________ P.M. Flight ________ to Reno will depart at P.M. from gate ________ Flight ________ to Monterey will depart at P.M. from gate ________. And Flight ________ to Sacramento will depart from gate ________ at ________ P.M.

Example 2: Picture Description

Test-takers hear:

Choose the correct picture. In my backyard I have a bird feeder. Yesterday, there were two birds and a squirrel fighting for the last few seeds in the bird feeder. The squirrel was on top of the bird feeder while the larger bird sat at the bottom of the feeder screeching at the squirrel. The smaller bird was flying around the squirrel, trying to scare it away.

Test-takers see:

Q1 Based on different types of listening performances describe in <A>, identify which type of listening performance is demonstrated in Example 1 and 2, respectively.

____

____

____

Q2 Then, support your choice using evidence from both <A> and <B>.

____

____

____

>> Possible Answers p.143

Key-concepts check-up : Reading

ACROSS ➡

❷ Open-ended, rapid-fire voluntary oral or written listing of ideas with no debate or evaluation by others.

❺ Students provides the text, through dictation, that serves as the basis of reading instruction. As a result, it is tailored to the learner's own interest, background knowledge, and language proficiency. (3 words)

❼ The reading material should interest the students as well as be relevant to their needs.

❽ The connection of ideas at the idea level. A text with this makes sense.

❾ A strategy of using the context of an unknown word to get clues.

⓫ A text with lexical and structural difficulty should challenge students, not overwhelming them.

DOWN ⬇

❶ A visual strategy of grouping ideas into meaningful cluster, providing some order to a long string of ideas or events from a text. (2 words)

❸ A text should facilitate the achievement of certain language and content goals and be integratable with other skills.

❹ The connection of ideas at the sentence level. In a text with this, its elements are connected.

❻ A text with this is written for "real world" purposes and audiences, like journal articles.

❼ _________ sentences is used to teach students coherence by making them divide a combination of two texts into two separate ones that make sense.

❿ A reading strategy to get the general sense of a passage, not specific details.

Answer

ACROSS ➡ **2.** brainstorming **5.** language experience approach **7.** suitability **8.** coherence **9.** guessing **11.** readability

DOWN ⬇ **1.** semantic mapping **3.** exploitability **4.** cohesion **6.** authenticity **7.** scrambled **10.** skimming

03 How to Improve Students' Reading Skills

1 Teacher's Preparation Before the Class

(1) Authentic Text or Simplified Text

Data Analysis

Authentic text is assumed to provide more natural language and more naturally occurring cohesion than the simplified text which excludes unnecessary & distracting, idiosyncratic styles to help learners easily comprehend the text. However, simplified text is thought to benefit low level learners because it contains increased redundancy & amplified explanation as well as it is lexically, syntactically, and rhetorically less difficult than authentic text.

Two teachers are evaluating two textbooks, Textbook A and Textbook B, in order to select the one that their students are going to use next year. This is part of their conversation.

T1 : So, why don't we start with the first criterion? I went with Textbook A.
T2 : May I ask you why?
T1 : I think that the illustrations and graphics in Textbook A portray people in the target culture more realistically.
T2 : Yeah! Textbook A contains very realistic visuals that can provide our students with cultural information more accurately.
T1 : Good! Then, what about the second criterion?
T2 : Well, I think Textbook B is the better of the two. I couldn't give Textbook A a good score, because it appears to aim at explicit learning with many contrived examples of the language.
T1 : Hmm... could you clarify your point a bit more?
T2 : Well, I mean the texts and dialogues in Textbook A are oversimplified.
T1 : I had the same impression, but don't you think that they may help our students by focusing their attention on the target features?

T2: You may be right, but I think that such texts might deprive them of the opportunities for acquisition provided by rich texts.
T1 : Oh, I see. That's a pretty good point.
T2: So, in my opinion, Textbook B can provide more exposure to language as it is actually used in the real world outside the classroom.
T1 : Yeah! From that point of view, Textbook B will be intrinsically more interesting and motivating to our students.
T2: I agree. Okay, then, I think we are ready to move on to the next evaluation criterion.

T=teacher

Q1 Fill in the blanks using the most appropriate words.

The teachers, T1 and T2 are mainly focusing on, first, the criterion of reality of visuals and then, the other criterion of ____________________.

>> Possible Answers p.143

(2) Six Pedagogical Basic Criteria of Selection of Reading Text

① **Authenticity**: Authentic material, i.e. material which is not adapted or intended for mere linguistic purposes, despite its complexity and the demand it puts on the readers, is highly recommended and should be provided enough room in the syllabus. Faced with authentic passages, the students are exposed to natural input, real-life language data where the text language, with all its system of references, repetition, redundancy, as well as discourse markers that learners draw upon when reading, is kept unchanged and unadapted.

② **Readability**: The reading passages selected should not only be linguistically and culturally accessible but also within the students' reach in terms of content, topic familiarity, and conceptual difficulty. However, over-explicit texts are to be avoided because they do not allow for adequate training in the different sub-skills and strategies especially inferencing. As a matter of fact, in many classrooms, texts are made increasingly easy for students in the mistaken belief that this supports struggling students who encounter problems in reading. However, oversimplification results in texts that lack any challenge, interest or exemplars of good writing. It is better to prepare students for a text and teach them how to read it until they can make those choices for themselves.

③ **Length / Size**: The texts that the students have to handle must be of reasonable length. The rationale behind this is to secure variations in reading speed rate and to process texts for different purposes.

④ **Suitability of content**: Here texts appealing to students' interest and chiming with their age, maturation, level, and knowledge of the world, etc, are highly recommended.

⑤ **Exploitability**: Exploitability is also a very important criterion that should be considered in text selection. Texts that do not lend themselves well to different forms of exploitation are useless for teaching intensive reading and ought to be discarded.

⑥ **Variety**: This criterion has to do with text types. The reason for exposing students to a variety of text types can be amply substantiated. First and foremost students are allowed exposure to and training in different types of text, such as narrative descriptive, argumentative, expository, etc. By the same token, the use of different text types makes different demands on the readers, requires different procedures and approaches, and calls for different reading strategies.

2 Level Differentiated Class

(1) Text Modifications

수준별 학습(level differentiated instruction)을 진행하기 위해 학생들의 영어 실력에 맞춰 기존의 text를 수정할 필요가 있다. 즉, low level 학생들을 위해 어휘나 문장 구조를 좀 더 단순하고 쉽게 구성하는 반면, upper level에 있는 학생들의 도전 의식을 심어주기 위해 어휘나 문장 구조를 원래의 수준보다 더 어렵게 구성할 수 있다.

Data Analysis

Ms. Park wants to modify the following original text for the level-differentiated classes, which consist of the 2nd year high school students.

Original

No sooner had my plane landed than I was charmed by Korea. I particularly like the outdoor street markets and the strength and openness of the people who work there.

A

When my plane landed I was charmed by Korea. I particularly like the outdoor street markets and the strength and openness of the people who work there.

B

No sooner had my plane landed than I was enthralled by Korea. I particularly like the outdoor street markets and the integrity and receptiveness of the people who work there.

Q1 Identify how Ms. Park modifies the original text depending on students' proficiency levels.

____

____

Q2 Support your answer using concrete evidence from the modified text.

____

____

» Possible Answers p.144

(2) Materials Adaptation

Data Analysis

A

There are always sound reasons for adapting materials in order to make them as accessible and useful to learners as possible. When adapting materials, having clear objectives is a necessary starting point. The objectives a teacher may hope to achieve by adapting classroom materials can be listed as follows:

- To cater to learners' language proficiency levels: The teacher can modify the difficulty of language features such as grammar and vocabulary in the materials.
- To reinforce learner autonomy: Through materials adaptation, the teacher can give students opportunities to focus on their own learning processes to become more independent learners.
- To enhance higher-level cognitive skills: The teacher can adapt materials in such a way as to require students to hypothesize, predict, or infer.
- To encourage learners to tap into their own lives: Through materials adaptation, the teacher can increase the relevance of the contents or activities in relation to the students' experiences.

B

Ms. Lee is teaching first-year high school students, and she is preparing for her English reading class next semester. Based on the results of a needs analysis, she has decided to adapt two chapters of the textbook materials to meet her students' needs. For Lesson 2, which is about career paths, she will use magazine pictures of various jobs like engineer, baker, and fashion designer, along with some pictures related to jobs in the textbook. She will use these pictures as a springboard to get students in groups to share their dream jobs. She thinks this adaptation will help students think about more varied jobs in the real world. For Lesson 5, there is a reading passage about Simon's adventure in Kenya in the textbook. However, she worries that there are only simple activities to check students' understanding of the story. So, she will edit the story, intentionally deleting a few sentences at the end. This will challenge the students to think about the story's structure and look ahead to possible endings, using the storyline.

Q1 Identify One objective that Ms. Lee aims to achieve through adaptation in Lesson 2 and another objective in Lesson 5.

____

____

____

Q2 Explain your answers with evidence from <A> and <B>.

____

____

____

>> Possible Answers p.144

(3) Classroom Organization

Example 1

Same Ability Grouping: Tiered Task

다음은 'The spirit of London'이라는 읽기 자료를 토대로 구성된 3개의 과업 자료이다.

Top Tier

Task A: for weaker students

1. How much of London's history does *The spirit of London* show?
2. How do you go around it?
3. What special effects does it have?
4. What can you see in the modern-day section?

Answers

ⓐ light, sound, music, and smells
ⓑ police, punks, and tourist
ⓒ more than 400 years
ⓓ in a taxi

Middle Tier

Task B: for midlevel students

1. How much of London's history does *The spirit of London* show?
   ⓐ 400 years ⓑ more than 400 years ⓒ 300 years
2. How do you go around it?
   ⓐ in a taxi ⓑ in a train ⓒ on foot
3. What special effects does it have?
   ⓐ lights ⓑ sound and music ⓒ smells
4. What can you see in the modern-day section?
   ⓐ police ⓑ punks ⓒ tourists

Bottom Tier

Task C: for stronger students

1. How much of London's history does *The spirit of London* show?
2. How do you go around it?
3. What special effects does it have?
4. What can you see in the modern-day section?

- **Matching work**: Task A gives all the answers on the page for support. They are jumbled for challenge. Weaker students manipulate the given material, and can use logic to help match the task items, together with the information in the reading text.
- **Multiple choice questions**: Task B gives multiple-choice answers to help the average students. This is slightly different from the conventional "one answer only is correct" multiple choice, since in questions 3 and 4 there are more than one correct answer.
- **Open questions**: Task C gives open questions—with no extra support—to challenge the stronger students in the group.

Example 2

Tiered task의 보다 간단한 형태로 학생들의 수준을 두 단계로 나눠 동일한 과업을 진행하되, 교사가 과업의 support를 다르게 제공한다. Dual-choice gapfill이 이에 속한다.

The Dead Sad Animal Rap		MISSING WORDS
Listen to the rap.	What are the missing words?	
Humans...	ⓐ ... the dear old dodo,	killed / shot
It was...	ⓑ ... It couldn' fly	easy / simple
Humans...	ⓒ ... all the passenger pigeons	hunted / shot
From the...	ⓓ ... American sky.	south / north

As they listen, weaker students circle one of the words in the box to fill each gap. Stronger students get the same task sheet, but with the missing words box cut off. The task is therefore more challenging for them.

Example 3

Mixed Level Grouping: Bias Task or Jigsawed Gapfill

다음은 학생들이 Penpal Ad Page를 읽고 진행할 과업들이다.

Task A: for weaker students
1. How many of the young people are 13 years old? (Three...)
2. How many boys are there?
3. Who doesn't eat meat?
4. Who likes football?
5. Who lives in the country?

Task B: for stronger students
Write questions for these answers, based on the Penpal Page.
1. How many of them are 13? Three of them are.
2. ______________________? There are four.
3. ______________________? Eloise doesn't.
4. ______________________? James does.
5. ______________________? Chris does.

With task A, weaker students answer questions about the text. With Task B, stronger students write questions for given answers related to the text. Because the answers to these two tasks are complementary, it would not be an efficient use of class time for the teacher to conduct post-activity feedback with the whole class. Instead, student-students feedback would be a good idea, with the students in AB pairs. The teacher should naturally be available as an arbiter if there are any questions of their own. If they are grammatically correct, and fit the given answers, the teacher should confirm them as also correct. This type of feedback, in weak/strong pairs, is very motivating for the weaker students. They have got the difficult questions that the strong students have struggled to reconstruct. For weak students, already knowing key information is a pleasant change from traditional whole-class oral feedback, which often turns into a dialogue between the teacher and the brightest and most forthcoming students.

Example 4

보다 간단한 형태의 bias task의 유형은 jigsawed gapfill의 형태이다. 주로 노래(song)나 이야기(short episode)를 들려주고 학생들에게 요약된 복사본을 주되, 학생들의 수준에 따라 higher-level students(Task sheet A)에게는 보다 많은 빈칸으로 된 복사본을 주고 weaker students(Task sheet B)에게는 빈칸이 상대적으로 적은 복사본을 제공하도록 한다. 이때 각 복사본 A, B의 빈칸은 서로 다른 장소가 지워져 있어야 한다.

The simplicity or complexity of the words you gap can also make the task easier or more difficult. A positive feature of this kind of bias activity is that because the jigsawed gaps are in different places, students are not necessarily aware of who has more gaps and who has fewer.

3 Lesson Procedure

(1) Reading Lesson A

Data Analysis

The reading passage, about 300 words long, is about a boy's adventure. The ending of the story is intentionally omitted by Ms. Park so that students can learn how to construct a cohesive and coherent text.

Pre-reading Activity

- Have Ss watch a 2-minute English video clip related to the reading passage and then answer questions about the clip.
- Give Ss half a minute to find previously learned discourse markers (e.g., *however, therefore, as a result*, etc.) in the passage while reading quickly through it.

· *activating schemata and stimulating students' interest*
· *using display questions*
· *encouraging scanning strategy*

While-reading Activity

Have Ss first read the story by themselves, complete the story in pairs by predicting the ending based on the storyline, and then write it down in about 50 words. While they carry out the task on their own, T circulates, offering feedback, suggestions, or language help Ss may need to accomplish the task.

· *engaging in collaborative learning*
· *stimulating top-down strategy*
· *using integrated skills(writing)*
· *playing roles of facilitator and resource person*

Post-reading Activity

- Have each pair make a presentation about their version of the ending of the story in English.
- Have Ss vote for the most interesting ending.

· *using integrated skills(presentation)*
· *promoting peer evaluation*

Q1 Complete the following table.

Lesson Objective	
Pre-reading Activity	• Question Types: • Focused Reading Strategy:
While-reading Activity	• Target Skills: • Required Reading Strategies: • Teacher Roles:
Post-reading Activity	Scoring method for students outcome:

>> Possible Answers p.144

(2) Reading Lesson B

Data Analysis

A

Worksheet

Family History

Group Name: ______________

Student Number & Name: ______________

Role	Assignment	Student Assigned
Discussion Leader	Keeping the conversation going if it falters	
Passage Chooser	Choosing three passages that are important to the story to discuss	
Word Master	Showing the meanings of new words	
Grammar Checker	Using syntactic clues to interpret the meanings of sentences	
Story Summarizer	Summing up the story briefly	
Online Manager	Posting the activity outcome to the web or social network service	

▪ Before Reading

Can you guess who will mention the following statements? Match the pictures of the characters in the story with their corresponding statements.

▪ While Reading

Based on the text about the Brown and the Garcia families, complete the following figure.

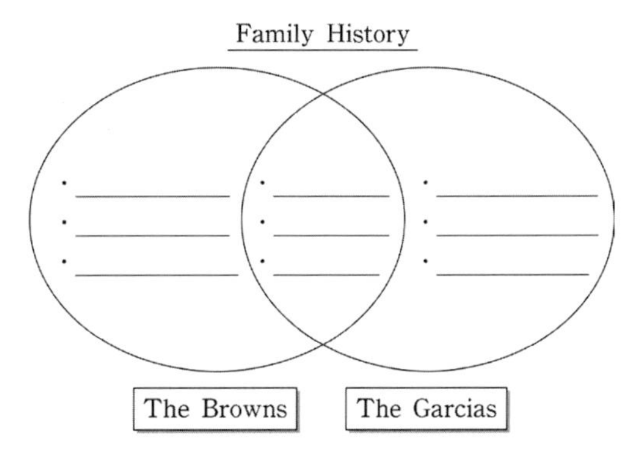

▪ After Reading

What do you think about the characters in the story? Complete the sentences.

1. I feel sorry for ________________ because ______________________.
2. I think ________________ is a nice person, but ________________.

B

Mr. Han's Class Observation Note

2. How did the teacher use teaching aids?	I set up a Reader's Club using a metaverse platform. While doing the reading activity in an online environment, each student took a specific role. I checked students' comprehension of the passage using the worksheet.
3. Did all the students participate actively?	The students looked absorbed in reading the three paragraphs of the text. After the reading activity, they actively participated in the discussion, carrying out their assigned roles. S1 managed the discussion and controlled each student's speaking time. S2 used an online dictionary when one student asked the meaning of a word, 'crane', and shared a picture of a crane with its meaning. S3 selected one linguistically complex sentence and explained its structure to the other students. S4 uploaded the summary that S5 wrote to the cloud and posted it on the class blog. Lastly, S6 selected another three paragraphs that they would read in the next class.
4. Did the students use suitable reading strategies?	During the discussion, students used various reading strategies such as activating schema, allocating attention, previewing, skimming, scanning, and criticizing. My students were pretty good at making guesses based on the pictures. I also noticed that using a graphic organizer helped students comprehend the story. By comparing and contrasting the two families, they extracted information from the text. My students understood the text very well based on the figure.

S=student

Q1 Complet the following table.

Before Reading Activity	• Purpose: • Focused Reading Strategy:
While/After Reading Activity	• Target Skills: • Required Reading Strategies: • Teacher Strategies for Students' Even Participation: ① ② • A Pedagogical Tool: • Required Comprehension Levels:

>> Possible Answers p.145

4 Reading Techniques

(1) Predicting

Before starting the text, encourage students to predict what the text will be about based on the title, images, or introductory paragraphs. This technique stimulates curiosity and motivates them to actively engage with the reading to see if their predictions were correct.

Example

Show the students the title and cover of the reading material and ask them to write or discuss what they think will happen in the story.

(2) Annotating the Text

Teach students to annotate by underlining or highlighting key ideas, new vocabulary, or important information while reading. They can also write short notes or questions in the margins.

Example

As students read, they mark any words they don't understand and note down questions about the story that they can later discuss in groups or with the teacher.

(3) Summarizing

After reading a section, have students summarize the main points in their own words. This ensures that they are actively processing and understanding the material.

Example

After each paragraph or page, students write one or two sentences summarizing what they read and then share their summaries with a partner.

(4) Questioning

Encourage students to ask questions before, during, and after reading. This keeps them actively engaged and allows them to think critically about the text.

Example

Provide students with a chart where they can write down questions they have while reading. Then, as a class or in small groups, discuss the answers to those questions after finishing the text.

(5) Think-Pair-Share

This strategy encourages interaction and engagement. After reading a section, students think about the material, pair up to discuss their thoughts, and then share their ideas with the class.

Example

After reading a paragraph, ask students to pair up and discuss what they think the author is trying to convey, then share their ideas with the class.

(6) Graphic Organizers

Use graphic organizers (e.g., mind maps, story maps, Venn diagrams) to help students visually organize information and ideas from the text. This technique helps them understand relationships between ideas, characters, or events.

Example

After reading a story, students complete a story map with details about the setting, characters, conflict, and resolution.

(7) Jigsaw Reading

In this technique, the class is divided into groups, and each group is responsible for reading and understanding a different section of the text. Afterward, they teach their section to the rest of the class, which promotes active reading and teamwork.

Example

Assign each group a portion of a long article. After reading, they discuss the main points in their group, then present their part to the rest of the class.

(8) Role-Playing or Dramatization

Have students act out or role-play scenes from the reading material. This makes the reading more engaging and helps them comprehend character motivations and plot developments.

Example

After reading a scene from a story, students take on the roles of different characters and act out the dialogue, focusing on key points and emotions.

(9) Post-Reading Reflection or Journaling

After reading, encourage students to reflect on the material by writing in a journal or engaging in a reflection activity. They can express how the text made them feel, what they learned, or any connections they made to their own lives.

Example

Students write a journal entry about how a character's experience in the story relates to something they've experienced in their own lives.

(10) Reciprocal Teaching

In this technique, students take turns being the "teacher" and guiding the reading discussion. This involves predicting, clarifying, questioning, and summarizing sections of the text.

Example

Assign students to lead discussions on specific sections of the text, encouraging them to ask their peers questions, summarize the key points, and clarify any confusing aspects.

(11) Language Experience Approach

- a process where students share an experience as a class, describe the experience out loud, write about it, and then read what they wrote
- a whole language approach that promotes reading and writing through the use of personal experiences and oral language
- Concrete experiences can be provided to help create the stories.
- Stories developed by students: motivational(intrinsic motivation), more meaningful

Example

- Students take turns giving dictation of experiences (school trip, school pets..)
- Teacher writes exactly what is said by students.
- Teacher reads the story back to students and tracks each word.
- Students take turns reciting the story.
- Each sentence is cut into strips. Students must reconstruct story.

These techniques encourage active engagement, promote deeper comprehension, and foster collaboration and critical thinking among middle school students. By using a variety of approaches, students are more likely to stay engaged and motivated throughout the reading lesson.

Data Analysis

Read the conversation between Minji and Youngho and follow the directions.

Minji : So in my group, we were assigned to read the first part of the article about climate change. We learned about the causes, like greenhouse gases and deforestation. We had to explain this section to the rest of the class. It was cool because I became the "expert" for that part. What did you do?

Youngho: Oh, that sounds interesting! For me, after reading a short story, I had to first think about the main conflict in the story on my own. Then I paired up with my classmate to discuss it. We both agreed that the main conflict was between the character and society, but we had slightly different ideas on why.

Q1 Identify the reading technique that Minji and Youngho participated in.

____

____

____

Q2 Explain your answers using evidence from the conversation.

____

____

____

>> Possible Answers p.145

Further Reading

After completing their respective tasks, Minji participated in the Jigsaw Reading activity, and Youngho did the Think-Pair-Share activity. They are now discussing what they learned.

Minji : So in my group, we were assigned to read the first part of the article about climate change. We learned about the causes, like greenhouse gases and deforestation. We had to explain this section to the rest of the class. It was cool because I became the "expert" for that part. What did you do?

Youngho: Oh, that sounds interesting! For me, we did Think-Pair-Share. After reading a short story, I had to first think about the main conflict in the story on my own. Then I paired up with my classmate to discuss it. We both agreed that the main conflict was between the character and society, but we had slightly different ideas on why.

Minji : That's interesting! How did you figure out the conflict?

Youngho: Well, when I was thinking alone, I thought the conflict was more about the character's internal struggle. But when I paired up with my partner, he pointed out that the society in the story had really strict rules that the character was pushing against. So after talking it out, we realized it was more of an external conflict with society.

Minji : I like that. Sometimes you need someone else's perspective to fully understand the story. In Jigsaw, it was similar but on a larger scale. My group was responsible for understanding and teaching the first part, but I had to rely on the other groups to explain the second and third parts. They talked about the effects of climate change and possible solutions. It was like fitting all the pieces together.

Youngho: That's so cool! I can see how Jigsaw reading makes you focus really deeply on your part because you know others are relying on you to explain it well.

Minji : Exactly! And it was interesting to hear the other groups' explanations. We all had to listen carefully because no one had the entire article on their own. I learned a lot from what they shared.

Youngho: That's similar to Think-Pair-Share too! I realized that discussing my ideas with my partner really helped me refine my understanding. At first, I wasn't sure about the conflict, but hearing another point of view made things clearer.

Minji : It seems like both methods helped us get a fuller picture by working with others. Do you think your partner helped you see something you missed on your own?

Youngho: Definitely. Our discussion made me notice details I had skipped when reading alone. I also liked that after we paired up, we shared our ideas with the class, so we heard even more interpretations.

Minji : That's great. I think these strategies really show how reading doesn't have to be a solo activity. You learn more when you collaborate with others.

Youngho: Agreed! Next time, I'd like to try Jigsaw reading. It sounds fun to be responsible for teaching part of the material.

Minji : You should! And I want to try Think–Pair–Share. It sounds like it gives you a chance to reflect before you discuss, which can really help clarify your thoughts.

Possible Answers

p.113

Q1 ① Because the news clip included too many unfamiliar and confusing expressions, students were unable to focus on the passive voice during the listening.
② Students felt confused due to the unfamiliar topic.
③ Students lacked equal opportunities to speak during the group discussion, which limited the effective exchange of ideas.

Q2 ① Ms. Kim should pre-teach difficult vocabulary and expressions before the students watch the clip.
② Ms. Kim should organize pre-listening activities, such as showing pictures or having a brief discussion to activate students' prior knowledge on the topic.
③ Ms. Kim should reorganize the groups of 8 into smaller groups of 4 or 5.

p.117

Q1 Both Examples 1 and 2 require selective listening.

Q2
- Selective Listening
  Students listen for specific information about the flight number, gate number, and departure time.
- Selective Listening
  Students listen for key points by identifying the differences between a squirrel and two birds at the bird feeder.

p.122

Q1 authenticity

p.125

Q1
- For low levels, Ms. Park simplifies a complicated structure(clause) from the original text into the simplified version in 〈A〉.
- For the advanced levels, Ms. Park modifies simple words into more complex ones in the modified text in 〈B〉.

Q2
- She simplifies "no sooner~ than" into "when".
- She modifies simple words such as "charmed", "strength", and "openness" into more complex words like "enthralled", "integrity", and "receptiveness".

p.126

Q1
- In Lesson 2, Ms. Lee adapts classroom materials "to encourage learners to tap into their own lives."
- In Lesson 5, Ms. Lee adapts classroom materials "to enhance higher-level cognitive skills."

Q2
- She asks students to share their dream jobs by relating them to their experiences, based on magazine pictures of real world jobs like engineer, baker, and fashion designer.
- She challenges students to predict or infer the intentionally deleted endings of a story.

p.131

Q1

Lesson Objective	Students will be able to write a cohesive and coherent text.
Pre-reading Activity	• Question Types: Display questions • Focused Reading Strategy: Scanning
While-reading Activity	• Target Skills: Reading & Writing skills • Required Reading Strategies: Inferencing and top-down strategy • Teacher Roles: Facilitator & Resource person
Post-reading Activity	Scoring method for students outcome: Peer evaluation

p.132

Q1

Before Reading Activity	• Purpose: Schema Activation, Attention allocation, Preview • Focused Reading Strategy: Prediction
While/After Reading Activity	• Target Skills: Reading, Speaking, and Writing Skills • Required Reading Strategies: Skimming, Scanning, Detailed Information • Teacher Strategies for Students' Even Participation: ① providing each student with an individual role ② controlling students' speaking time • A Pedagogical Tool: a graphic organizer, particularly, Venn Diagram • Required Comprehension Levels: literal, inferential, and critical comprehension levels

p.140

Q1 Minji participated in Jigsaw Reading while Youngho did a Think-Pair-Share activity.

Q2 Minji's group read the first part of the text on climate change and explained it to the class as experts. Meanwhile, Youngho reflected on the main conflict in the story and discussed it with his partner, leading to shared insights on the conflict between the characters and society.

Key-concepts check-up : Speaking (1)

ACROSS ➡

❷ Driving some new information from given information through processes of inference, deduction, practical reasoning, or a perception of relationships or patterns.

❸ The difference between what I can say and what I should say.

❻ To resolve communication breakdowns and to work toward mutual comprehension.

❾ Specific kind of information gap task, that is a task that requires learners to communicate with each other in order to fill in missing information and to integrate it with other information.

❿ To make students use language to express their own ideas, feelings, preferences and opinions.

DOWN ⬇

❶ Output that students use accurately and appropriately within a specific context when they respond and interact in the target language.

❹ This is a type of a drill. This is a further extension of meaningful communicative practice found in form-focused communicative practice.

❺ A drill is repetitive oral practice of a language item, whether a sound, a word, a phrase or a sentence structure. This drill has only one correct response from a student and has no implied connection with reality.

❼ A transfer of given information from one person to another.

❽ Segmentals consist of the phonemes of the language, or its smallest meaning units. Discrimination of one consonant or vowel.

Answer

ACROSS ➡ **2.** reasoning-gap **3.** notice the gap **6.** meaning negotiation **9.** jigsaw **10.** personalization

DOWN ⬇ **1.** comprehensible output **4.** communicative drill **5.** mechanical drill **7.** information gap **8.** minimal pairs

Key-concepts check-up : Speaking (2)

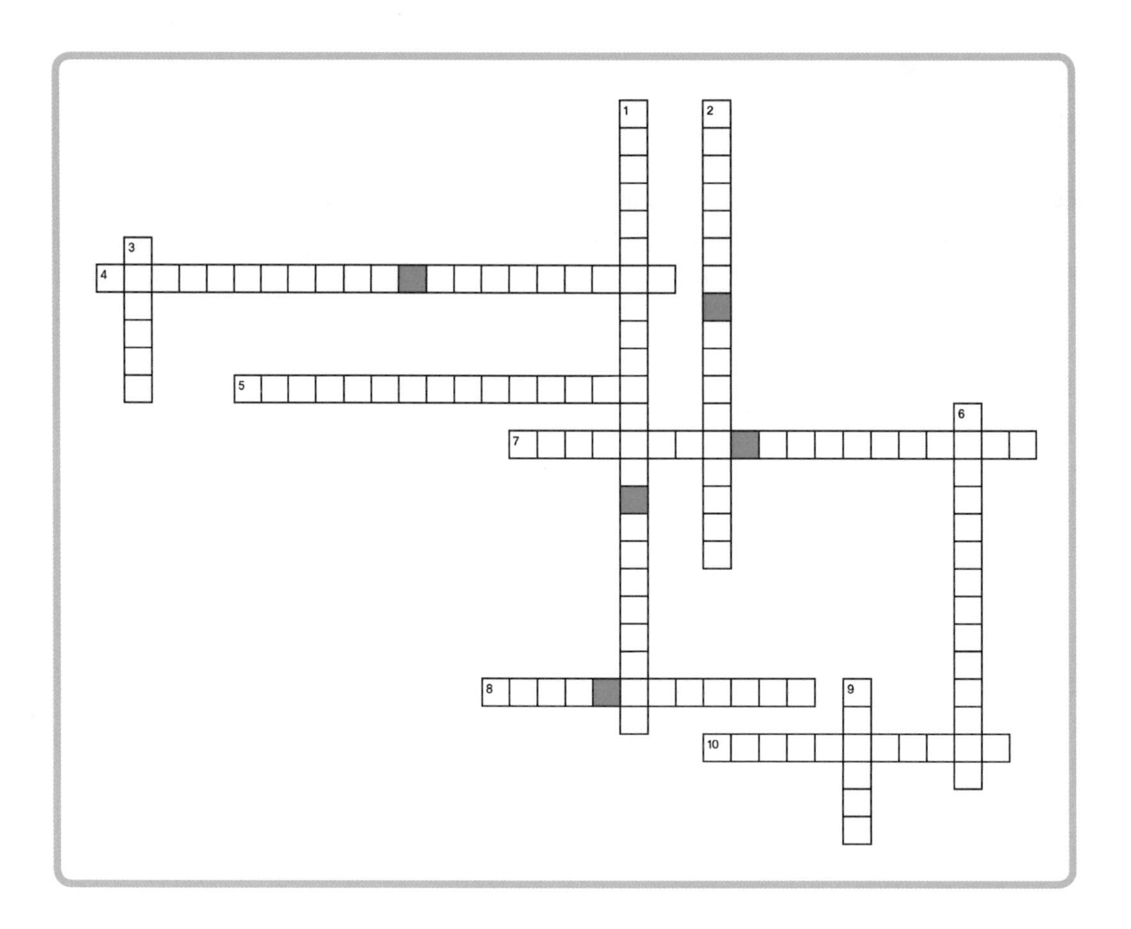

ACROSS ➡

❹ This type of question require answers which contain information unknown by the teacher, and they are frequently used to call for evaluation or judgment.

❺ It includes intonation, rhythm, and stress. These features can have an even greater impact on intelligibility than the mispronunciation of sounds.

❼ The teacher directly tells a student what a mistake was and provides the correct answer. She might say, "Oh you should say...," or "the correct form of this verb form is..."

❽ Creating a nonexisiting L2 word based on a supposed rule, such as vegetarianist for vegetarian.

❿ Another strategy involves pausing. The instructor repeats the learner's utterance up to the point of the error, where the student needs to self-correct.

DOWN ⬇

❶ It contains either comments or information regarding the accuracy of a student's utterance without providing the correct form.

❷ They seek answers in which the information is already known by the teacher. They are an important tool in the classroom, not only for the teacher to be able to check and test their learners, but also as a source of listening practice.

❸ A teacher reformulates all parts of a student's utterance minus the error.

❻ Describing or exemplifying the target object of action.

❾ It is defined in their work "student's utterance that immediately follows the teacher's feedback and that constitutes a reaction in some way to the teacher's feedback."

Answer

ACROSS ➡ **4.** referential questions **5.** suprasegmentals **7.** explicit correction **8.** word coinage **10.** elicitation

DOWN ⬇ **1.** metalinguistic feedback **2.** display questions **3.** recast **6.** circumlocution **9.** uptake

Chapter 02

How to Teach the Productive Skills

01 How to Teach Students' Oral Skills

1 Communicative Competence

① ______	______ ②
Understanding and using: • vocabulary • language convention (e.g, grammar, punctuation, spelling) • syntax (e.g, sentence structure)	Using techniques to: • overcome language gaps • plan and assess the effectiveness of communication • achieve conversational fluency • modify text for audience and purpose
Having awareness of: • social rules of language (e.g., formality, politeness, directness) • nonverbal behaviors • cultural references (e,g., idioms, expressions, background knowledge) ______ ③ ______	Understanding how ideas are connected through: • patterns of organization • cohesive and transitional devices ______ ④ ______

Communicative Competence

the ability to understand and use language effectively to communicate in authentic social and school environment

Answer

① Grammatical ② Strategic ③ Sociolinguistic ④ Discourse

Data Analysis

Read the conversation between two teachers in a language classroom.

T1 : What are you doing?
T2: I'm writing a recommendation letter for Miri.
T1 : She is a good student, but she doesn't know how to adapt her conversational style when making a request.
T2: Does she?
T1 : Last time, when she approached me, she said, "Hi, teacher, can you write me a recommendation letter?"
T2: That's right! Some of my students also seem to have trouble making their speech style appropriate to the situation.
T1 : If so, how about offering a special lecture on this topic?
T2: That sounds great!

Q1 Identify the component of Communicative Competence that the two teachers are concerned about in this conversation.

____

____

____

Q2 Explain your choice using the concrete evidence from the conversation.

____

____

____

>> Possible Answers p.218

2 Teaching Principles

(1) Plan speaking tasks that involve negotiation for meaning

Reasoning-gap tasks involve some new information from given information through processes of inference, deduction, practical reasoning, or a perception of relationships or patterns.

Example

This is Mary's budget and her list to interest, favourite leisure activities. Listen to four holiday packages given, note down the key details and choose the one that in your opinion best suits her and say 'Why'.

In the Classroom

Activity Procedure : Jigsaw

Step 1	• T places various information on a different job in each of the four corners in the classroom. (Each corner is labelled with a different letter, A, B, C, D.) • T assigns individual Ss a letter(A, B, C, D) in order to create four groups of four Ss, each of which is a base group composed of A to D.
Step 2	• T provides Ss in each base group with handouts. (Each handout has a set of questions about four different jobs.) • T helps Ss understand that they should be interdependent upon one another not only for their own learning but also for the learning of others throughout the activity. • T informs Ss which corner to go to based on their letter in order to form four different expert groups.
Step 3	• Ss move to their expert groups and find out information about different jobs through discussions and answer the questions on the handouts. • T circulates within the groups and makes sure each of the Ss has all the answers.
Step 4	• Ss return to their initial base groups and exchange the information through discussing what they learned in the expert groups. • All the base groups present their findings to the whole class and decide which job they would like most.

Activity 1	I'd like you to practice the dialog you've learned. Get into pairs and pretend that you were these people.
Activity 2	Someone has to think of an object, a thing, an animal, for "Twenty Questions". And then, everyone else has to guess what it is. Remember, this activity is designed to derive information through a process of inference.
Activity 3	Let's go over some expressions that might be useful for conversation. Why don't you practice the patterns you've learned today? Please repeat after me.
Activity 4	I'd like you to look at the picture, and describe whatever is in the picture to your partner. Your partner has to identify the similarities and differences. You're not supposed to look at your partner's page.

Data Analysis

Topic-based & Task-based Activity

Read Activities 1 and 2 carefully, and follow the instructions.

Activity 1

Talk about your hobbies and interests in small groups. You have 15 minutes.

Activity 2

How do you like to spend your time on the weekend? Circle three things you like to do. Cross out three things that you never do. Write three other things you like to do in your free time.

swim visit family listen to music go to the library
garden visit friends cook for friends and family watch TV
take walks exercise go to cinema

Three other things you like to do: ______________________

Now talk to the other students in class and find the person who has the most things in common with you. Ask that person the following questions:

How often do you do that activity? / What do you like about that activity?

Q1 Choose one of Activity 1 or 2 which increases students' active engagement and interaction.

____

____

____

Q2 Explain your choice by comparing and contrasting the two activities.

____

____

____

____

>> Possible Answers p.218

▶ How to Give Clear Directions.

- "Just do it" represents the need for teachers to demonstrate, or do an activity rather than explain it.
- "Less is more": The fewer words used, the better. Lengthy or multiple steps explanations are difficult for beginning level learners to follow.

Data Analysis

Read the Lesson Procedures chose by Mr. Kim and Ms. Park and follow the directions.

Mr. Kim

Lesson objectives: Students will be able to say their future job and find the peer who wants to have common jobs by asking questions.

1. Show a short video clip about the future jobs to students.
2. Distribute the handout to the class.

Handout

1) What do you want to be in the future? Circle three jobs you want to be. Cross out three that you don't want to be. Write three other jobs you would like to be.

architect	artist	baker	businessperson	carpenter
engineer	firefighter	gardner	lawyer	model
doctor	nurse	police officer	soldier	teacher
veterinarian	writer	musician	babysitter	florist

Three other jobs you would like to be ______________________.

2) Now talk to other students in class and find the person who has the most jobs in common with you. Ask that person the following questions:
– What do you like about the job?
– What skills do you need for the job?
– What job you can do in your country that you can't do in U.S.?

3. Explain how to do the activity with the handout.

Mr. Kim talk: Now you are going to talk about jobs you want to have in the future. I want you to circle three jobs you want to be, cross out three you don't want to be, and add three more jobs you want to be. After you finish, talk to people in class and find the person who wants to have jobs the most in common with you. Ask them the questions at the bottom of your handout.

4. Ask students to do this activity.
5. Walk around and observe their performance. Take note about their mistakes if they make any.
6. Check their answers by asking questions.
7. Provide feedback for their mistakes.

Ms. Park

Lesson objectives: Students will be able to say their job of the future and find the peer who wants to have common jobs by asking questions.

1. Show a short video clip about the future jobs to students.
2. Demonstrate how to do the activity with the handout by interacting with students.

Ms. Park :	Jinah, what do you want to be in the future?
Jinah :	I want to be a teacher.
Ms. Park :	So do I. (*Ms. Park places sample handout on overhead and circles 'teacher.'*) Do you want to be a babysitter?
Jinah :	No.
Ms. Park :	Neither do I. (*Ms. Park crosses off 'babysitter.'*) (*Distribute the handout to class*)
Ms. Park :	Minchul, what do you want to be in the future?
Minchul :	Soccer player.
Ms. Park :	Hum . . . do you see soccer player on the list? (*Ms. Park points to overhead.*)
Class :	No.
Ms. Park :	Minchul, write the job in on the blank. Do you see the long blank?
Minchul :	Yes! OK.
Ms. Park :	Everyone, read the instructions aloud together. (*Class is reading the instructions.*)
Ms. Park :	What do you circle?
Class :	Three jobs that we want to do.
Ms. Park :	What do you cross out?
Class :	Three jobs that we don't want to do.

3. Ask the students to do number 1 individually and demonstrate how to do number 2 with interaction like step 2.
4. Ask the students to do number 2.
5. Walk around and observe their performance. Take note about their mistakes if they make any.
6. Check their answers by asking questions.
7. Provide feedback for their mistakes.

Q1 Choose One of the two lesson procedures that gives clear directions for students' active engagement.

Q2 Explain your choice by comparing and contrasting how directions are given each lesson procedure.

>> Possible Answers p.218

(2) Personalize the content of speaking activities whenever possible

In the Classroom

After reading about sports, in pairs, students talk about what their favorite sports are and whether they prefer to play or watch.

Advantages

- Personalization makes language **relevant to students**.
- Personalization makes communication activities **meaningful**.
- Personalization helps **memorisation**.

Data Analysis

Read the classroom conversation between the two teachers who discuss how to manage classroom activities for students' active engagement.

Mr. Choi : You know, I've noticed my students aren't really engaging in some of the activities I've been doing lately. It's like they're just going through the motions.

Ms. Park : Yeah, I've had that problem before too. However, I fixed it. When students can relate the material to their own lives, they tend to pay more attention and participate more.

Mr. Choi : That's a good point. I've been doing more structured exercises, but I guess they're not really connecting with the content. How do you make it more personal, though?

Ms. Park : It's simpler than it sounds. For example, instead of just practicing vocabulary in isolation, I have them use it in sentences about their own experiences. Like if we're talking about hobbies, I ask them to share what they actually do in their free time, instead of just repeating phrases from the book.

Mr. Choi : I see. That definitely makes it more real for them. And I guess it makes communication activities feel more natural too, right?

Ms. Park : Exactly. When they're talking about themselves, it's not just language practice anymore—it's an actual conversation. Plus, they're more likely to remember what they've said because it's personal to them.

Mr. Choi : That makes sense. I always notice they struggle with memorization when the material feels too disconnected from their lives. But if they're using it to talk about things that matter to them, it probably sticks better.

Ms. Park : Yeah, and it doesn't have to be complicated. Even just asking them to use new vocabulary to describe something they like—whether it's a favorite movie, place, or even a personal goal—helps them internalize the language faster.

Mr. Choi : I like that. I think I'll try tweaking my next lesson. Maybe I'll have them talk about their future plans using the future tense instead of just working with those fill-in-the-blank exercises.

Ms. Park : That's a great idea! It'll get them talking, and they'll feel like they're using the language for something real, not just for an exercise. You'll probably see a difference in how engaged they are.

Mr. Choi : I hope so! Thanks for the tip—I'll let you know how it goes

Q1 Based on the conversation between the two teachers, fill in the blank with the most appropriate term.

> In this more authentic conversation, the teachers casually discuss how ______________________ makes language activities more engaging and memorable by connecting content to students' real lives, leading to better participation and retention. The second teacher offers practical examples that are easy to implement in the classroom.

>> Possible Answers p.218

(3) Provide opportunities for learners to notice the gap

Noticing the gap, a concept integral to language learning, refers to the process by which learners become aware of the differences(gap) between their language use (what they can say) and the target language norm or model (what they want to say). This awareness is crucial *for self-correction and language development*. Here are several strategies for providing opportunities for learners to notice the gap in classroom settings:

① Comparative output analysis: Engage students in activities where they compare their spoken or written output with that of peers, native speakers, or model outputs provided by textbooks or the teacher. This can be done through peer review sessions or by analyzing recordings/ transcripts of native speakers followed by self-recording of the same task. Highlighting differences helps learners notice gaps in vocabulary, grammar, pronunciation, and usage.

② Recasts and explicit correction: When learners make errors during speaking activities, provide immediate feedback in the form of recasts (repeating the incorrect sentence correctly) or explicit correction. Encourage learners to repeat the corrected form. This immediate feedback helps students notice discrepancies between their interlanguage and the target language.

③ Dictogloss activities: Use a **dictogloss** activity, where learners listen to a short text, read aloud at normal speed, try to write down everything they hear, and then work in groups to reconstruct the text. This activity forces learners to notice the gap in their listening comprehension and language production skills compared to the original text.

In the Classroom

In my classes, I put the **present passive simple in context** using a text about the olive harvest. After creating interest in the theme of the lesson, I read at a natural speed:

There ***are estimated*** *nine million olive trees in Palestine, which can produce tons of oil. Green ripe olives* ***are picked*** *in October by thousands of Palestinian farmers who work daily for over a month. More than half of the Palestinian population participate in the olive harvest. Once the harvest* ***is completed****, fresh olives* ***are sent*** *to the press. Olive oil* ***is*** *then* ***extracted*** *from the olives and packaged in yellow gallons. The product* ***is*** *not only* ***sold*** *in Palestine but also* ***shipped*** *around the world.*

I checked learners' general understanding of the text, then I re-read it. This time learners wrote down key words. **In groups**, they tried to **reconstruct** the text. Then they compared their version with another group, and worked together to agree on one version. Finally, I **showed the original version** on an interactive whiteboard.

During the activity, **the learners used their linguistic knowledge and worked out the meaning and form of the emerging target language**. This is **how they 'notice' the gaps in their current version of English**. The process can lead to a restructure in their mental picture of the language system.

(4) Maintain the balance between focus on accuracy and a focus on fluency

While fluency may in many communicative language courses be an initial goal in language teaching, accuracy is achieved to some extent by allowing students to focus on the elements of phonology, grammar, and discourse in their spoken output: task-based instruction, giving some feedback on students' errors

① **Fluency-based activity**: Fluency refers to how well a learner communicates meaning rather than how many mistakes they make in grammar, pronunciation and vocabulary. In other words, the ease with which a learner can speak and how well they can communicate without pauses or hesitations, without needing to search for words or phrases, without having to consider the language of what they are about to say.

It's important to note that a person who is fluent may not necessarily be 100% accurate but they are generally still comprehensible. Fluency activities focus not so much on how the students are communicating but what they are communicating. Examples of fluency activities are *conversations, roleplays, debates and projects.*

Data Analysis

Read the passages in <A> and <B> and follow the directions.

A

Task Difficulty

English teachers have several factors to consider when creating classroom tasks. One of the key considerations is whether the activity is appropriately challenging for our students—neither too difficult nor too easy. The following are factors that teachers should consider when creating tasks, along with corresponding questions:

Factors	Questions
Text	• How dense/complex are the texts that learners are required to process? • How relevant/irrelevant is the content to the learners' experience? • How much contextual support is provided?
Task	• How many steps are involved in the task? • How relevant and meaningful is the task? • How much time is available? • What degree of grammatical accuracy is required? • How much rehearsal time is available?
Learner	• Learner confidence • Motivation of learners • Prior knowledge of content • Degree of linguistic knowledge • Skill level and extent of cultural knowledge • Degree of familiarity with task type itself

B

T1 : Hi there, Ms. Jin! Shall we discuss our problem-solving task?
T2: Hello, Mr. Lee. Yes, let's start.
T1 : I believe our topic, 'Traffic Congestion in Front of the School,' is closely related to students' real lives, and the text we've chosen clearly outlines the problem.
T2: I agree. The level of vocabulary and grammar is accessible for them. Regarding the task process — from understanding the problems to deciding on a solution — the steps are clear and logical.
T1 : My concern is whether we're providing enough time for presentation practice.
T2: Presentation practice is essential. We should allocate more time for it, ensuring students feel confident about their actual presentations.
T1 : You're right. So, let's adjust the plan to include about half an hour for students to feel ready. What do you think?
T2: Perfect! Also, we need to consider if students have enough background knowledge on the topic.
T1 : True. The topic 'Traffic congestion in front of school,' while relevant, might be challenging without previous knowledge. Perhaps, we should provide additional materials for a better understanding.
T2: A background video followed by a Q&A session could bridge that gap and engage students.
T1 : Excellent idea. I'll look for a suitable video and share it with you for review. We'll add it to our lesson plan.
T2: Sure, let's work on it together.

T=teacher

Q1 Based on the information provided in <A>, identify the TWO factors that teachers in <B> consider to reduce the task difficulty.

____

____

Q2 Explain how the strategies related to these factors will support students in completing the task, using concrete evidence from both <A> and <B>.

____

____

>> Possible Answers p.218

② **Accuracy-based activity:** Accuracy refers to how correct learners' use of the language system is,including their use of grammar, pronunciation and grammar. In other words, accuracy is the correct use of tenses, verb forms, collocations and colloquialisms, among other things.

Accuracy activities are activities which will concentrate on the nitty gritty of the language construction to ensure that the language item is produced 100% accurately-such *as grammar exercises, gap fills, drilling or noticing activities*. These usually take place in the controlled practice stage of the lesson. There is not a lot of variation in these activities, as there is a right and a wrong answer.

For many EFL learners, accuracy is considered very important, and one of the main responsibilities of an EFL teacher is thought to be to correct errors and ensure the highest level of accuracy. However, while, of course, a certain degree of accuracy is needed for all communication, classroom tasks should not be geared towards more accuracy activities than fluency, because fluency is just as important.

Data Analysis

Activity 1

In my class I taught grammatical structures as follows:

T : Good morning, class, Summer vacation is coming soon. I will go to Jeju Island and travel around. Kim, what will you do this vacation?
S1: I go to Granma's house in Busan.
T : Kim, I go to Gramma's house?
S1: Oh... eh... I will go to Gramma's house.
T : Perfect! What about Bora? Do you have any plans?
S2: Um.. I.. take guitar lessons.
T : I take guitar lessons?
S2: Uh... I will take guitar lessons.
T : Good! What a great plan! Why do you want to do that?

Activity 2

- T has Ss form groups of three.
- T asks Ss to think of a job that they would like to have in the future.
- Ss use "If I were..." to share their opinions about their future dream jobs.
- Assuming that their dreams come true, two Ss take a reporter's role and interview the other S asking how he or she feels about his or her job.
- Ss take turns and continue the activity.

Q1 Read the following and discuss how these TWO activities differ from traditional accuracy-based activities.

____

____

____

>> Possible Answers p.219

(5) Train students to use strategies

① Learning strategies

Data Analysis

Read the passage in <A> and the dialogue in <B>.

A

While styles are preferred ways of processing information, strategies are conscious mental and behavioural procedures that people engage in with the aim to gain control over their learning process. Although the definitions and boundaries of learning strategies can be varied, there are several categories of strategies that have generally been agreed upon, as shown below.

Strategy	Definition	Examples
Metacognitive	Learners being consciously aware of their thought processes and cognition	• Planning • Monitoring • Evaluating
Cognitive	Learners using their brains to manipulate or transform L2 input in order to retain it	• Keyword technique • Repetition • Inferencing • Visualization
Social	Learners involving others in their L2 learning processes	• Having conversations in L2 with other speakers • Practicing L2 with other classmates
Affective	Learners engaging their own emotions to facilitate L2 learning	• Rewarding oneself for studying • Intentionally reducing anxiety

B

Mina : Hi, Junho. Is everything going well?
Junho: Hey, Mina! Good to see you here. Can I ask you something?
Mina : Sure. What's up?
Junho: I know you are a good English learner and I'd like to get some tips.
Mina : Sure. Will you tell me how you study?
Junho: I try to set schedules for learning. For example, I decide what I should study first and what I can study at a later time.
Mina : That's a good way. Anything else you do?
Junho: While studying, I sometimes stop to check my comprehension.
Mina : Okay. In my case, I usually create pictures in my mind to remember the things I've studied.
Junho: Oh, you do? I've never tried to create mental images when I study.
Mina : Actually, it helps me remember things a lot longer.
Junho: That makes sense. I think I need to try it.
Mina : And, whenever I find some difficult English expressions I'm not familiar with, I talk in English with native speakers to find out exactly what those expressions mean.
Junho: I usually use my online dictionary. But I often find the dictionary explanation is rather difficult for me.
Mina : That happens a lot. I think asking questions to others is one of the best ways to clarify the meaning.
Junho: I quite agree. I'll apply your advice to my English learning immediately. Thanks for your tips!

Q1 Identify TWO strategies in <A> that Mina recommended to Junho in <B>.

____

____

____

Q2 Support your answers with evidence from <B>.

____

____

____

>> Possible Answers p.219

② **Communication strategies**: prefabricated patterns, circumlocutions, literal translation, code-switching, word coinage, appeal to the authority, nonlinguistic signals, approximation, time-gaining strategies, foreignizing, avoidance

Data Analysis

Read the passages and follow the directions.

A

Below is a student's writing and a conversation with his teacher about the writing.

Student Writing

Someone first showed the bicycle to the public in the late 18th century. People first thought it was not safe or comfortable. But many creative people improved it. So, many people use the bicycle widely as a form of transportation or for exercise today. Bicycle makers manufacture lighter, faster and stronger bicycles now than before. Because of that, more people ride the bicycle around the world these days than any time in the past. But they used some unique types of cycles in the old days like the four-cycle.

Teacher-student one-on-one Conference

T: What is this writing about?
S: It's about the bicycle. Do you ride a bicycle?
T: Yes, I sometimes do. So your writing is not about people who produce or use the bicycle.
S: That's right.
T: OK, the main theme is the bicycle. But none of the sentences has the bicycle as its subject.
S: I know. But if the bicycle becomes the subject, then I have to use many passives. They are complicated and difficult. So I tried not to use them.
T: But it would be better to use the bicycle as the subject in most sentences. That way, it will become clear that the main focus of your writing is the bicycle.
S: Well, okay. I'll try.
T: You used the word "manufacture." Did you know this word?
S: No, I didn't. At first, I wanted to use "make" but then the sentence looked a bit awkward because the subject is "makers." It would go like "Bicycle makers make."

T: I see.
S: So I looked up a different word in a dictionary that has the same meaning as "make."
T: That works. What about this word "four-cycle?" What do you mean? Are you trying to describe a bicycle but with four wheels?
S: Yes, I am. I added "four" to "cycle" just like "bi" is put before "cycle" in bicycle.
T: Oh, it is called "quadricycle." "Quadri" means four just as "bi" means two.

T=teacher, S=student

B

When writing as well as speaking in a second language, learners who have limited command of the second language may have to use a variety of strategies that can compensate for their lack of knowledge of the target language grammar and vocabulary in order to effectively get their intended meaning or message across to a reader or listener. Strategies employed for this purpose include avoidance, code switching, word coinage, appeal to authority, and using prefabricated patterns. As these strategies constitute a significant part of strategic competence, advances in the learners' ability to effectively use them play a considerable role in promoting their communicative competence.

Q1 Based upon the students' writing and his dialogue with the teacher in <A>, identify THREE strategies the student used from those mentioned in <B>.

____

____

____

Q2 Provide corresponding evidence for each identified strategy from <A>.

____

____

____

>> Possible Answers p.219

③ Pair work

Data Analysis

Read the conversation and follow the directions.

Students are talking about their favorite dish in pairs.

S1: What is your favorite dish?
S2: Well, I like pig meat.
S1: Pig meat? You mean pork?
S2: That's right! I mean pork. What about you?
S1: Well, I don't like meat. In fact, I never eat meat.
S2: Are you a vegetarianist?
S1: Not quite. I eat fish burgers. Do you like burgers, too?
S2: Yes, and I love the potatoes that you eat with them.
S1: Do you mean French fries?
S2: That's right, French fries. Why do I keep forgetting that word?
S1: Don't worry. I could understand what you meant.

Q1 Based on the conversation, identify the types of communication strategies S2 uses to prevent a communication breakdown, citing concrete examples for each.

____

____

____

>> Possible Answers p.219

(6) Encourage students to take responsibility for their own learning

- Providing each role for students during group work: Jigsaw
- Arranging students to write their learning log after finishing speaking lessons

In today's English class, students were asked to retell the story to their partners after reading a newspaper article together. Their performance was video-recorded. The following is one of learning logs after a student watched the video.

Student's Learning Log

1. Mistakes and difficulties I had during the task

The newspaper article had a lot of new words that I've never seen before. I was worried if I could accurately retell the story.

2. Strategies I used to complete the task

Since I didn't have time to look up words in the dictionary, I had to guess their meanings based on the context. I thought I understood the story. When I didn't have enough words to describe it, I simply used Korean words.

3. Overall assessment of my performance on today's task

I paused a lot without speaking while I was telling the story because I didn't know what to say in English. When I was listening, I didn't understand my partner's story clearly. But I didn't ask her to repeat it because I wasn't sure if it was okay.

4. Strategies I will practice

In the past, I wrote down new words at least ten times to memorize them. It didn't work very well, but I don't know how else I can remember the words I will try to read more so I can learn more new words.

(7) Check up the levels of the students and their perceived needs

- Arranging students to take a diagnostic test before the lesson
- Choosing topics relevant to students' real lives(needs analysis)
- Providing level-differentiated task
- Setting appropriate grouping strategies
- No lengthy explanations/ Having a meaningful conversation(checking questions) with the students as a teacher demonstrates the activity

Data Analysis

Read the passage in <A> and the email in <B>.

A

Ms. Hong, a new English teacher, had a hard time getting her students to talk in her English speaking class. She investigated the issue and found a checklist related to the problems that hinder the students' active engagement in speaking. The checklist consisted of seven categories with descriptions: no preparation time, uneven participation, poor listening ability, lack of speaking strategy use, mother-tongue use, nothing to say, and inhibition. Based on her observations, she evaluated how often her students struggled with the problems in the checklist during her English speaking class.

Class Observation Checklist

Descriptions	Scale		
	1	2	3
1. Students need some quiet time before they are engaged in a speaking activity.		✓	
2. In group activities, some of the students free-ride without contributing to the discussion.		✓	
3. Students have listening difficulties when engaged in speaking activities.	✓		
4. Students are not aware of speaking strategies and need to develop their own.			✓
5. When students speak the same mother tongue, they tend to use it in group work, especially when the teacher is far away.			✓
6. Students complain that they cannot think of anything to say.		✓	
7. Students are often inhibited from trying to say things in English in the speaking class.			✓

1=seldom, 2=sometimes, 3=often

Ms. Hong gave careful thought to six, out of the seven problems, that she checked as "sometimes" or "often" in the checklist. She came up with satisfactory solutions to four of the problems; but for the other two, she decided to ask for help. She sent an email about the two problems to Mr. Park, a head teacher, in order to seek some advice. He replied as in <B>.

B

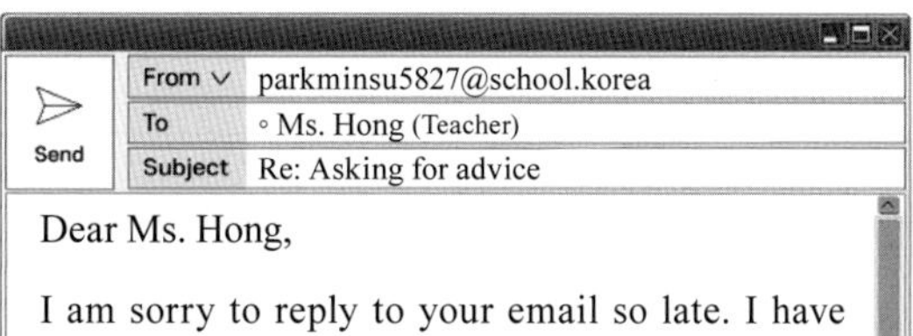
Send
From parkminsu5827@school.korea
To ◦ Ms. Hong (Teacher)
Subject Re: Asking for advice

Dear Ms. Hong,

I am sorry to reply to your email so late. I have thought about the two problems you mentioned in your email, and my suggestions for the problems are, in brief, as follows:

The first problem arises quite often in speaking classes. If the task you want to do in class is based on group work, I think you need to choose a task such as jigsaw that we talked about the other day. When I included that activity in my English speaking class, the students' participation increased significantly overall while they were pooling all their information in groups.

The second problem is another one that happens frequently in English speaking classes. Why don't you appoint one of the group members as monitor? I think the very awareness that someone is monitoring helps the students put more effort into using the target language.

I hope these suggestions work well in your class. If you have any more questions or problems, please feel free to talk to me.

Best regards,

Park, Min-su

Q1 Based on <A> and <B>, identify the TWO problems Ms. Hong asked for Mr. Park's advice about.

____

____

____

Q2 Explain why he made the suggestions for her two problems, respectively. Do NOT copy more than FOUR consecutive words in <A> and <B>.

____

____

____

>> Possible Answers p.219

Plus +

Suggestions for Teachers in Teaching Speaking

Here are some suggestions for English language teachers while teaching oral language:

- Provide maximum opportunity to students to speak the target language by providing a rich environment that contains *collaborative work, authentic materials and tasks, and shared knowledge.*
- Try to involve each student in every speaking activity; for this aim, practice different ways of student participation, for example, students can be given group roles during the group work.
- Reduce teacher speaking time(TTT) in class while increasing student speaking time (STT). Step back and observe students: a teacher plays roles *as a facilitator or a resource person.* Circulate around classroom to ensure that students are on the right track and see whether they need your help while they work in groups or pairs.
- Ask eliciting questions such as "What do you mean? How did you reach that conclusion?" in order to prompt students to speak more.
- Provide written feedback like "Your presentation was really great. It was a good job. I really appreciated your efforts in preparing the materials and efficient use of your voice…"
- Do not correct students' pronunciation mistakes very often while they are speaking. Correction should not distract student from his or her speech.
- Involve speaking activities not only in class but also out of class; ask students to join a speech club or conversation club.
- Provide the vocabulary beforehand that students need in speaking activities.
- Diagnose problems faced by students who have difficulty in expressing themselves in the target language and provide more opportunities to practice the spoken language; provide *a rehearsal time* before their presentation or public display.

3 Classroom Talk

(1) Questioning Techniques

Questioning techniques in the language classroom are essential for promoting engagement, improving language skills, encouraging critical thinking, and supporting student interaction. When used effectively, questioning not only enhances comprehension and language production but also motivates students to participate, reflect, and communicate in meaningful ways.

① **Display questions**: Display questions are questions where the teacher already knows the answer. The main goal of these questions is to assess students' knowledge or check comprehension.

② **Referential questions**: Referential questions, on the other hand, are questions where the teacher does not know the answer in advance. These questions are typically more open-ended and encourage students to provide personal opinions, experiences, or interpretations.

• Key Differences Between Display and Referential Questions •

Aspect	Display Questions	Referential Questions
Purpose	To check comprehension or recall information	To encourage communication and fluency
Teacher's Knowledge	Teacher knows the answer.	Teacher doesn't know the answer.
Type of Response	short, factual responses	extended, personal or opinion-based responses
Focus	accuracy and form	fluency and meaning
Examples	"What color is the sky?"	"What did you do last weekend?"

Data Analysis

A

Ms. Park and her students are reviewing a story they just read in class.

Ms. Park : Okay, class, let's start by reviewing the story. Can someone tell me, what is the name of the main character in the story?
Student 1 : Her name is Sarah.
Ms. Park : Good! Now, where does Sarah live?
Student 2 : She lives in New York.
Ms. Park : Exactly. What was Sarah's problem in the story?
Student 3 : She lost her job.
Ms. Park : Yes, that's right! Now, I want you to think about Sarah's situation. If you were in Sarah's shoes, what would you do?
Student 4 : I think I would look for another job, maybe something that I like more.
Student 5 : I would probably talk to my family to get advice before making a decision.
Ms. Park : Great ideas! Now, how do you think Sarah felt when she lost her job?
Student 6 : She was probably really scared and worried about what would happen next.

B

Ms. Park's Reflection Journal

I started with ______①______ questions to check my students' understanding of the basic facts from the story. I asked simple questions like, *"What is the name of the main character?"* and *"Where does she live?"* These questions helped me assess whether the students had retained key information and understood the fundamental aspects of the plot. I find that display questions are particularly useful when I want to make sure everyone is on the same page, especially for lower-proficiency students who might struggle with more complex language tasks. The short, direct responses allow all students to participate without feeling overwhelmed. It's also a good way to introduce the lesson and build a foundation before moving on to deeper discussions.

However, I realize that these questions alone can make the interaction feel a bit mechanical at times. The students' answers tend to be brief, and the focus is more on ______②______ than on engaging in meaningful conversation. So, while these questions are effective for reviewing factual information and checking comprehension, they don't really push students to think critically or express themselves fully. I try to use them sparingly, as a stepping stone toward more dynamic interactions. After the first type of questions, I shifted to ______③______ questions, like *"If you were in Sarah's shoes, what would you do?"* and *"How do you think Sarah felt when she lost her job?"* These questions really changed the atmosphere in the classroom. Suddenly, the students were eager to share their own thoughts, and their responses were much longer and more expressive. I love how these questions encourage personal reflection and real communication. The students aren't just recalling facts—they're using the language to think, hypothesize, and share their own perspectives.

What I found particularly rewarding was how these questions gave my more advanced students the opportunity to engage in critical thinking and use more complex language. They were able to discuss hypothetical situations, express emotions, and even debate different points of view. This really helped to build their ______④______ and confidence in speaking. It also fostered a more interactive and student-centered environment, where the conversation flowed naturally. In reflection, I think today's lesson was a success because I managed to create a lesson that focused both on accuracy and meaningful use of language. It reinforced my belief that using both types of questions in tandem offers a well-rounded approach to language teaching, catering to students' needs at different levels of proficiency.

Q1 Based on the classroom conversation in <A> and Ms. Park's reflection journal in <B>, fill in the blanks with appropriate words.

① ________________________________

② ________________________________

③ ________________________________

④ ________________________________

>> Possible Answers p.220

(2) IRE & IRF

① **IRE** (Initiation-Response-Evaluation): This type of classroom interaction is where the teacher initiates with a question, the student responds, and the teacher evaluates the response. This is more of a traditional, teacher-centered approach, often used to check for understanding and give feedback on correctness.

> ▶ **Purpose**: IRE is often used for quick checks of understanding or to confirm facts. It's useful for reviewing known material or assessing students' factual knowledge.

Example

Teacher: What's the capital of France?
Student : Paris.
Teacher: Correct! Great job.

② **IRF** (Initiation-Response-Feedback): In this interaction, the teacher initiates with a question, the student responds, and instead of just evaluating, the teacher provides feedback that extends the conversation. This fosters more student-centered communication and encourages further thinking or elaboration.

> ▶ **Purpose**: IRF promotes more active learning and allows students to explore topics in greater depth. It's valuable for developing critical thinking, communication skills, and deeper comprehension. The feedback encourages extended interaction, allowing the conversation to grow beyond simple recall of facts.

Example

Teacher: That's right! Now, can you tell me what's famous about Paris? Why do so many people visit the city?
Student : I think people visit because of the Eiffel Tower and the museums.
Teacher: Exactly! The Eiffel Tower is a major attraction, and Paris has a lot of art museums, like the Louvre. Have you ever learned about any of the famous paintings in the Louvre?
Student : Yes, I know about the Mona Lisa.
Teacher: Great! The Mona Lisa is one of the most famous paintings in the world. What do you think makes it so special?

4 Error Treatment

It refers to how teachers respond to students' mistakes in order to help them improve their language skills. Error treatment involves understanding what errors to correct, when to correct them, and how to provide feedback in a way that promotes learning without discouraging students.

(1) What to Correct

When deciding what to correct, teachers need to consider the types of errors students make. There are generally two main types of errors:

① **Global errors**: These are errors that affect overall understanding of the message.

② **Local errors**: These are minor errors that do not disrupt the meaning, such as mispronunciations or small grammatical mistakes (e.g., forgetting an article, like "a" or "the").

What to correct often depends on the learning objectives. For example, if the focus of the lesson is on fluency, teachers might prioritize communication over accuracy and avoid interrupting students for small errors. However, if the focus is on accuracy (e.g., a grammar lesson), teachers might focus on correcting specific structures or vocabulary.

(2) When to Correct

Timing is crucial in error correction, as it can affect a student's confidence and learning process. There are different options for when to correct errors:

① **Immediate correction**: This involves correcting errors as they happen. This method is useful in controlled practice activities, such as grammar drills or pronunciation practice, where the goal is accuracy. However, if used too often in fluency activities, it can interrupt the flow of conversation and discourage students from speaking.

② **Delayed correction**: This means waiting until after the activity to address errors. It is especially effective during communicative tasks like discussions or role-plays, where the focus is on fluency and communication. Teachers can take notes during the activity and address common errors afterward, either individually or as a class.

③ **Self-correction or Peer-correction**: Teachers can allow students to correct their own mistakes or have their peers help. This encourages autonomy and reduces the pressure from constant teacher correction. For example, after an error is made, a teacher can say, "Can you try that again?" or ask a peer to suggest a correction.

(3) How to Correct

How a teacher provides feedback is key to ensuring that correction is constructive and supports learning. There are several methods to correct errors in a language classroom:

① **Explicit correction**: The teacher directly points out the error and provides the correct form. This method is clear and effective, but overusing it can be demotivating, especially in a fluency-focused activity.

Ex | Student : He go to the store yesterday.
Teacher: Actually, we say 'He went to the store yesterday.'

② **Recasting**: The teacher repeats the student's sentence correctly without explicitly pointing out the mistake. This is a less intrusive way to correct errors, especially in fluency-focused activities, but students may not always notice the correction.

Ex | Student : He go to the store yesterday.
Teacher: Yes, he went to the store yesterday.

③ **Clarification request**: The teacher asks the student to clarify what they meant, indirectly signaling that there was a mistake. This method encourages self-correction and student reflection.

Ex | Student : He go to the store yesterday.
Teacher: Sorry? Could you say that again?

④ **Elicitation**: The teacher prompts the student to correct the error by asking leading questions or repeating part of the sentence with a pause, allowing the student to fill in the correct form.

Ex | Student : He go to the store yesterday.
Teacher: He...?
Student : He went to the store yesterday.

⑤ **Metalinguistic feedback**: The teacher gives comments or questions that guide the student to think about the structure of the language and self-correct the error.

Ex | Student : He go to the store yesterday.
Teacher: What tense do we use for actions that happened in the past?

⑥ **Repetition**: The teacher repeats the part of the student's sentence that contains the error, often with stress or a rising intonation, to signal that something needs to be corrected. It encourages the student to notice their mistake and self-correct.

Ex | Student : He go to the store yesterday.
Teacher: go?
Student: Oh, sorry. He went to the store yesterday.

Data Analysis

Script A

T: What did you do last Sunday?
S: Movie.
T: Excuse me?
S: I see a movie.
T: You saw a movie?
S: Yes, I see a movie.
T: But you saw a movie LAST SUNDAY, and last Sunday is in the past, right?
S: Oh, yes, right.
T: So, the correct verb is SAW, not SEE.

Script B

T: And what do you think?
S: He is coming lately.
T: He's coming...?
S: Later.
T: That's right!
S: He is coming later.

Q1 Read Script A and B and analyze feedback types.

Feedback types	Scrip A	Scrip B
Clarification request		
Recast		
Metalinguistic feedback		
Explicit correction		
Elicitation		

>> Possible Answers p.220

5 Factors to Consider in Error Treatment

(1) Student's Proficiency Level

Lower-level students might need more explicit correction and support, while more advanced learners might benefit from techniques that encourage self-correction and critical thinking.

(2) Activity Focus (Accuracy vs. Fluency)

In accuracy-focused activities (e.g., grammar exercises), immediate and direct correction might be more appropriate. In fluency-focused activities (e.g., discussions), delayed or subtle correction like recasting works better to maintain the flow of communication.

(3) Affective Factors

Some students may be more sensitive to correction, so it's important to create a positive and supportive learning environment. Encouraging students to see errors as part of the learning process helps reduce anxiety.

Effective error treatment in the language classroom involves knowing what errors to correct, when to correct them, and how to do so in a way that promotes learning without discouraging students. By balancing correction techniques with the objectives of the lesson and the needs of the students, teachers can help learners improve both their accuracy and fluency in a supportive and communicative environment.

6 How to Teach the Pronunciation – Segmentals & Suprasegmentals

Ms. Park's Reflection Journal on Teaching Pronunciation

In today's lesson, I focused on ways to improve my students' oral skills through the teaching of both **segmentals** and **suprasegmentals**. I've realized that balancing these two aspects is crucial in helping students develop not just accurate pronunciation but also natural-sounding, fluid speech.

While segmentals are important for clarity, I noticed that focusing too much on individual sounds can make students overly conscious and hesitant when speaking. I want to avoid making them feel too self-conscious, so I will incorporate more **communicative activities** where they can practice segmentals in context, rather than isolated drills.

Additionally, I realized that suprasegmentals are often overlooked but play a key role in making speech **intelligible** and **fluent**. Students can memorize vocabulary and grammar, but if they don't use proper intonation or stress, their speech sounds robotic or unclear. The students seemed to enjoy the rhythm exercises, and I plan to incorporate more of these **interactive**, **playful activities** to make learning suprasegmentals engaging.

Overall, teaching segmentals and suprasegmentals together is essential to developing my students' oral skills. Focusing on one without the other leaves gaps in their communication abilities. Moving forward, I will incorporate a variety of activities that target both aspects, ensuring that my students not only speak clearly but also sound natural and expressive. This holistic approach will undoubtedly contribute to their overall **fluency** and **communication skills** in English.

(1) Teaching Segmentals

Segmentals refer to the individual sounds or phonemes in a language, such as consonants and vowels. I believe that a strong foundation in segmental pronunciation is essential for my students, especially at the beginner and intermediate levels. When students mispronounce key sounds, it can lead to misunderstandings and difficulty in communication, even if they have a good grasp of grammar and vocabulary.

Approach to Segmentals

Today, I worked on teaching specific troublesome sounds that my students tend to struggle with, such as distinguishing between /r/ and /l/, or pronouncing /th/ sounds, which don't exist in their native language. I started by modeling these sounds for them and using **minimal pairs** (like "rice" vs. "lice" or "think" vs. "sink") to help them hear the difference. After some guided practice, I had them use the words in simple sentences to integrate the pronunciation into real communication.

(2) Teaching Suprasegmentals

Suprasegmentals include features like intonation, stress, rhythm, and pitch, and are just as important for effective oral communication. I find that even when students can pronounce individual sounds accurately, they often struggle with making their speech sound natural because of improper intonation or stress patterns. Without proper suprasegmental skills, even perfectly articulated words can sound awkward or difficult to understand.

Approach to Suprasegmentals

In today's lesson, I incorporated activities that focused on sentence stress and intonation. For example, we worked on stressing the right syllables in multi-syllabic words and using rising or falling intonation in yes/no and wh- questions. I used **dialogues and short role-plays**, where students practiced how changing the stress or intonation could change the meaning of a sentence (e.g., "You're going to the party?" vs. "You're going to the party.").

I also did a fun rhythm activity where students had to clap along with the stress patterns in sentences. This made them more aware of how stress and rhythm give natural flow to their speech.

(3) Balancing Segmentals and Suprasegmentals

In teaching both segmentals and suprasegmentals, I understand the need to strike a balance between the two. While segmentals are the building blocks of clear speech, suprasegmentals give language its natural rhythm and flow, which is essential for students to sound more fluent and native-like. I need to integrate both into my lessons, so students can work on accurate pronunciation (segmentals) while also mastering the prosody of the language (suprasegmentals).

▶ Next Steps: I plan to use more **integrated activities** where students can practice both segmentals and suprasegmentals in context, such as **through storytelling, dialogues, and role-plays**. These activities will allow students to focus on both the individual sounds and the overall melody of the language, helping them become more confident and fluent speakers.

Activity: "Find Someone Who..."

- Objective: Practice the correct pronunciation of specific target sounds while engaging in a communicative, interactive activity.
- Target Segmentals: /i/ and /i:/ (short "i" as in "ship" and long "ee" as in "sheep")
- Instructions: Prepare a handout with a list of prompts that include words with the target sounds. For example:
  - Find someone who likes **ea**ting pizza.
  - Find someone who has been on a s**hi**p.
  - Find someone who has a pet sh**ee**p.
  - Find someone who enjoys reading b**oo**ks.
  - Find someone who likes s**wi**mming.

- Introduction (3–5 minutes)
  - Begin by reviewing the target sounds with the class, focusing on the difference between /i/ and /i:/ sounds. Give examples like "ship" (short i) vs. "sheep" (long ee) and model the correct pronunciation.
  - Practice the sounds with the class by repeating pairs of words (e.g., "ship" vs. "sheep," "swimming" vs. "reading").

- Activity (15–20 minutes)
  - Hand out the "Find Someone Who..." worksheet to each student.
  - Tell students they need to move around the classroom and ask their classmates questions based on the prompts (e.g., "Do you like eating pizza?" or "Have you been on a ship?"). Encourage students to use the target words while asking the questions.
  - The goal is for students to find someone who matches each description and write that person's name next to the prompt.
- Feedback and Reflection (5–10 minutes)
  - Once students have completed the activity, gather them back together and review the answers.
  - Ask a few students to share their findings, focusing on the correct pronunciation of the target sounds (e.g., "I found someone who has been on a ship").
  - Provide corrective feedback or model the correct pronunciation if needed, but keep the focus on the communication that occurred during the activity.

Activity Analysis

- Communicative Focus
  The activity emphasizes real communication through peer interaction, not just isolated pronunciation drills. Students have to ask each other meaningful questions, which encourages natural use of the target sounds.
- Contextualized Practice
  Instead of focusing only on sounds in isolation, students practice pronouncing the segmentals in a communicative context (e.g., using "ship" or "sheep" in a real question).
- Engagement
  The interactive nature of the activity keeps students engaged and focused on both pronunciation and communication. It also provides plenty of opportunities for repetition and practice without feeling repetitive.
- Feedback in Context
  After the communicative part of the activity, students receive feedback on how well they used the segmentals during the interaction, promoting awareness of accurate pronunciation within real-world communication.

By integrating segmental practice into this kind of communicative activity, students can improve their pronunciation while also developing their overall speaking and listening skills in a meaningful context.

7 ICT Classroom

(1) Digital Literacy

Digital literacy refers to the ability to effectively find, evaluate, create, and communicate information using digital technologies. It involves not just basic computer skills, but also understanding how to critically use online resources, navigate different digital platforms, create digital content, and participate responsibly in online environments. In the context of education, digital literacy equips students with the skills they need to succeed in an increasingly digital world.

(2) Classroom Example to Build an ICT Classroom

- Project: Creating a Collaborative Digital Presentation
- Objective: Develop students' digital literacy by using digital tools to create and present a project collaboratively.
- Tools: Google Slides, Online Research Tools (e.g., Google Scholar, educational websites), and a Classroom Learning Management System (LMS) like Google Classroom or Microsoft Teams.
- Activity Procedure:

  ① Topic Selection and Research: The teacher assigns students to groups, and each group is given a broad topic (e.g., environmental issues, historical events, or cultural diversity).
  Students must conduct online research using credible sources to gather information on their topic. The teacher guides them on how to evaluate reliable sources and avoid misinformation, thus building their critical digital literacy skills.

② Collaborative Work on Google Slides: Each group creates a collaborative Google Slides presentation, where all members contribute from their devices. They work on text, images, videos, and charts that illustrate their research findings.
Throughout the process, students learn how to embed videos, hyperlink resources, and cite online references. This step enhances their technical digital skills as they work with multimedia.

③ Feedback and Peer Review: Students upload their work to Google Classroom (or another LMS). The teacher and peers review and comment on each group's presentation, giving feedback using digital collaboration tools.
This develops their ability to communicate effectively and responsibly in a digital space, an important aspect of digital citizenship.

④ Final Presentation: Students present their final projects using digital tools in the classroom, such as interactive whiteboards or projectors. The focus is on how they use technology to communicate their ideas clearly and creatively.
The teacher assesses not just content knowledge but also digital literacy skills, such as proper source citation, multimedia integration, and collaborative work.

▶ **Rationale:** This activity builds a strong ICT(Information and Communication Technology) classroom by integrating digital tools into the learning process. Students practice researching, collaborating, and creating content using digital technologies, thereby enhancing their digital literacy in a meaningful, practical way.

Data Analysis

Examine the evaluation results of a teaching tool by a review committee in <A> and read Ms. Jang's comments in <B>. Then, follow the directions.

A

Evaluation of Three CMC tools

<table>
<tr><th colspan="2">Criteria</th><th>Tool A</th><th>Tool B</th><th>Tool C</th></tr>
<tr><td rowspan="2">User Experience</td><td>user-friendly design</td><td>Good</td><td>Okay</td><td>Good</td></tr>
<tr><td>Supportive features for diverse learners (e.g., subtitles, text-to-speech technology)</td><td>Okay</td><td>Good</td><td>Poor</td></tr>
<tr><td rowspan="2">Content Quality</td><td>Accuracy and relevance of the educational content</td><td>Poor</td><td>Good</td><td>Poor</td></tr>
<tr><td>Alignment with curriculum standards and learning objectives</td><td>Good</td><td>Good</td><td>Good</td></tr>
<tr><td rowspan="2">Engagement and Interactivity</td><td>Variety and effectiveness of interactive elements</td><td>Good</td><td>Okay</td><td>Good</td></tr>
<tr><td>Real-time feedback support</td><td>Poor</td><td>Good</td><td>Poor</td></tr>
<tr><td rowspan="2">Assessment and Tracking Features</td><td>Availability and variety of assessment tools</td><td>Poor</td><td>Okay</td><td>Good</td></tr>
<tr><td>Detailed analytics for educators</td><td>Okay</td><td>Good</td><td>Good</td></tr>
<tr><td>Security and Privacy</td><td>Security features to protect user data</td><td>Okay</td><td>Good</td><td>Okay</td></tr>
</table>

B

Ms. Jang's Comments

To enhance English interaction among my students, I plan to integrate a Computer-Mediated Communication(CMC) tool into my lessons. The ideal CMC tool must meet specific criteria: it should support students with relatively low proficiency levels by offering comprehensive support features, such as providing subtitles and assistive technology that reads the text aloud. Additionally, I seek a tool that provides instant feedback so that students can promptly recognize language errors and self-correct them. Furthermore, the tool should offer comprehensive analytics on each student's performance and learning progress, allowing me to give personalized instruction tailored to individual needs. With these key features, I am confident that the chosen tool will cultivate a dynamic and inclusive learning environment, ensuring every student's success.

Q1 Considering the information in <A> and <B>, choose the ONE CMC tool you would recommend for Ms. Jang.

____

____

____

Q2 Provide THREE reasons for recommending it based on its characteristics.

____

____

____

>> Possible Answers p.220

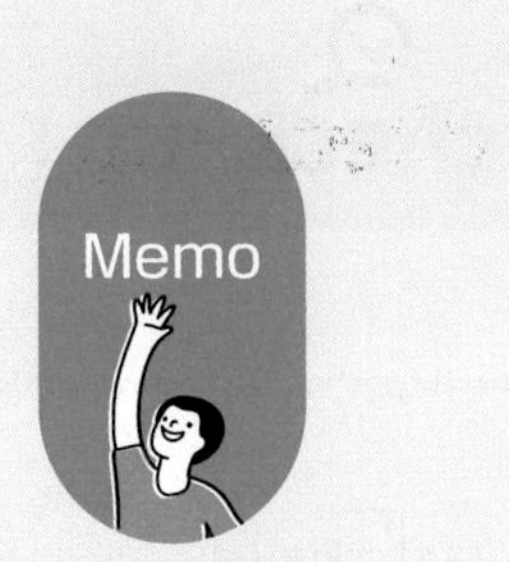
Memo

Key-concepts check-up : Writing

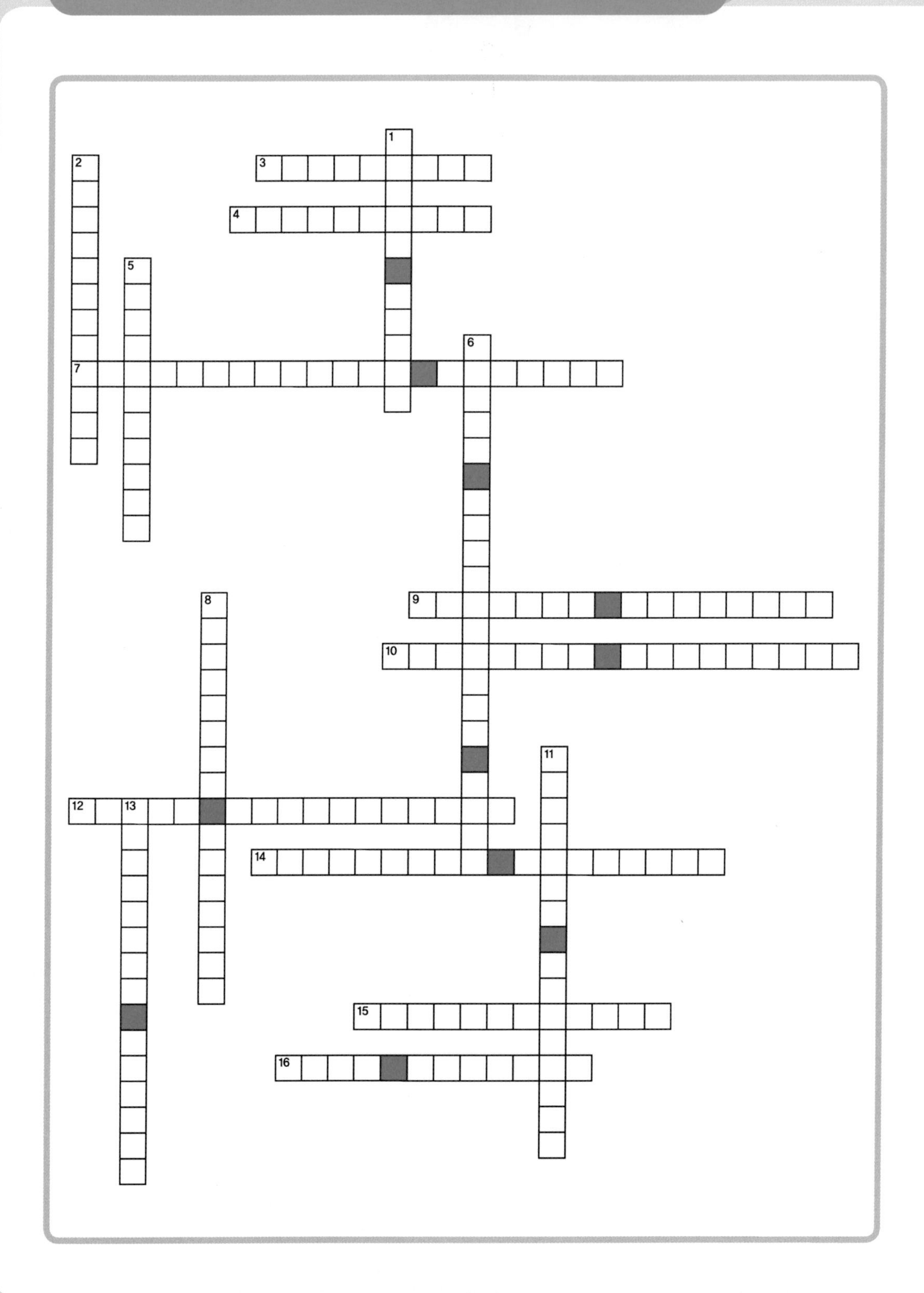

ACROSS ➡

❸ It means the utterances in a text go together even though there are no explicit cohesive links between the utterances.

❹ This activity begins with a key word or central idea placed in the center of a page around which the student jots down in a few minutes all of the free associations triggered by the subject matter. The words or phrases generated are put on the page or board in a pattern which takes shapes from the connections the writer sees as each new thought emerges.

❼ This writing can be quite motivating. It enables the stronger students to help the weaker ones.

❾ This is a mixture of online and face-to-face course delivery. For example, learners might meet once a week with a teacher face-to-face for an hour, and do a further two hours' work weekly online.

❿ This encourages a writer to take two or more short, choppy sentences and combine them into one effective sentence.

⓬ A paragraph is read at normal speed, usually two or three times. Then the teacher asks students to rewrite the paragraph to the best of their recollection of the reading.

⓮ Information which is given to the student, either in written or recorded verbal form, about the present state of their learning.

⓯ This reflects writing activities that are performed in real life outside the class such as: writing telephone message, texting on the phone, writing facebook messages, etc.

⓰ This allows students to identify each other's strengths and weaknesses in their writing skills while being less reliant on the teacher. When students experience this, they become more empowered, and more objective in their writing.

DOWN ↓

❶ This writing approach mainly concerned on teaching particular genres that students need control of in order to succeed in particular situations. This might include an emphasis on the content of the text as well as the context in which the text is produced.

❷ As the class writes, the teacher can talk with individual students about work in progress. Through careful questioning, the teacher can support a student writer in getting ideas together, organizing them, and finding appropriate language.

❺ The teacher's role of encouraging students to participate and makes suggestions about how students may proceed in an activity. The teacher should be helping students only when necessary.

❻ When students still favor comments on the grammatical and lexical correctness of their work, the teacher can use this. This serves to highlight the error but still requires the students to reflect on what the error actually is.

❽ This enables students and teachers to interact on a one-to-one basis at any level and in any learning context. They are very useful communicative events at the early stages of learning to write in a new language.

⓫ This approach focuses on the steps involved in creating a piece of work. A writer will get closer to perfection by producing, reflecting on, discussing, and reworking successive draft of text.

⓭ These are words or phrases that show the relationship between paragraphs or sections of a text or speech. These are words like 'For example', 'In conclusion', 'however' and 'moreover'. - **write in singular form**

Answer

ACROSS ➡ **3.** coherence **4.** clustering **7.** collaborative writing **9.** blended learning **10.** sentence combining **12.** dicto-composition **14.** narrative feedback **15.** authenticity **16.** peer-editing

DOWN ⬇ **1.** genre-based **2.** conferencing **5.** facilitator **6.** error correction code **8.** dialogue journal **11.** process-oriented **13.** cohesive device

02 How to Teach Students' Writing Skills

1 Product vs. Process-oriented Writing Approach

- Writer-based prose / Reader-based prose
- an error-free coherent text / successive draft of text

(1) Classroom Activity: Dicto-comp

> The teacher played a short news clip from the website, "BBC English Online" three times successively and then asked students in a group to rewrite the news story in their own words.

(2) Classroom Activity: Process-oriented Writing Activity

> The teacher provides background information about artificial intelligence and Ss watch videos related to the topic. Then, students discuss the topic in groups and brainstorm. They sketch their ideas and write the first drafts, focusing on content. The teacher reviews Ss' drafts and provides meaning-focused feedback. Based on the feedback students revise their drafts once, and then hand in their final drafts to the teacher.

Data Analysis

Read the passages in <A> and <B>, and follow the directions.

A

In planning a comprehensive writing lesson, it's crucial for teachers to be familiar with the structured steps designed to enhance students' writing skills effectively. Below are the structured steps for general process-oriented writing lessons.

- Start with brainstorming: Students think of as many ideas as they can.
- Make a mind map: This helps show how the ideas are connected.
- Provide a model text: This serves as an example of quality writing, enhancing students' comprehension of the teacher's instructions.
- Write the first draft: Students put their ideas into sentences and paragraphs.
- Provide language supports: the teacher can answer questions on structure, lexical items, etc.
- Do peer editing: Students work in pairs to give and receive feedback to improve each other's drafts.
- Write the second drafts: Students revise their first drafts better using their partner's advice.
- Provide Teacher's feedback: The teacher reviews students' second drafts and gives more feedback for improvement.
- Write the final drafts: Students complete their final draft, using all the advice they received to make their writing the best it can be.

B

Below is the part of the writing lesson plan that Ms. Kang, a middle school English teacher, has designed for her low-intermediate level students following the structured steps for writing lessons.

Lesson Procedure

Step 1	• T asks students to share simple actions they can take to help the environment. • Ss call out ideas on how they can contribute to environmental conservation in their daily lives. • T writes down students' ideas on the board.
Step 2	Ss create a mind map, linking their conservation ideas and how they impact the environment.
Step 3	T asks Ss, in groups, to discuss the structure and required content of an essay about personal environmental actions.
Step 4	Ss begin writing their draft, focusing on what actions they take for conservation and why these are important.
Step 5	T walks around the classroom and gives advice regarding structure, vocabulary, and other related topics.
Step 6	In pairs, Ss exchange their drafts and provide constructive feedback to each other.
Step 7	With the feedback in mind, Ss refine their work and write the second draft.
Step 8	T asks Ss to read their second draft by themselves and fix any punctuation, spelling, or writing convention errors.
Step 9	Ss write their final essay and post it on the class blog.

Q1 Considering information in <A> and <B>, identify the TWO steps from the lesson plan in <B> that differ from the logical sequence provided in <A>.

____

____

____

Q2 Then explain your answers with evidence from <A> and <B>.

____

____

____

>> Possible Answers p.220

2 How to Support the Lower Level Students

(1) Teaching Principles

- Scaffold Writing Tasks
  Break down writing tasks into manageable steps. For example, start with brainstorming, then move to outlining, and finally proceed to sentence or paragraph writing. This step-by-step approach makes writing less intimidating and helps students build confidence as they progress.

- Use Sentence Starters and Frames
  Provide sentence starters and writing frames to help students structure their thoughts. For example, prompts like "I think that..." or "One reason is..." guide students in forming complete sentences and coherent thoughts without struggling with language formulation.

- Provide Vocabulary and Phrase Banks
  Offer a list of key vocabulary and useful phrases related to the writing topic. This helps lower-level students express ideas without needing to search for the right words, allowing them to focus on organizing their thoughts.

- Focus on Simple Sentence Structure
  Encourage the use of simple sentences before moving to complex structures. Teaching subject-verb-object(SVO) sentences initially helps students gain clarity and reduces errors, laying a strong foundation for more advanced writing.

- Model Writing
  Show examples of good writing, such as teacher-written samples or student models. By breaking down these examples together, students can observe structure, tone, and word choice, giving them a clearer idea of expectations and the process of crafting written pieces.

- Emphasize Content over Grammar

  Focus on content and clarity in early drafts, and address grammar and syntax in later revisions. Encouraging students to prioritize their ideas first helps them feel more comfortable writing and prevents grammar concerns from stifling expression.

- Provide Frequent, Specific Feedback

  Give constructive feedback on specific aspects of their writing, such as organization or idea clarity, and celebrate small successes. Short, clear feedback on a few focus areas helps students identify growth points and motivates them to improve.

- Encourage Peer Support

  Use peer review sessions where students can read each other's work and provide simple feedback. Working with peers can make writing feel less isolating, and feedback from classmates may feel less intimidating.

- Integrate Visual Aids and Graphic Organizers

  Use visual aids like mind maps, flowcharts, or graphic organizers to help students plan and organize ideas before writing. This support is particularly helpful for visual learners and assists students in structuring their work effectively.

- Build Writing Confidence Through Positive Reinforcement

  Reinforce positive aspects of each student's writing and celebrate progress, even small ones. Confidence-building is crucial for lower-level students, as feeling successful encourages them to take on more challenging writing tasks over time.

(2) Classroom Writings

The teacher gives each of the students a short story of a dog and a set of four sequential pictures showing its storyline. All students read the story silently for 3 minutes. After reading it high level students return the story and pictures to the teacher but low-level students keep the pictures. If necessary, also, they get some key words from the story. While high level students write the story as accurately and closely as they can remember, low level students write the story with the aid of the pictures and key words.

Teaching Procedure

- Ss write down all the ideas that come to mind in connection with the given topic. (brainstorming)
- Ss extend their ideas into a mind map or clustering.
- T provides a model text and Ss read it by focusing on coherence and cohesion of a model text.
- In pairs, Ss write the first draft of their texts. (reader and writer)
- When Ss co-construct texts, T moves around the classroom, providing feedback or answering questions on structure and lexical items, etc.
- Ss edit their text. (self-editing / peer editing)
- Ss write the second draft based on self-and peer editing. Then, T responds to students' second drafts suitably.
- T returns the drafts and then Ss write the final draft based upon teacher feedback.

3 How to Respond to Students Writing

(1) Narrative Feedback

Meaning-focused feedback on content and organization in terms of strengths and weakness by giving specific examples and if possible, suggesting practical solutions

(2) Form-focused Feedback

• Error Correction Code: simply indicate where the errors occur •

Advantages	1. Promotes Student Autonomy ECC allows students to take ownership of their learning by identifying and correcting their own mistakes, fostering a habit of self-editing and reducing reliance on the teacher. 2. Improves Error Awareness Over time, students become more aware of specific language aspects they struggle with. ECC helps students target these problem areas, leading to gradual improvement in accuracy.
Limitations	1. May Be Confusing for Lower-Level Students Without adequate language proficiency, lower-level students may struggle to understand certain error codes and how to correct their errors, potentially leading to frustration rather than learning. 2. Limited Focus on Content and Expression Error Correction Codes typically address language form (grammar, spelling, punctuation) rather than content quality or expressive style, which could limit students' broader writing development. 3. Can Lead to Overemphasis on Error-Free Writing Focusing on error correction can make students overly concerned with producing perfect grammar at the expense of creativity and fluency in writing.

(3) Classroom Feedback

① Narrative(written comments) & ECC

The following excerpts are two students' writing samples with feedback from their teachers:

Sample 1

Do you remember your middle school's life? Well, compared to high schools, middle schools end up more earlier. Also, middle school students don't worry about their future as much as high schoolers. However, there is a big similarity between middle school and high school, which is both students have to study a lot, and the fact that most of them go to academy.

Teacher comments

Nice work! You started with an attractive question, which is a good organizational skill for the introduction of an essay. When you rewrite, please try to add your own story about your school life to make the essay more appealing.

Sample 2

All Koreans enters school, and learns many things. They entered
Agr Agr Tns
elementary school, Middle school, High school. Total, there is twelve
Agr
grade. In elementary school, Koreans learned six year. In middle
Agr Tns Agr
school, they learned three year and same in high school.
Tns Agr

Agr=Agreement, Tns=Verb tense

② Checklist

Teacher's Reflection

This semester I have been using a checklist in my English writing class to help my students revise their drafts by themselves. The checklist I provide for my students covers the following areas: content, organization, grammar, vocabulary, and mechanics. Below is a part of the checklist.

Areas	Indicators	Yes	No
(1) Grammar	I use correct subject and verb agreement.		
	I use verb tense correctly.		
(2) Mechanics	I put a period at the end of every sentence.		
	I use capital letters correctly.		
	I spell the words correctly.		

At first, the checklist didn't seem feasible because there was little improvement, especially in organization in writing. To find the reason, I held group conferences with the students and discovered that the indicators for organization were too complicated for them to understand. Some of them included more than one aspect to check simultaneously. So, I divided those indicators into two or three separate sentences so that one indicator assesses only one aspect. Since the revision of the indicators, the students' organization has gotten much better.

However, some students still had problems using the checklist appropriately. So, I ran a couple of training sessions to teach the students what the indicators meant and how they should be utilized. First, we read the indicators and I asked if they made sense. Then, I had them practice checking particular errors with a sample paragraph I had prepared. Since the training sessions, the students have been making significantly fewer errors. Overall, the use of the checklist has worked well in the revision process.

③ Writing conference

Mr. Min, a middle school English teacher, is talking with his student, Jinhee, about her writing.

T : Jinhee, I think you put a lot of effort into this first draft.
S : Yeah. But I think I made many mistakes.
T : Don't worry. I'll give you some comments on the categories you need to improve so that you can revise your draft. Can you do that?
S : Yes.
T : Great. Let's begin with content. I like your story, but it'll be better if you add more details here. Do you remember that we discussed how to use supporting details last week?
S : Yes, I do.
T : Good. I also saw that you had problems with organization.
S : You're right. Many events are popping up in my mind, but I can't put them logically.
T : One way to solve the problem is to use linking words such as *and, so, but, however, then, thus*, and so on, in order to show a logical sequence of events.
S : I see.
T : Two more categories are vocabulary and grammar. These two expressions here need to be changed. Look up the appropriate expressions in a dictionary. In addition, *swimed* here and *very not much* here are not correct. Think about how you can correct them.
S : Okay.
T : If you have any questions, just let me know. I'm looking forward to reading your second draft.
T : Thank you.

T=teacher, S=student

Data Analysis

Read the passages in <A> and <B> and follow the directions.

A

When correcting students' errors during writing activities, it's crucial for teachers to do so in a manner that promotes learning and development. Here are some guidelines that teachers should follow:

- Promote self-correction: encourage students to identify and correct their own mistakes.
- Prioritize global errors for correction: focus initially on errors that significantly hinder comprehension.
- Balance corrections with praise: recognize students' strengths alongside areas needing improvement.
- Maintain consistency in feedback: use consistent symbols for making errors, allowing students to easily understand.
- Wise use of technology: instruct students on the effective use of tools like a spell checker, while emphasizing the importance of their own judgment.

B

Below is a student's writing piece about her school life and the teacher's feedback.

Teacher's Feedback

I am Ana and going to school every days. In school, I has lots of friends
SV
and we play soccer lunch. Science is best class it teach us about space
SV V!
and the animal world. Homeworks is sometimes too difficult and makes
S!
me confuse. Teacher is helping me if I don't get something. Weekend
times, watching movies and reading books is what I do for fun. On
FORM
Sundays, I visit my favorite friend's houses for a family dinner.
PL

Note:
- *Words/phrases containing errors are marked with '____' but not specifically pointed out by the teacher.*
- *Only subject-verb agreement and plural errors are pinpointed.*

Teacher's Comments

Great job on your writing! Your ideas are captivating, and your vocabulary is diverse. I've made some corrections, but there are still a few errors left for you to discover and learn from. For assistance with basic grammar, some Grammar apps could be beneficial. They offers real-time suggestions for improvements. However, it's crucial to understand the rationale behind the suggested corrections to genuinely enhance your writing skills. Should you have any questions or require further assistance, feel free to reach out!

Q1 Based on the information in <A>, identify TWO guidelines for correcting errors in writing lessons that the teacher's feedback in <B> does not follow correctly.

____

____

____

Q2 Then, explain your choices with evidence from <A> and <B>.

____

____

____

>> Possible Answers p.221

4 Classroom Writing Activities (Controlled to Free Writing)

(1) Dicto-comp

A paragraph is read at normal speed, usually two or three times. Then the teacher asks students to rewrite the paragraph to the best of their recollection of the reading.

(2) Guided Writing

As an extension of controlled writing, it is less controlled than the controlled writing in that it gives students some but not all of the content and form of the sentences they will use.

(3) Dialogue Journals

- An informal written conversation between teacher and student about topics of mutual interest.
- Reinforcing learning while forming bonds between two people(S-S, S-T).
- Generating some personal input and receiving the teacher's direct feedback on it.
- Emphasizing meaning rather than form.

Data Analysis

Read the passages in <A> and <B>, and follow the directions.

A

Dialogue journals serve as a powerful pedagogical tool, fostering interactive, reflective, and personalized communication between students and their teacher. At the core of dialogue journals are several key principles.

Principle about Topics:
In dialogue journals, the topics are typically not assigned in advance, allowing students the freedom to write about subjects that are personally meaningful to them. By letting students choose their own topics, they take greater ownership of their writing.

Principle about Contents:
Dialogue journals allow students to express personal thoughts, ideas, and reflections, giving them a chance to share their experiences in a safe and supportive environment. In turn, the teacher responds with direct, individualized feedback. This interaction not only helps students to clarify their thinking but also supports language development by providing meaningful feedback on their writing.

Principle about Grading:
The writing in dialogue journals should not be graded, scored, or corrected using standard codes, as the goal is to encourage free expression without the fear of making mistakes. Grading could inhibit the student's willingness to take risks in their writing or explore more complex ideas.

Principle about Confidentiality:
It is essential for teachers to maintain the confidentiality of the students' writing in dialogue journals. Teachers should promise to keep the content private and not share it with third parties, which helps to build trust between the student and teacher.

Principle about Language in Response:
The language input that the learner receives from the teacher should be comprehensible and level-appropriate; Correct grammatical forms should be taught indirectly by modeling them in the feedback.

B

Below is a journal from a low-intermediate level student, who was free to choose the topic, along with a teacher's comments responding to the journal.

Student's Journal

Dear Diary,

Today was just a regular school day, but something cool happened between me and my friend Alex. In the morning, we got all mixed up about who was supposed to bring what for our science project. He thought it was my turn to bring the materials, and I thought it was his. We both got pretty annoyed because it meant we couldn't work on our project in class. When lunchtime rolled around, I really didn't want a tiny mix-up to mess things up between me and Alex. (ellipsis)

Teacher's Comments

Well done on handling the situation with Alex using strong communication skills and empathy. Your coherent articulation*, despite minor grammatical slips such as using 'me and Alex' instead of 'Alex and I,' and your ability to maintain verb tense consistency, is noteworthy*. Your adeptness in problem-solving and a reflective approach to learning are admirable* traits, which will refine your already substantial writing abilities. Also, the content of your journal will remain private between us, so you don't have to worry about it. Keep up your great work, and I will continue to support you as you improve.

Warm regards,
Ms. Shin

P.S.: If the words with '' in my feedback must be unfamiliar to you. So, please look them up in a dictionary. I use some challenging words to help expand your vocabulary.*

Q1 From the principles described in <A>, identify the ONE specific principle that is not followed in <B>.

____

____

____

Q2 Then, support your answers with specific evidence from both <A> and <B>.

____

____

____

>> Possible Answers p.221

Data Analysis

Read the passage in <A> and the activities in <B>, and follow the directions.

A

When it comes to learning how to write well, there are three main types of writing exercises that can help us get there: *controlled writing, guided writing*, and *free writing*. Each type has its own unique approach and purpose. First up is controlled writing. In *controlled writing*, we follow specific rules and patterns. It's all about practicing the basics, like grammar and spelling, to make sure we're getting them right. Next, we have *guided writing*. This is where we start to have a bit more fun and get a little creative. Guided writing provides helpful instructions on what to write or how to write. This guidance may include pictures, examples, or specific instructions to assist the writer in organizing and articulating their thoughts and ideas more effectively. Lastly, there is *free writing*, which offers the ultimate creative freedom. In free writing, there are no strict rules or patterns to follow and we can write about whatever we want. It's all about letting our ideas flow and seeing where our imagination takes us.

B

Activity 1

Instructions: Write one paragraph about the given picture below.

a. Begin your first paragraph by describing the classroom: table, chairs, clock, TV, white board, window, etc.
b. Start your second paragraph by describing the teacher: what is she doing? Then write sentences about students: how many are there? What are they doing?

Activity 2

Instructions: Read each sentence carefully. Each one describes an activity from a perfect day but is missing a verb. Fill in the blanks with the correct past tense form of the verb given in parentheses.

Sentences to Complete:
a. After breakfast, I ________ (go) for a long walk in the park.
b. I ________ (meet) an old friend for coffee.
c. In the afternoon, I ________ (read) my favorite book.
d. For dinner, I ________ (cook) a delicious meal.
e. Before bed, I ________ (watch) a funny movie to relax.

Q1 Based on the information in <A>, identify the type of writing of Activity 1 and Activity 2, respectively, from <B>.

____

____

____

Q2 Then, explain your choices with evidence from <A> and <B>.

____

____

____

>> Possible Answers p.221

5 Genre-based Writing Approach – What is a genre?

(1) A genre is primarily recognised by its communicative purpose, which shapes how a text is realised.

(2) Texts that belong to a genre share similar characteristics, such as target audience, organisation of ideas and language choices.

(3) For example, a thesis statement is obligatory in an argumentative essay because the communicative purpose of this genre is to argue for or against a position.

Data Analysis

Read the passage in <A> and the activities in <B>, and follow the directions.

A

One of the reasons we can communicate successfully, especially in writing, is because we have some understanding of genre, socially recognized ways of using language for particular purposes. Genre represents the norms of different kinds of writing shared among people within a particular community. The emphasis on the social dimension of genre is a major characteristic of genre-based approaches to teaching writing.

A genre-based writing instruction involves students in an in-depth analysis of texts in the genre in which they are going to be writing. In particular, students are asked to analyze three essential features of the genre using example texts: 1) the *context*, which includes the situation and audience, 2) the *content*, which indicates the information and message conveyed, and 3) the *construction*, that is, how the texts of the genre are typically constructed in terms of the layout and language. When students are done with this task, they are in a position to create their own writing within the genre.

B

Activity 1

After conducting a reading lesson about volunteering, a middle school English teacher prepares a poster-making activity for recruiting volunteers. He plans to have his students analyze the features of the poster genre before they make their own posters.

- Ask the students to share their volunteering experiences.
- Have the students examine the poster and answer the questions in the worksheet.

Worksheet

1. Why are some words capitalized?
2. Does the poster use full sentences? If not, why?

Activity 2

Believing writing reviews is an important skill that her students should be equipped with, a high school English teacher prepares a genre-analyzing kit with which the students figure out the characteristics of the book review genre.

- Tell the students they are going to read a book review.
- Have the students use the genre-analyzing kit while reading the book review.

Book Review

"I Really Want the Cup Cake"
Written by Philip Kent
Illustrated by Terra Wang
Ages 3—5 | 20 Pages
Publisher: Green Books | ISBN: 978-1-338-95941-2
What to expect: Rhyme, Dessert, Self Control
(or lack thereof)

Honestly, who of us hasn't wanted to dive in, just a teeny, tiny bit, to that delicious-looking cup cake left on the table? Just a bite couldn't hurt, could it? In this hilarious story about a little boy and his dog, that's exactly what they are trying not to do.

Reviewers' Genre-Analyzing Kit

1. Who do you think the review is aimed at?
2. When would people write this kind of text?

Q1 Based on <A>, identify ONE essential feature of the target genre that each activity in <B> focuses on, respectively.

____

____

____

Q2 Then, explain your answers with evidence from <B>.

____

____

____

>> Possible Answers p.221

Possible Answers

p.151

Q1 Two teachers are concerned about their students who lack sociolinguistic competence.

Q2 According to them, their students have trouble adjusting speech style to fit the situation.

---

p.153

Q1 Activity 2 is the best for increasing students' engagement and interaction.

Q2 Activity 2 is more structured, ensuring all students can participate. It has a clear goal and encourages multiple interactions as students move around the classroom, engaging with everyone rather than just a small group. In contrast, in Activity 1, verbal students may dominate the discussion due to the lack of clear outcomes or specific direction.

---

p.154

Q1 Ms. Park's lesson procedure gives students clear instructions.

Q2 It avoids lengthy explanations, demonstrates how to do the activity, and includes meaningful conversation with students through comprehension questions. In contrast, Mr. Kim's lesson procedure merely describes the activity with lengthy explanation lacks modeling.

---

p.158

Q1 personalization

---

p.162

Q1 The teachers consider two factors—'Task' and 'Learner'—to adjust the difficulty of the task.

Q2 First, they help students build confidence for the actual presentation by providing a 30-minute rehearsal period. Additionally, they aim to bridge the students' knowledge gap and increase engagement by showing an additional video clip followed by a Q&A session.

p.164

Q1 These two activities enable students to engage in more active and meaningful interaction in real communication, unlike traditional accuracy-based activities that focus on rote learning and mechanical drills.

p.166

Q1 Mina recommends both cognitive and social strategies to Junho.

Q2 First, she advises visualizing what he has studied in his mind. Second, she suggests that he have conversations with native speakers of English (or ask questions to others) to work out the exact meaning whenever he encounters an unfamiliar expression.

p.168

Q1 The student used three communications strategies as follows : avoidance, appeal to authority, and word coinage.

Q2 First, the student avoids using 'bicycle' as the subject to avoid constructing a sentence in the passive voice. Next, to find a synonym of the verb 'make,' the student refers to a dictionary. Finally, instead of using 'quadricycle', he creates a non-existing word 'four-cycle'.

p.170

Q1 S2 uses literal translation by saying 'pig meat', word coinage by creating a non-existing word 'vegetarianist', and circumlocution by saying 'the potatoes that you eat with them'.

p.172

Q1 Ms. Hong seeks Ms. Park's advice regarding two problems, 'uneven participation' and 'mother-tongue use.'

Q2 A jigsaw significantly increase overall student participation. Additionally, she believes that the awareness of being monitored encourages students to use the target language instead of their mother-tongue.

p.177

Q1 ① display ② accuracy ③ referential ④ fluency

p.183

Q1

Feedback types	Script A	Script B
Clarification request	Excuse me?	
Recast	You saw a movie?	
Metalinguistic feedback	But you saw a movie LAST SUNDAY, and last Sunday is in the past	
Explicit correction	the correct verb is SAW, not SEE.	
Elicitation		He's coming...?

p.191

Q1 Tool B is best for Ms. Jang.

Q2 First, it is equipped with supportive feature, such as subtitles and text-to-speech technology, which are beneficial for low-level students.
Second, it offers real-time feedback to help students self-correct.
Lastly, it provides detailed analytics on students' performance and learning progress, which is valuable for educators.

p.199

Q1 In the lesson plan, Steps 3 and 8 diverge from the sequence in ⟨A⟩.

Q2 In Step 3, instead of the teacher presenting a model text, students discuss essay structure and required content. Additionally, Step 8 replaces teacher feedback on students' second drafts with student self-editing (proofreading) for punctuation, spelling, and writing conventions.

p.208

Q1 The teacher does not follow two key guidelines: Prioritize global errors for correction and Maintain consistency in feedback.

Q2 Firstly, the teacher focuses on correcting simple grammatical errors, such as subject-verb agreement, and plurals, rather than addressing global errors that significantly affect comprehension. Additionally, the teacher does not use consistent error correction symbols, alternating between 'PL' or 'S!' for plural errors, and 'SV', 'V!', or 'FORM' for subject-verb agreement errors.

p.211

Q1 Ms. Shin violates 'Principle about Language in Response'.

Q2 She directly corrects the student's grammatical error, changing 'me and Alex' into 'Alex and I,' rather than modeling grammatical correct form indirectly. Additionally, she uses challenging words, such as 'articulation' and 'noteworthy,' which are not level-appropriate for low-intermediate students.

p.213

Q1 Activity 1 demonstrates guided writing, while Activity 2 exemplifies controlled writing.

Q2 Activity 1 provides specific instructions based on a classroom picture, guiding students on what to describe in the first and second paragraphs. Conversely, in Activity 2, students fill in blanks with the correct past verb forms to reinforce basic grammar rules.

p.215

Q1 Activity 1 focuses on 'construction,' while Activity 2 focuses on 'context.'

Q2 In Activity 1, students pay attention to capitalized words and incomplete sentences on the poster, analyzing its layout and language. In Activity 2, students identify the audience and situation of the book review by determining for whom and when to write it.

Key-concepts check-up : Vocabulary

ACROSS ➡

❺ Various researchers have asserted that learners should receive explicit instruction and practice for the first two or three thousand high-THIS words and beyond this threshold level, most low THIS words will be learned implicitly while reading or listening.

❼ _________ knowledge. THIS is knowledge about something. THIS enables a student to describe a rule of grammar and apply it in pattern practice drills.

❽ _________ knowledge. THIS is knowledge of how to do something. THIS enables a student to apply a rule of grammar in communication.

❾ __________ vocabulary learning. Learning that occurs with awareness of the L2 feature that is being learned and with an intention to learn that feature. THIS often results in explicit knowledge; however, it is arguably possible for THIS to contribute to implicit knowledge.

⑩ THIS is a computer program that automatically constructs a concordance. The output of THIS may serve as input to a translation memory system for computer-assisted translation, or as an early step in machine translation.

⑪ The ability of the same form to appear in many meanings

⑫ __________ of vocabulary knowledge. THIS is defined as a learner's level knowledge of various aspects of a given word, or how well the learner knows this word. That is, THIS focuses on the idea that for useful higher-frequency words learners need to have more than just a superficial understanding of the meaning.

DOWN ⬇

❶ __________ vocabulary learning. THIS is learning that occurs when the mind is focused elsewhere, such as on understanding a text or using language for communicative purpose.

❷ _________ strategies. How to determine the meaning of unknown word. Help students learn to recognize clues to _________ word meaning (low frequency vocabulary) from context; provide rich authentic texts with enough adequate clues.

❸ ① Look for prefixes that may give clues. ② Look for suffixes that may indicate what part of speech it is. ③ Look for roots that are familiar.

❹ __________ method. THIS is called a "mnemonic device," which helps to link a word form and its meaning and to consolidate this linkage in memory.

❻ An activity that helps bring into consciousness relationship among words in a text and helps deepen understanding by creating associative networks for words. A text is chosen based on the words to be learned and students are asked to draw a diagram of the relationships between particular words, found in the text.

Answer

ACROSS ➡ **5.** frequency **7.** declarative **8.** procedural **9.** intentional **10.** concordance program **11.** polysemy **12.** depth

DOWN ⬇ **1.** incidental **2.** guessing **3.** vocabulary analysis **4.** keyword **6.** semantic mapping

Chapter 03

How to Develop the Vocabulary and Grammatical Knowledge

01 How to Develop Students' Vocabulary Knowledge

Most teachers says that the most significant handicap for especially reading comprehension is not lack of reading strategies but insufficient vocabulary in English. Students, also, point out lack of adequate vocabulary as one of obstacles to text comprehension.

1 Breadth vs. Depth of Vocabulary Knowledge

Vocabulary knowledge comprise two dimensions, which are vocabulary **breadth**, or size, and **depth** or quality of knowledge.

A

Knowing a word does not simply mean knowing its surface meaning. Rather, it involves knowing diverse aspects of lexical knowledge in depth including phonological and morphological forms and syntactic and semantic structures. Therefore, activities that integrate lexical knowledge of form, meaning, and use should be included in class.

B

Teacher's Journal

Ms. Kang and I read an article on teaching vocabulary and discussed how we can improve the way we teach vocabulary. We realized that we have been heavily focused on expanding the size of our students' vocabulary. As a result, they seem to know a lot of words but do not understand or use them properly in context. So, we came up with the following activities that we believe help our students develop depth of vocabulary knowledge across form, meaning, and use.

Vocabulary activities to be implemented:

- Trying to pronounce the target words by listening to a recorded text
- Analyzing parts of the target words (e.g., prefixes and suffixes)
- Guessing the meanings of the target words using contextual cues
- Studying concordance examples to see various contexts and collocation patterns
- Writing a short story using the target words

2 Lexical Knowledge: Polysemy / Collocations / Synonymy & Antonymy / Word family

(1) Polysemy / Collocation

Below is a sample interaction from an activity used in a middle school English classroom.

S1 : I have to do a diet.
(*T indicates an error by facial expression.*)
S1 : I have to do a diet.
T : (*Writes 'diet' on the board.*) What verb do we usually use when we start a diet?
S2: 'Go on'.
T : Yes, that's right. (*Writes 'go on' on the board.*) How about if you've already started a diet?
S2: 'Be on'.
T : Yes, if you are trying to loose weight by eating less food, then you are on a diet. (*Pause*) What did you eat for breakfast?
S1 : Rice, eggs and vegetables.
T : Sounds like you ate a balanced diet.
S1 : 'Balanced'?
T : Yes. (*Writes 'Balanced' on the board.*) If you eat all of the things you need to eat, we say you eat a balanced diet. What adjectives can we use with 'diet'?
S2: 'Healthy'.

T : And?
S1 : 'Unhealthy'.
T : Yes. You can also use 'poor'. (*Writes 'healthy,' 'unhealthy', and 'poor' on the board.*)

T=teacher, S1=student 1, S2=student 2

(2) Collocations

Activity Procedure

1. Work in pairs and choose one of the three verbs that most likely appears before each phrase.

do	make	take	
	√		a lot of noise
			family photographs
			a lot of mistakes
			the housework

2. Check your answers with another student.
3. Using a concordancing program on the Internet, find other phrases that can be used with the three verbs.
4. Make your own conversation about a familiar topic (e.g, family life) using the phrases you have found on the Internet, and practice it in pairs.

(3) Synonymy & Antonymy

① 어휘상 대체 가능한 어휘 모음: start, begin / complete, end, finish
② 의미상 반의어: wet-dry, light-dark
맥락 안(in context)에서 지도할 필요가 있다. 그렇지 않을 경우 overgeneralization of meaning의 우려가 있기 때문이다.

(4) Word Family: a group of words that may share a common root word with different prefixes and suffixes in morphology

Ex walk, walks, walking, walked

3 Intentional vs. Incidental Vocabulary Learning

(1) Intentional Learning

Students engage in activities that focus direct attention on vocabulary.

① **What to teach**: high frequent words / word family- talk, talked, talking, talks(inflections or derivation)

What do the following prefixes in bold mean? · **re**play / **re**do · **dis**belief / **im**polite / **il**logical / **un**usual / **ir**responsible / **in**visible · **under**estimate / **under**weight · **ex**-husband / **ex**-president

② **How to teach**:

- **Word family**: by highlighting word families in a particular context, students can see the relationships. Also, students can observe how the forms change according to discourse functions.
- **Corpus data & Concordancing program**: context, collocation, frequency
- **Word map**: building up vocabulary knowledge using what students know
- **Keyword method**: linking a word form and its meaning and consolidating this linkage in memory
- **Realia**: using a type of supplementary materials to attract students' attention and to aid understanding and retention of key vocabulary to be taught

Case 1

A corpus is a collection of texts of written or spoken language from various sources presented in electronic form. It provides evidence of how language is used in real situations, from which lexicographers can analyze millions of examples of each word to see how real language behaves. Many contemporary dictionaries, therefore, incorporate the features derived from the analyses of corpus data, some of which are shown below.

1. **Frequency**: statistical data on how often words are used in the language
2. **Collocation**: information on what other words commonly occur with the word in focus
3. **Context**: information on which particular field (e.g., law, engineering, medicine) or social situation (e.g., formal vs. informal) a word is used in
4. **Authentic example sentences**: sentences from what users of the language actually write or say in books, newspapers, speeches, or recorded conversations, etc.

Examples

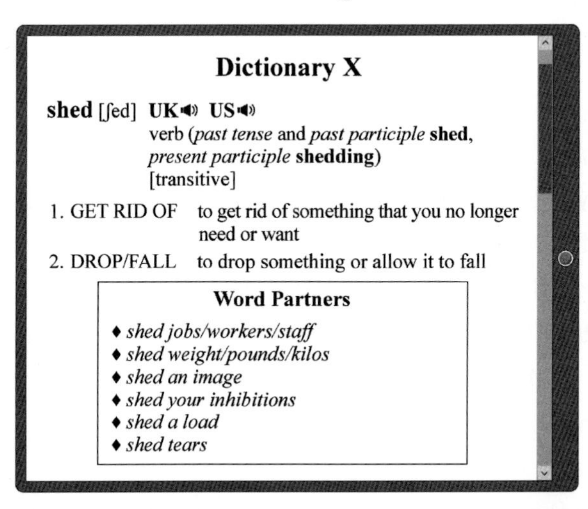

Dictionary X
shed [ʃed] UK US
verb (past tense and past participle shed, present participle shedding)
[transitive]
1. GET RID OF to get rid of something that you no longer need or want
2. DROP/FALL to drop something or allow it to fall
Word Partners
♦ shed jobs/workers/staff
♦ shed weight/pounds/kilos
♦ shed an image
♦ shed your inhibitions
♦ shed a load
♦ shed tears

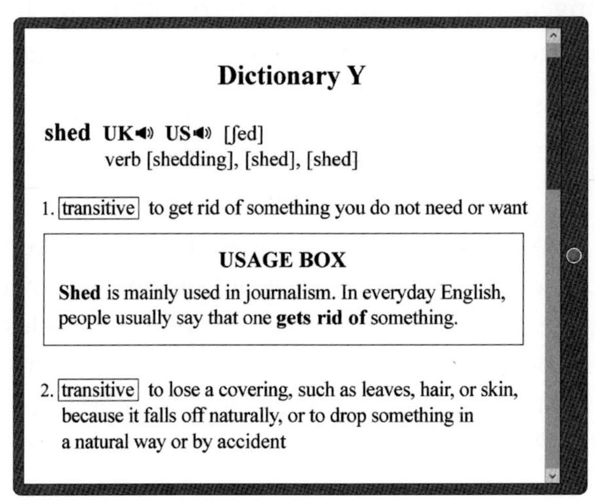

Dictionary Y
shed UK US [ʃed]
verb [shedding], [shed], [shed]
1. transitive to get rid of something you do not need or want
USAGE BOX
Shed is mainly used in journalism. In everyday English, people usually say that one gets rid of something.
2. transitive to lose a covering, such as leaves, hair, or skin, because it falls off naturally, or to drop something in a natural way or by accident

T : Today, we are going to read a text about cooking. Are you interested in cooking?
Ss: Yeah.
T : Great. Let's study today's key words first. (*The teacher brings out kitchen utensils from a box.*) I brought some cooking utensils.
S1: Wow! Are those yours?
T : Yes, they are. I use them when I cook. (*showing a saucepan*) You've seen this before, right?
S2: Yes. My mom uses that when she makes jam.
T : Good. Do you know what it's called in English?
S3: It's a saucepan.
T : Excellent, it's a saucepan. Everyone, repeat after me. Saucepan.
Ss: Saucepan.
T : And, (*showing a cutting board*) what's this in English?
S4: A board?
T : Right, it's a cutting board. Good job. I also brought a couple of things from my refrigerator. This is one of my favorite vegetables. (*The teacher holds up an eggplant.*)
S5: Umm.... It's an egg...
T : Nice try! It's an eggplant.

T=teacher, S=student

Data Analysis

Read the passage in <A> and the teaching procedures in <B>, and follow the directions.

A

The basic aspects the students need to know about a lexical item are its written and spoken forms, and its denotational meaning. However, there are additional aspects which also need to be learned, as are described in the following table.

Aspects	Descriptions
Grammar	A grammatical structure may be lexically bound, and lexical items also have grammatical features.
Collocation	Collocation refers to the way words tend to co-occur with other words or expressions.
Connotation	The connotations of a word are the emotional or positive-negative associations that it implies.
Appropriateness	Students need to know if a particular lexical item is usually used in writing or in speech; or in formal or informal discourse.
Word formation	Words can be broken down into morphemes. Exactly how these components are put together is another piece of useful information.

B

Teaching Procedure 1

1. Present the following expressions in the table. Ask students to choose which expressions are possible.

do my homework	(O/X)	make my homework	(O/X)
do some coffee	(O/X)	make some coffee	(O/X)
do the laundry	(O/X)	make the laundry	(O/X)

2. Ask students to find more examples using do and make, referencing an online concordancer.

Teaching Procedure 2

1. Ask students to identify countable and uncountable nouns.

advice	employee	equipment	facility
information	money	proposal	result

2. Tell students to choose the expression of quantity that does NOT fit with the noun in each sentence.

(a) The researchers found [*a significant proportion of* / *some of* / *most of*] the results were not corroborated by other sources.

Q1 Identify ONE aspect in <A> that each teaching procedure in <B> focuses on, respectively.

Q2 Then, explain your answers with evidence from <B>.

>> Possible Answers p.254

(2) Incidental Learning

Through my teaching experience, I've learned that different students learn in different ways. Considering the current trend in teaching and learning, I believe that students should be provided with more opportunities to be exposed to the **incidental** learning condition. Minsu's case may illustrate that point. At the beginning of the semester, Minsu introduced himself as a book lover. He wanted to read novels in English but was not sure if he could. I suggested that he didn't have to try to comprehend all the details. Indeed, Minsu has benefited a lot from reading novels. He said he learned many words and expressions even though he did not make attempts to memorize them. I will continue observing his progress as his way of learning is of great interest.

▶ Extensive reading for vocabulary learning according to students' levels

① low levels - graded readers

② intermediate levels - read numerous authentic texts, but all the same topic

③ advanced levels - read a wide variety of authentic texts

4 Vocabulary Strategies

(1) Guessing Strategies

- to guess word meaning from context using some clues
- to provide rich authentic texts with enough adequate clues

(2) Vocabulary Analysis

Example ①

Roots

S: What does ***subsequently*** mean?
T: What part of speech do you think it is?
S: Adverb?
T: Why?
S: It's got –ly on the end.
T: Good. Look at the co-sentences which contains ***subsequently***. If we took away ***subsequently***, what other words could we put there to join the two sentences.
S: ***Then? Next?***
T: Great! That's the meaning of subsequently. The ***sequ*** part means "to follow".

Example ②

Prefixes

What do the following prefixes in bold mean?
Example: *re-* means 'again.'

a. **re**play / **re**do
b. **dis**belief / **im**polite / **il**logical / **un**usual / **ir**responsible / **in**visible
c. **over**crowded / **over**charge
d. **under**estimate / **under**weight
e. **post**graduate / **post**mortem
f. **ex**-husband / **ex**-president
g. **sub**marine / **sub**way

Example ③

Grammatical Relationghip

Looking at the relationship between this clause or sentence and other sentences or paragraphs. Signals to look for might be a coordinating or subordinating conjunction such as *but, because, if, when* or an adverbial such as *however*, or *as a result*.

a. She was excited **but** fatigued when arriving at home. ('fatigued' is inferred as 'tired')
b. There was a horrible **and** atrocious murder case in this town. ('atrocious' is inferred as 'wicked' or 'cruel')

5 Vocabulary Teaching Principles

Example

After reading about whales, Ms. Park is asking 2nd grader of a middle school for the main idea.

Ms. Park: Who can tell us what the main idea of the passage is- What is the gist?
S1 : Certain types of whales are being endangered.
(Another student immediately raises his hand.)
S2 : What does "endangered" mean?
Ms. Park: *(encouraging him to take a guess)* Is there any part of the word "endangered" that you recognize? What do you think it might mean in the context of passage about whales?
S2 : *(pausing, thinking for a minute)* The whales, they are disappearing?
Ms. Park: Yes. Scientists are worried that whale will disappear if conditions do not get better. Well done!!

Memo

Key-concepts check-up : Grammar

ACROSS ➡

❷ Unlike inductive and deductive reasoning, learners come to understand hidden rules of language use through the process of exploring hypothesis and inferences.

❸ THIS refers to the practice of explicitly drawing students' attention to linguistic features within the context of meaning-focused activities. In other words, communication comes first, and attention to form second.

❺ THIS is an approach to grammar instruction that guides learners to process what they see or hear. This approach helps learners connect language forms with their intended meanings.

❻ Students are asked to infer the rule from the partial information. THIS makes students overgeneralize and leads them into error. They are more likely to learn the exceptions to the rule to memorize in advance.

❼ The teacher presents the grammar rule and then gives students exercises in which they apply the rule in this approach.

❾ THIS is the application of a grammatical rule in cases where it doesn't apply. For example, a young child may say "foots" instead of "feet". THIS is one of the examples of intralingual transfer.

❿ According to THIS, second language learners cannot begin to acquire a language feature until they have become aware of it in the input. Therefore the learner should be provided with plenty of meaningful input through authentic L2 materials.

⓭ When students produce utterances with error, they receive corrective feedback from teachers/peers explaining the correct use of the form. Such error correction can provide "THIS," facilitating learners' noticing of the correct form.

DOWN ⬇

❶ THIS is a technique for getting students to notice the grammar item by using materials that contain a lot of target items.

❹ THIS type of task helps to develop learners' own understanding of language and to build confidence as learners. Allowing the learners to take responsibility for discovering target rules favorably affects retention. Students are provided with L2 data in some form and required to perform some operation on or with it.

❽ THIS is a technique for getting students to notice the grammar item that the teacher wants to introduce with highlighting, underlining, or coloring.

⓫ The teacher presents samples of language, and the students have to infer the rule in this approach.

⓬ "Is there a set order for language development in the brain, in which case formal instruction may be ineffective if the student is not at the appropriate stage?" THIS hypothesis proposes that second language learners will not acquire a new structure until they are ready to do so.

Answer

ACROSS ➡ **2.** abduction **3.** focus on form **5.** input processing **6.** garden path **7.** deductive **9.** overgeneralization **10.** noticing hypothesis **13.** negative evidence

DOWN ⬇ **1.** input flooding **4.** consciousness raising **8.** input enhancement **11.** inductive **12.** teachability

02 How to Develop Student's Grammatical Knowledge

1 Form-focused Instruction: Focus on Forms vs. Focus on Form

It means all the activities emphasizing the features of particular grammar points to develop language accuracy.

(1) **Focus on Forms**: traditional formal instruction where students are presented with grammar rules, examples, and practice exercises

> My students often tell me that they feel overwhelmed by a number of grammatical structures they have to learn. While thinking about ways to help students develop grammatical competence, I decided to teach grammar explicitly in class. Today, I spent most of the class time on explaining grammatical rules using metalinguistic terms. Although some of the students initially showed some interest in learning about the rules, many of them got bored, with some dozing off after ten minutes or so.

(2) **Focus on Form**: indirect approaches to grammar instruction, where students are supposed to use grammar forms communicatively if instruction is then followed by opportunities to encounter the instructed grammar point frequently in communicative usage

> Most of my students find grammatical rules difficult and boring. So I decided to implement a new approach. For this approach, I typed up the reading passage in the textbook and deliberately italicized the target structures, hoping that this would help my students notice how the target structures function. After I passed out the reconstructed reading passage, I had my students read it by themselves and then work together in groups, cross-checking their understanding.

① Negative evidence

- **context**: if students receive corrective feedback from teacher/peers explaining the correct use of the form or if the teacher/peer "recast" or repeats the utterance so that the correct form is used.
- **roles**
  - facilitating learners' noticing of the correct form
  - building form-meaning relationships
  - pushing students' output further in the direction of improved accuracy

S: I am very worried.
T: Really? What are you worried about, Minjae?
S: Math exam for tomorrow. I don't studied yesterday.
T: You didn't study yesterday?
S: No, I didn't study.
T: Please tell me why. What happened?
S: I did volunteering all day long. So I don't had time to study.
T: Well, Minjae, "don't had" is not the right past tense form.
S: Uh, I didn't have time, time to study.

T=teacher, S=student

② **The teachability hypothesis**: Second/foreign language learners will not acquire a new structure until they are developmentally ready to do so.

▶ **current approach**: Practice of language points can lead to automatization, thus bypassing natural order/teachability consideration.

2 Deductive vs. Inductive vs. Abduction – how learners process linguistic form to acquire rules that govern its use

(1) Deductive Approach

Teacher A's Class

- T explains to Ss that past tense verb forms should be used in sentences with *if* clauses to describe hypothetical situations.
- T asks Ss to complete sentences with appropriate verb forms to show hypothetical situations.

> 1. I ______(can) fly to you, if I ______(be) a superhero.
> 2. If he ______(have) a time machine, he ______(will) go back in time.

- T asks Ss to read a short text with sentences describing hypothetical situations.

> If I had a spaceship, I would fly to Mars. I would also build my own house there and live forever, if there were both oxygen and water. Unfortunately, I don't have lots of money to buy a spaceship. . . .

- T asks Ss to write a paragraph starting with the given expression.

> If I lived on Mars, . . .

(2) Inductive Approach

Teacher B's Class

- T gives back the written texts about hypothetical situations Ss produced in the previous class and provides their reformulated texts T has produced at the same time. Only incorrect verb forms in Ss' writings are changed in T's reformulation as in the examples below.

<A student's original writing>

If I have last year to live over again, I will exercise more and eat less junk food because I can be healthier. I will spend more time with my friends and have better grades, if I am more active and watch less TV. . . .

<The teacher's reformulated text>

If I had last year to live over again, I would exercise more and eat less junk food because I could be healthier. I would spend more time with my friends and have better grades, if I were more active and watched less TV. . . .

- T asks Ss to compare T's reformulated sample with their writings and to underline all the words in the sample that are different from those in their writings.
- T asks Ss to find what the underlined words have in common and in what way they differ from the ones used in their original writings in terms of language form.
- T asks Ss to work out the rule that applies to all their underlined words based on their findings in the previous step.

(3) Abduction

Learners come to understand hidden rules of language use through the process of exploring hypothesis and inferences.

Step 1

Ms. Park presents an authentic text that incorporates the target structure "should+have+pp" she wants to highlight.

> Kate travelled across the Australian desert. She made no preparations. She didn't take a map, and she didn't take a cell phone. Soon after she set off, she got lost and got trapped in a flash flood. Later, looking back on it, she said, "I **should have taken** a map. I **should have taken** a cell phone...."

Step 2

Ms. Park designs an information-gap activity that focuses on "should+ have+pp". She asks students to talk about their previous journey.

Step 3

Ms. Park asks students to work in groups and note the target structure "should+ have+pp" they observe.

Step 4

Students report their findings to the class.

3 Grammar Techniques in Language Classroom

(1) Input Enhancement: getting students to notice the grammar item by highlighting, underlining, or coloring

Example

For Third Person Singular Possessive Determiner

Once upon a time there was a king. **He** had a beautiful young daughter. For **her** birthday, the king gave **her** a golden ball that **she** played with everyday. The king and **his** daughter lived near a dark forest...

(2) Input Flooding: using materials that contain a lot of target items

Example

1. Read the following about your country.

> In this country, you have to start school at the age of 7. You can drive when you are 17, but you can't buy alcohol until you are 18. You also have to wait until you turn 18 before you can vote. Men have to serve in the military, but women don't have to.

2. Listen to a similar conversation about England.
3. Mark the differences between your country and England on the worksheet.

➡ The activity helps students notice the target structure through input flooding.

(3) Input Processing

- guiding students to process what they see or hear
- helping students connect language forms with their intended meanings through structured input activities

Teaching Procedure

1. Explicit Explanation
Explain how a past tense sentence is constructed in English. Then inform students of why they tend not to notice the past tense marker *-ed* and thus misinterpret past tense sentences.

2. Structured Input Activity
Have students read six sentences and decide whether they describe an activity that was done in the past or usually happens in the present. Then, check the answers together.

Sentences	Present	Past
(1) They watched television at night.	□	□
(2) They watch television at night.	□	□
(3) I walk to school on Mondays.	□	□
(4) I walked to school on Mondays.	□	□
(5) We played soccer on weekends.	□	□
(6) We play soccer on weekends.	□	□

(4) Consciousness-raising Tasks

① Type: awareness-raising inductive approach

② Process: Students are provided with L2 data in some form and required to perform some operation on or with it. Finally, they arrive at an explicit understanding of some linguistic properties.

③ Activity example

In pairs, do the following tasks in English:

1. Talk about the differences between adjectives ending in *-ed* and *–ing*.

We felt moved by his story.
* We felt moving by his story.
It was a really exhausting day.
* It was a really exhausted day.

2. Indicate whether the sentences below are grammatical or ungrammatical, focusing on the underlined words.

1. They seemed pleasing with the outcome.
2. I saw the most amazed film yesterday.
3. He felt disappointed about the test results.
4. The most annoyed thing was her rude attitude.
5. The incident could be embarrassing for him.

3. Write a rule that can explain the differences between the two types of adjectives.

(5) Garden Path

- giving students information about structure without giving them the full picture
- students inferring the rule from the partial information and committing overgeneralized errors
- giving students disconfirming evidence and asking them to modify their hypothesis

In the Classroom

T: Look at these examples for forming superlative adjectives. (*Write on the board, cute → the cutest, grand → the grandest*) Now make superlatives out of 'beautiful, outrageous, expensive.' OK, now, what have you written? Sonia?

S: **Beautifulest, outrageousest, expensivest.**

T: No, for these words, the superlative forms are 'the most beautiful, the most outrageous, and the most expensive.' Now, I want you to get into groups and figure out the rule.

T: Who thinks they have the answer? Jose's group.

S: **It's about how big the word is. If it's a big word, you use 'most.'**

T: Big. How do we measure the size of words?

S: **The number of syllables.**

T: OK. How many syllables do 'beautiful, outrageous, and expensive' have?

S: Three.

T: Three. OK, so who can state the rule?

S: Adjective with three syllables form the superlative with 'most.'

➡ The teacher intentionally leads the student to commit an error (overgeneralization).

Data Analysis

Read Ms. Lee's opinions about the grammar lesson in <A> and the sample lesson plan in <B>, and follow the directions.

A

Ms. Lee's Opinions

I think teachers should keep in mind that the ultimate goal of any grammar lesson is to build up communicative ability. In order to achieve this goal, I believe that classroom activities should not focus on practicing structures and patterns in a meaningless way. Instead, they should be designed to involve students in real communication. By doing so, grammar lessons will be able to encourage the students' interest in learning and elicit more active and meaningful interaction with others in the classroom.

B

<table>
<tr><td>Subject</td><td colspan="2">High School English</td><td>Students</td><td>1st-year students</td></tr>
<tr><td>Title</td><td colspan="2">Lesson 9 My Dream</td><td>Date</td><td>Nov. 24th</td></tr>
<tr><td>Objectives</td><td colspan="4">• Students will familiarize themselves with the expression "If I were ... ."
• Students will be able to communicate using the expression "If I were ... ."</td></tr>
<tr><td colspan="5">Teaching-Learning Activities</td></tr>
<tr><td rowspan="3">Introduction</td><td>Greeting & Roll-call</td><td colspan="3">• T and Ss exchange greetings.
• T checks if all the Ss are present.</td></tr>
<tr><td>Review</td><td colspan="3">T reviews materials from the previous lesson.</td></tr>
<tr><td>Stating the Objectives</td><td colspan="3">T introduces the objective of the lesson.</td></tr>
<tr><td rowspan="3">Development</td><td>Activity 1</td><td colspan="3">• T hands out a text that contains several instances of "If I were ... ."
• Ss scan the text and highlight all the sentences including "If I were ... ."
• Ss check the ones they highlighted with T.
• T tells Ss to pay attention to the verb form "were."</td></tr>
<tr><td>Activity 2</td><td colspan="3">• T tells Ss that she is going to read a passage on "My Dream."
• T explains difficult words in the passage.
• T reads the passage at a normal pace.
• Ss jot down the key words in the passage as T reads.
• Ss reconstruct the passage individually.
• T hands out the original text to Ss.</td></tr>
<tr><td>Activity 3</td><td colspan="3">• T has Ss form groups of three.
• T asks Ss to think of a job that they would like to have in the future.
• Ss use "If I were ... " to share their opinions about their future dream jobs.
• Assuming that their dreams come true, two Ss take a reporter's role and interview the other S asking how he or she feels about his or her job.
• Ss take turns and continue the activity.</td></tr>
</table>

	Activity 4	• T hands out a worksheet. • Ss put together sentence fragments to form complete sentences. • T reads out complete sentences and each Schecks their own answers. • T writes three more sentences using "If I were ..." on the board. • T asks Ss to read the sentences.
Consolidation	Review	T reviews what Ss learned.
	Closure	• T hands out homework and announces the next lesson. • T says goodbye to Ss.

T=teacher, S=student

Q1 Based on <A>, choose the ONE most appropriate activity in the development stage that reflects Ms. Lee's opinions.

Q2 Then, support your choice with evidence from <B>. Do not copy more than FOUR consecutive words from the passage.

>> Possible Answers p.254

Data Analysis

Read the passages in <A> and <B> and follow the directions.

A

Ms. Park's Teaching Log

The grammar teaching technique I am planning to use offers advantages over traditional rote learning methods. Unlike rote learning, which often emphasizes memorization without understanding, this approach helps learners identify the gap between their current grammatical usage and the accepted norms. By focusing on this gap, students gain a clearer, more explicit understanding of target grammar rules. Another key benefit of this method is its learner-centered approach, which encourages students to discover and understand grammar through analysis and reflection, rather than simply memorizing and applying rules presented by the teacher. This often leads to deeper comprehension and more natural language use, whereas traditional methods tend to be more structured and focused on accuracy through direct rule teaching.

B

Below is a lesson procedure designed by Ms. Song, tailored for intermediate-level students. This lesson plan utilizes a proven educational strategy that enhances language awareness and deepens understanding through active engagement.

Lesson Procedure

1. T puts Ss in groups of three.
2. T hands out the table below to each group. The table illustrates proper and improper uses of relative pronouns in sentences. Incorrect sentences are extracted from the students' written work.

	Correct sentences	Incorrect sentences (extracted from students' writing works)	Explanation of incorrect sentences
A	This is the house **that** I bought.	This is the house in **which** I bought.	Avoid using ________ relative pronouns like 'in which' when the verb does not require a preposition, and a relative pronoun like 'that' is sufficient and more appropriate for the context.
B	The teacher **whom** I respect is retiring.	The teacher **who** I respect *him* is retiring.	Don't use ________ pronouns after relative pronouns. The word "him" is redundant and grammatically incorrect after "who."

3. T tells each group to look at the table above, explaining that the relative pronouns are in bold, and personal pronouns are italicized.
4. T asks each group to read through the table.
5. T tells each group to fill in the blanks in "Explanation of incorrect sentences". Also, T asks students to work on the following sentences and determine whether they are *correct* or *incorrect*:

> a. This is the book in which I read. (①)
> b. The actor who I expect him to win the award. (②)

6. T asks each group to try to find out rules of relative pronouns.
7. T clarifies their findings, providing additional examples or corrections as needed.

Q1 Fill in the blanks (①) and (②) with "correct" or "incorrect."

Q2 Identify the name of grammar teaching technique that Ms. Park has designed in TWO words.

Q3 Explain TWO main benefits of the identified technique that differ from traditional grammar teaching methods with evidence from <B>.

>> Possible Answers p.254

Possible Answers

p.230

Q1 Teaching procedures 1 and 2 focus on collocation and grammar, respectively.

Q1 Teaching procedure 1 presents words that commonly co-occur with 'do' and 'make.' Conversely, Teaching procedure 2 asks students to identify countable and uncountable nouns and choose appropriate expressions of quantity.

---

p.248

Q1 Activity 3 aligns best with Ms. Lee's opinion on how the grammar lesson should be taught.

Q2 In Activity 3, students are asked to use the target phrase 'If I were…' by exchanging their future job ideas in groups. Additionally, by interviewing in pairs, they engage in more active and meaningful interaction.

---

p.251

Q1 ① incorrect ② incorrect

Q2 The grammar teaching technique in ⟨B⟩ is a consciousness-raising task.

Q3 First, unlike traditional rote learning, it helps students notice gaps in their knowledge by comparing correct and incorrect sentences of relative pronouns extracted from their writing. Additionally, it encourages a learner-centered approach by guiding students to discover the rules of relative pronouns on their own, rather than direct instruction.

Memo

Key-concepts check-up : Assessment (1)

ACROSS ➡

❷ It provides students information of useful diagnoses of strengths and weaknesses.

❻ ___________ testing: A view of testing that incorporated the whole of a communicative event, considered to be greater than the sum of its linguistic elements.

❽ ___________ testing: It is designed to give test-takers feedback on specific course or lesson objectives.

❾ __________ validity criterion in such cases is not to measure concurrent ability but to assess a test-taker's likelihood of future success.

❿ If a test actually samples the subject matter about which conclusions are to be drawn, and if it requires the test-taker to perform the behavior that is being measure.

⓬ ___________ testing: This measures one knowledge or skill at once and, testing knowledge of specific elements in phonology, grammar and vocabulary to determine proficiency in the isolated skill areas of listening, reading, speaking and writing.

DOWN ⬇

❶ ___________ assessment. It aims to measure and summarize what a student has grasped.

❸ This is defined as the degree of correspondence of the characteristics of a given language test task to the features of a target language task. For this in a test, a task is likely to be enacted in the real word.

❹ ___________ testing: instrument in which each test-taker's score is interpreted in relation to a mean, median, standard deviation, and/or percentile rank.

❺ Reliability associated with scoring.

❼ This asks, "Does this test actually tap into the theoretical construct as it has been defined?"

❽ A test has __________ validity if its results are supported by other concurrent performance.

⓫ ___________ assessment. Ongoing informal evaluation serving the purpose of facilitating improvement in a student's performance.

Answer

ACROSS ➡ **2.** washback **6.** integrative **8.** criterion-referenced **9.** predictive **10.** content validity **12.** discrete point

DOWN ⬇ **1.** summative **3.** authenticity **4.** norm-referenced **5.** rater-reliability **7.** construct validity **8.** concurrent **11.** formative

Key-concepts check-up : Assessment (2)

ACROSS ➡

❷ ____________ test: The most important reason of this test is to find out how well the students have mastered the language areas and skills which have just been taught. If we test what has recently been taught and practiced, then we should expect students to score fairly high marks. If most of the students fail to score high marks, something must have been wrong with the teaching, the syllabus or the materials.

❻ THIS is the extent to which an item is easy or difficult for the proposed group of test-takers. THIS is a number, typically printed as a decimal, ranging from 0.0 to 1.0.

❽ If a test is given to a large group of people, the discriminating power of an item can be measured by comparing the number of people with high test scores who answered that item correctly with the number of people with low test scores who answered the same item correctly.

❾ THIS is a purposeful collection of students' work that demonstrates to students and others their efforts, progress, and achievements in given areas.

⓫ Scoring method classroom evaluation of learning is best served through THIS, in which as many as major elements of writing are scored, thus enabling learners to capture their weakness and strengths.

⓬ THIS is a log of one's thoughts, feelings, reactions, assessments, ideas, or progresses toward goals, usually written with little attention to structure, form, or correctness.

DOWN ⬇

❶ Every multiple-choice item consists of a stem and either three, four, or five answer options. One, and only one, of the options is correct, and the rest is called THIS. / Incorrect alternatives in a multiple-choice question.

❸ Students are asked to assess themselves each week according to the most appropriate grades listed on a simple form. The students then show their forms at the end of the week and briefly discuss their results individually with a teacher.

❹ Scoring method THIS uses a rubric for scoring oral production holistically. Each point on a holistic scale is given a systematic set of descriptors, and the reader-evaluator matches an overall impression with the descriptors to arrive at a score.

❺ ____________ test: An assessment instrument designed to analyze a test-taker's strengths and weaknesses in terms of grammar, pronunciation, fluency, discourse, or other targeted linguistic features.

❼ In THIS, the second half (according to the number of letters) of every other word is deleted, leaving the first and the last sentence of the passage intact. Within THIS, a clue (half the word) serves as a stimulus for respondents to find the other half.

❿ ___________ test: In THIS, a sentence with a word left out should be filled with a calculated guess, using linguistic expectancies and background knowledge. THIS is an integrative measure not only of reading ability but also other language abilities.

Answer

ACROSS ➡ **2.** progress **6.** item facility **8.** item discrimination **9.** portfolios **11.** analytic **12.** journals

DOWN ⬇ **1.** distractor **3.** self-assessment **4.** holistic **5.** diagnostic **7.** C test **10.** cloze

Chapter 04

All About the Assessment

01 How to Manage the Classroom Testing

1 The Constructive View of Language Testing

① an opportunity for interaction between a teacher and students
② helping students improve their skills
③ The test criteria are clear to students.
④ Test takers are trained in how to take tests (unfamiliar formats).
⑤ The tests are returned promptly.
⑥ The results are discussed.

2 Principle of Assessment – practicality, reliability, validity, authenticity, washback

Data Analysis

Mr. Kim, a head teacher of high school English, wanted to evaluate the achievement test of English reading in order to find to what extent the five major principles of language assessment (practicality, reliability, validity, authenticity, and washback) were applied to the test.

Test Evaluation Checklist

Test-takers: 2nd year high school students

Content	Scale		
	1	2	3
Subjectivity does not enter into the scoring process.	□	□	■
Classroom conditions for the test are equal for all students.	□	□	■
Test measures exactly what it is supposed to measure.	■	□	□
Items focus on previously practiced in-class reading skills.	■	□	□
Topics and situations are interesting.	□	□	■
Tasks replicate, or closely approximate, real-world tasks.	□	□	■

1=poor, 2=average, 3=good

Post-Exam Reflection

I studied really hard for the test because I wanted to move to a higher level class. But I got 76 and I was so disappointed. Since there were no errors in scoring, my score was dependable, I think. The topics were very relevant to my real life. But what was the problem? Did I use the wrong study skills? Actually I was very surprised when I first saw the test. Lots of tasks were very unfamiliar and I believe I've never done those kinds of tasks in class. Furthermore, after the test I actually expected the teacher to go over the test and give advice on what I should focus on in the future. It never happened. No feedback or comments from the teacher were given. I was not sure which items I got wrong. I will have the same type of test next semester and I'm not sure how I can improve my reading skills and get a better grade.

Q1 Identify TWO well-applied principles and TWO poorly-applied principles among the five principles of language stated above based on all the data.

____

____

____

Q2 Support each of your choices with details from the post-exam reflection ONLY.

____

____

____

>> Possible Answers p.286

(1) Inter-rater Reliability

At a high school English writing contest, contestants were given the instructions in the box and completed their compositions.

> Listen to a taped radio interview of Barbara Carrel, a famous writer, about her adventure to Africa. While listening, take notes. Then using the notes, write a story about her adventure. You will be given 30 minutes to complete the story.

Each contestant's composition was evaluated by two English teachers using the same rating scale. Below is a part of the two teachers' scoring results.

Ratings of Contestants' Compositions

Students	Criteria	Teacher A	Teacher B
Giho Lim	Content	2	5
	Organization	1	4
	Vocabulary	3	4
	Grammar	2	5
Bomi Cho	Content	3	1
	Organization	5	1
	Vocabulary	4	2

1=lowest ↔ 5=highes

Comment

The procedure used in the contest exemplifies **integrative** testing in terms of the number of skills assessed. One potential problem with the scoring process is low **inter-rater** reliability, which is most likely due to the subjectivity of the raters.

(2) Intra-rater Reliability

T1 is the head teacher, and T2 is teaching English writing this semester at the school.

T1 : Good morning, Mr. Lee. How are your writing classes going?
T2: Good morning, Ms. Park. They're going well, but I find scoring students' writing quite challenging.
T1 : What makes you say that?
T2: I rated my students' writing assignments last night. But when I look at them today, I feel I would give different scores.
T1 : Why do you think that happened?
T2: Well, I'm pretty sure it was because I was doing it late at night. I think I was too tired.
T1 : Mmm... I don't grade my students' writing assignments when I'm tired. That way, I can avoid being inconsistent. I just put them away until the next day.
T2: I bet that would be very helpful with keeping scoring reliable.
T1 : Yeah, it helps.
T2: Another issue is that over time, I tend to stray from the rating criteria. I need to find a way to stick to it for consistency in scoring.
T1 : Well, why don't you go back every once in a while and check the last few essays you've marked to see that you're still following the rating criteria?
T2: That's a good idea. It'll help keep me on track.
T1 : Exactly.
T2: Thanks for your advice.

T=teacher

Data Analysis

Read the passage and follow the directions.

An English proficiency test was administered to 3rd graders (n=300) of a middle school. In order to check how well the test components contribute to the construct that is being measured, Ms. Kim, who is an English teacher, did the following with the test results:

1. She divided the questions into even and odd numbers.
2. She scored each half of the test for each student.
3. She found the correlation coefficient for the two halves to learn how strong a relationship between two halves there was.

Figure 1. Score of each student

Student	Score	Even questions	Odd questions
1	42	22	20
2	66	36	30
3	88	46	42
4	90	50	40
5	60	38	22
6	100	50	50
7	45	23	22
8	68	38	30
9	80	46	34
10	85	45	40

(ellipsis)

Figure 2. Correlation graph (r=0.87)

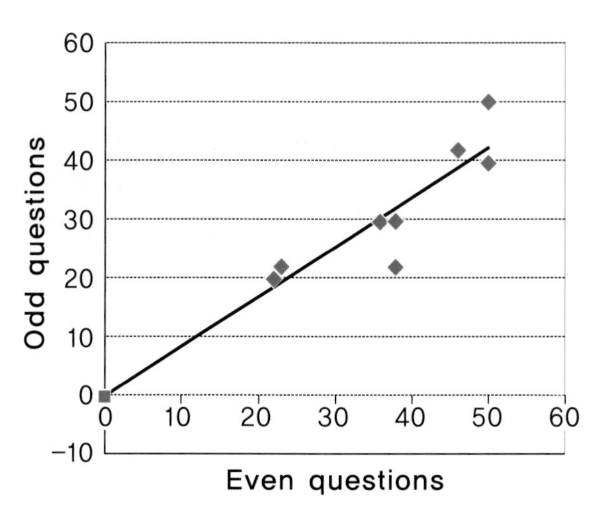

Q1 Fill in the blanks with the ONE most appropriate word in common.

Given the information and figures provided in the text, Ms. Kim intends to measure internal consistency of the English proficiency test using the ______________ method. For example, Figure 1 shows the scores of each student on even and odd questions, providing the data needed for the ______________ reliability calculation. Figure 2 presents the correlation graph, illustrating the strength of the relationship between the two sets of scores. This approach helps ensure that the test items consistently reflect the construct being measured, thereby validating the test's reliability.

>> Possible Answers p.286

(3) Construct Validity

Data Analysis

A high school teacher wanted to develop a test in order to assess his students' English reading ability. He developed the test based on the following procedures:

- Step 1. Construct Definition
  He started by clarifying what his test was intended to measure. He defined the construct of his English test as the ability to infer meanings from a given reading passage.

- Step 2. Designing Test Specifications
  According to the construct definition in Step 1, he specified the test as consisting of a total of 20 multiple-choice items: 1) 10 items asking test-takers to infer meanings and fill in the blank with the most appropriate words or phrases (i.e. Fill-in-the-Blank), and 2) 10 items for finding the best order of scrambled sentences (i.e. Unscrambling).

- Step 3. Developing Test Items & Piloting
  He finished item development. He piloted the test to examine whether the items had satisfactory test qualities.

- Step 4. Analyzing Item Facility & Item Discrimination
  He analyzed item difficulty. To increase internal consistency, he removed the items with a high value of item discrimination.

- Step 5. Analyzing Reliability & Validity
  Reliability was assessed by Cronbach's coefficient alpha. To investigate the concurrent validity of the test, he asked his colleagues to review the given test based on the test specifications.

- Step 6. Administering the Test
  After making the necessary revisions, he administered the test to his students.

Q1 Based on the passage above, identify TWO steps out of the six that have a problem in the process of test development.

____

____

____

Q2 Support your answers with evidence from the passage. Do Not copy more than FOUR consecutive words from the passage.

____

____

____

>> Possible Answers p.286

(4) Predictive Validity

Mr. Lee wants to determine how well the scores from the College Entrance Exam(CEE) predict academic success in college. The scatter plot below includes high school seniors' CEE scores from 2014 and their college Grade Point Averages(GPAs) in the fall of 2016. Their CEE scores are placed on the horizontal axis and their college GPAs on the vertical axis.

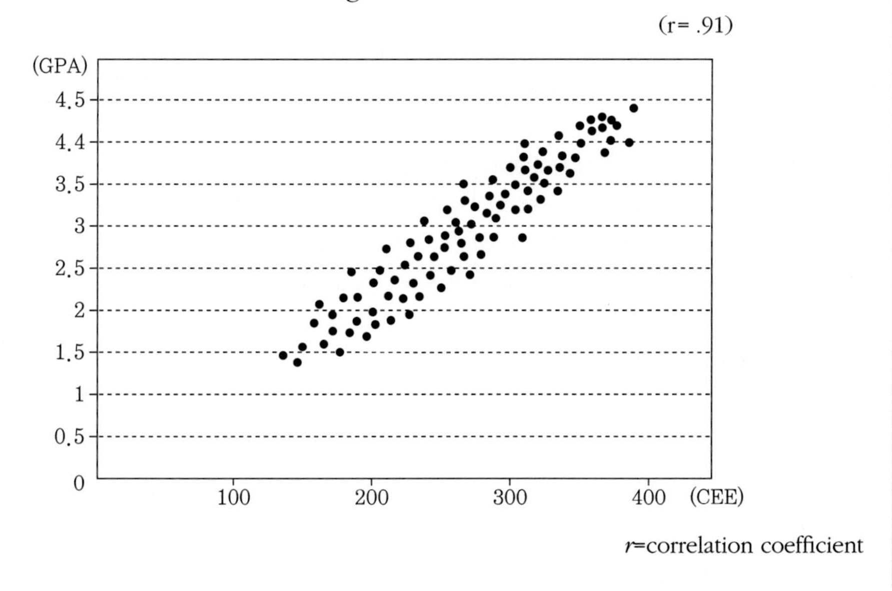

r=correlation coefficient

Students	CEE (Fall 2014)	GPA (Fall 2016)
A	389	4.43
B	246	2.58
C	304	3.15
D	322	3.27
E	211	2.10
F	328	3.62
G	314	3.18
H	288	2.83
I	372	4.00
J	368	3.85
.	.	.
.	.	.
.	.	.

Data Analysis

Read the passage and follow the directions.

Ms. Park aimed to investigate how well her classroom tests in Speaking, Writing, and Reading, reflect students' actual language proficiency as measured by a validated assessment like the TOEFL. She compared her students' classroom test scores from 2024 with their TOEFL scores from the same period to evaluate the ____________ of her tests. A total of 30 second-year high school students participated, and they were grouped into three levels based on their classroom test performance. For each level, the corresponding TOEFL skill test score ranges were also analyzed. The comparison revealed a strong correlation between the students' performance on the classroom tests and their TOEFL scores, indicating that the classroom tests have strong ____________ in measuring students' language proficiency. The results are as follows.

Classroom Tests	LEVEL	TOEFL Score in each section (out of 30 points)
Classroom Test 1 (Speaking)	Advanced	25-28 points
	Intermediate	18-24 points
	Low intermediate	10-17 points
Classroom Test 2 (Writing)	Advanced	24-29 points
	Intermediate	17-23 points
	Low intermediate	10-16 points
Classroom Test 3 (Reading)	Advanced	22-30 points
	Intermediate	15-21 points
	Low intermediate	7-14 points

Q1 Fill in the blanks with the TWO most appropriate words in common.

>> Possible Answers p.286

(5) Washback Effect

Ms. Ahn's Journal

I think I need to change my approach to teaching speaking skills. In my conversation class, I usually have my students listen to dialogues and then practice the main expressions using pattern drills, which I thought would help them speak with both accuracy and fluency. However, when I assessed their speaking performance last week, most students had difficulties speaking fluently. They frequently had long pauses in their speech, but were quite accurate. In order to address this issue, I'm going to add more fluency activities such as discussion, role-plays, and information-gap activities.

Nayun's Journal

Today, I got my final exam results. Compared to the mid-term exam, my score has improved a lot. I'm very proud of myself because I studied a lot for the test. My English teacher usually includes lots of reading comprehension questions on exams, so this time I read all the reading texts in the textbook multiple times and took many practice tests. However, I'm a bit disappointed with the test in a way. I really want to improve my English writing skills, but I just don't have time to practice them. Well... I don't know.... I want to change how I'm studying, but I can't give up on getting good English test scores.

➡ The above two journal entries demonstrate washback effect in that the teacher and the student each write about what they do for their teaching and studying with regard to tests.

3 Formative vs. Summative Assessment

Mr. Kim : What about assessment this semester?
Ms. Park: Students just took one major test at the end of the semester. I regret that I evaluated only their learning product.
Mr. Kim : You mean just once over the semester? At the end of the semester?
Ms. Park: Yes, I thought it was impossible to assess their speaking performance regularly by myself and I gave one major test to the students. So I was actually unable to gather information on the developmental process of their speaking abilities.

4 Norm-referenced vs. Criterion-referenced Testing

(1) Norm-referenced Testing

English teachers are looking for a standardized test. They will use the test results to award scholarships to the top 10%. With this in mind, they are looking over the test manual of a standardized test. After the test students will receive a total score for the reading section and a percentile rank.

(2) Criterion-referenced Testing

The teacher has been working with first year high school students and decides to test their speaking ability using an oral task. The students who get over 10 out of 16 will pass the conversation course.

Procedure

1. The students are divided into five groups and each group writes a script for an English drama.
2. Each group hands in a copy of the script and rehearses.

3. On the evaluation day, each group takes turns performing in front of the class.
4. The teacher observes the performance and scores each student according to the following criteria:

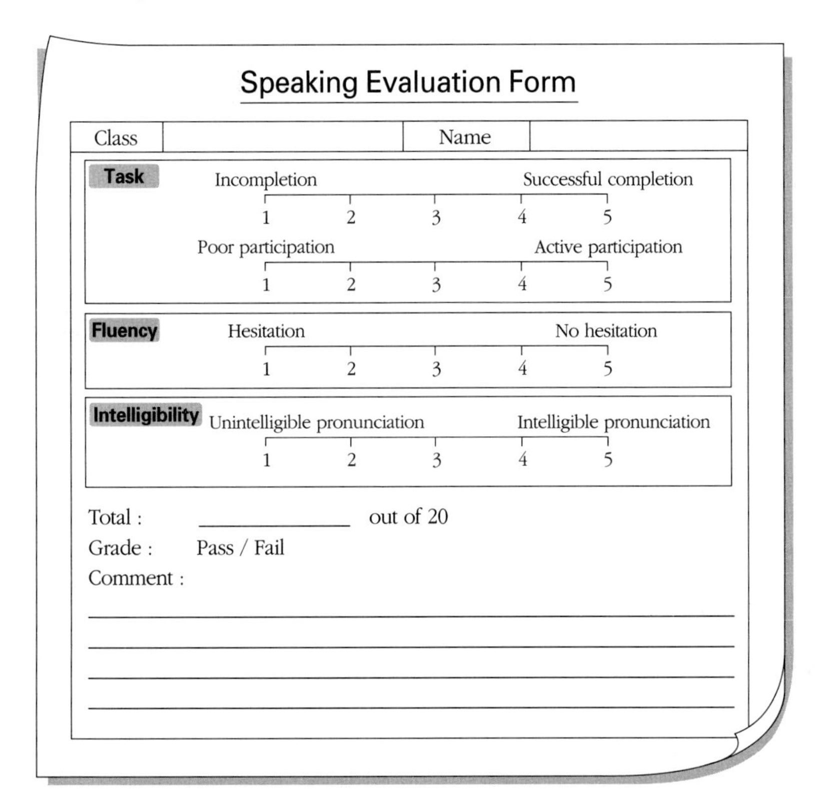

Speaking Evaluation Form

Class		Name	

Task

Incompletion — Successful completion
1 2 3 4 5

Poor participation — Active participation
1 2 3 4 5

Fluency

Hesitation — No hesitation
1 2 3 4 5

Intelligibility

Unintelligible pronunciation — Intelligible pronunciation
1 2 3 4 5

Total : ______________ out of 20
Grade : Pass / Fail
Comment :

5. The teacher reports the grades as 'PASS' or 'FAIL' and gives comments to each student.

5 Discrete-point Testing vs. Integrative Testing

(1) Multiple Choice Item Testing

① Basic rules of multiple choice Items

A

The following are guidelines for constructing multiple choice items to assess knowledge of word meanings:

1. Make sure there is only one correct answer for each item.
2. Make sure the distractors are the same grammatical class as the key.
3. Do not provide inadvertent clues to the key which allow students to answer an item correctly without knowledge of word meanings.
4. Make sure the key cannot be selected based on students' world knowledge.

B

Below are some examples of multiple-choice items that are intended to measure students' knowledge of word meanings.

Choose the one that best fits in each blank.

a. I want to be a poet. I have had an _______ in writing poems, since I was a child.
① interest ② doubt ③ concern ④ worry

b. I was hungry, so I went home ________ to eat dinner.
① run ② rate ③ quickly ④ rapid

c. I usually go to the dentist to have my teeth ______ once a year.
① examined ② checked ③ seen ④ fixed

d. Inventors are always coming up with new ideas because they are very _______.
① creative ② sad ③ lazy ④ guilty

e. When tourists from Seoul go to Jeju on vacation, they travel ______.
① north ② west ③ east ④ south

Data Analysis

Read the passages in <A> and <B>, and follow the directions.

A

A high school English teacher, Mr. Choi, wanted to learn how to write selected-response items (e.g., multiple-choice items) more efficiently. He wrote several items before the workshop began, and found some of them were flawed according to the guidelines he learned during the workshop. The following are some of the guidelines along with examples of flawed items.

General Guidelines for Writing Selected-response Items

① Make certain that there is only one, clearly correct answer.
② State both the stem and the options as simply and directly as possible.
③ Present a single clearly formulated problem to avoid mixed content.
④ Avoid negative wording whenever possible. If it is absolutely necessary to use a negative stem, highlight the negative word.

Item 1

My forehead itches every day during the summer. Using sunscreen hasn't helped much. I think I'd better go to the __________ to get my skin checked.

a. dentist
b. optometrist
c. pediatrician
→ d. dermatologist

Item 2

Where did Henry go after the party last night?

a. Yes, he did.
b. Because he was tired.
→ c. To Kate's place for another party.
d. He went home around eleven o'clock.

Item 3

I never knew where __________.

a. had the boys gone

→ b. the boys had gone

c. the boys have gone

d. have the boys gone

Item 4

According to the passage, which of the following is not true?

a. My sister likes outdoor sports.

b. My brother is busy with his plans.

→ c. My sister and I often do everything together.

d. My brother is more energetic and outgoing than I.

Note: '→' indicates the key; '?' indicates a possible answer.

B

After the workshop, to improve the quality of the items, the teacher revised some items according to the guidelines. The following are the revised items.

Item 1

I think I'd better go to the _________ to get my skin checked.

a. dentist

b. optometrist

c. pediatrician

→ d. dermatologist

Item 2

Where did Henry go after the party last night?

a. Yes, he did.

b. Because he was tired.

c. It was about eleven o'clock.

→ d. To Kate's place for another party.

Item 3

I never knew ________.

a. where had the boys gone

→ b. where the boys had gone

c. the boys where had gone

d. the boys had gone where

Item 4

According to the passage, which of the following is NOT true?

a. My sister likes outdoor sports.

b. My brother is busy with his plans.

→ c. My sister and I often do everything together.

d. My brother is more energetic and outgoing than I.

Q1 Based on <A>, identify the ONE most appropriately revised item in <B> according to guideline ②, and the ONE most appropriately revised item according to guideline ③.

Q2 Explain each of the item with evidence from <A> and <B>.

>> Possible Answers p.286

② Item facility & Item discrimination

Below are the results from a 10-item test that Mr. Park gave to his 11 students to compare their English abilities. Based on the test results, Mr. Park divided the students into three groups–upper, middle, and lower. He wanted to determine the effectiveness of the test by examining item facility(IF) and item discrimination(ID). To calculate IF, Mr. Park divided the number of students who correctly answered a particular item by the total number of students who took the test. ID indicates the degree to which an item separates the students who performed well from those who did poorly on the test as a whole. Mr. Park used the following formula to calculate the ID for each item:

$ID = IF_{upper} - IF_{lower}$.

Test Results

Groups	Students	Items										Total
		1	2	3	4	5	6	7	8	9	10	
Upper	A	1	1	1	1	1	1	1	1	1	1	10
	B	1	0	1	1	1	1	1	1	1	1	9
	C	1	0	1	0	1	1	1	1	1	1	8
	D	1	1	0	1	1	1	1	0	1	1	8
Middle	E	0	1	0	1	1	1	1	1	0	0	6
	F	1	0	1	1	1	0	1	0	1	0	6
	G	1	1	0	0	1	0	1	0	1	1	6
Lower	H	1	1	0	0	1	0	1	0	0	0	4
	I	0	0	0	0	1	1	0	0	1	1	4
	J	0	1	1	0	0	0	0	0	1	1	4
	K	1	0	0	1	1	1	0	0	0	0	4
Total		8	6	5	6	10	7	8	4	8	7	

1=a correct response, 0=an incorrect response

③ Distractor analysis

Mr. Lee's English listening test consisted exclusively of four-option, multiple-choice items. After scoring the test, he calculated the response frequency for each item. Part of the results is presented below.

	Upper Group (N=100)				Lower Group (N=100)			
Item \ Option	A	B	C	D	A	B	C	D
1	50%*	27%	13%	10%	10%*	45%	25%	20%
2	13%	10%	70%*	7%	25%	27%	28%*	20%
3	20%	25%	18%	37%*	21%	26%	16%	37%*
…								
17	4%	0%	61%	35%*	66%	0%	29%	5%*
…								

* indicates the correct response

(2) Integrative Testing: Cloze Assessment Task

T1: My students are having trouble with plural nouns. I'm thinking of trying a new assessment task.
T2: What's your idea?
T1: I'm planing to give a short text where every seventh word is blanked out. Students have to guess the correct word for each blank to make a complete sentence.
T2: Well, that might be a bit difficult for beginning level student. I did a similar activity last semester. I gave a text where I blanked out only plural nouns so that students could focus on them.
T1: Oh, I see.
T2: You can also give students only parts of words in the blanks and ask them to restore each word in the text.
T1: Hmm, that seems interesting. Well, then, for my students, I'll try to use only plural nouns in the written text and ask my students to fill in the blanks.

6 Classroom Testing – proficiency test, diagnostic test, placement test, achievement test, progress test

T: Come here, Sumin. How was your vacation?

S: Pretty good. Thank you, Ms. Kim. Actually, I'm so happy to be taking English classes from you this year.

T: Good! You're really welcome in my class. Okay, then, let's talk about the test you had.

S: You mean the reading test you gave us in the first class? Actually, I was wondering why you gave us a test instead of going directly into the textbook.

T: Right, your class hasn't had a lesson yet. It was mainly to see how much you are ready for this semester and give you individual attention for any strong and weak points you have.

S: I see. So, how were the results?

T: Hmm... Overall, you did quite well. Especially, you did well on the grammar questions. But it appears you had a bit of trouble with some words in the reading texts.

S: You're right. Some words are really hard to memorize although I keep trying.

T: I understand. Well, why don't you try to learn them through a context particularly relevant to you? That will be helpful, I believe.

S: Thank you for your advice, Ms. Kim.

T=teacher, S=student

7 Alternative Assessment

(1) **Portfolios**: a collection of student work

- including essays, reports, journals, video or audio-recorded learner language data, students' self-assessment, teachers' written feedback, homework, conference forms, etc.
- leading students to have ownership over their process of learning
- allowing teachers to pay attention to students' progress as well as achievement

Student—Teacher Meeting

T: Well, looking back over the last twelve weeks, I can see that you have written many drafts for the three essay writing assignments.
S: Yes, I have. I have a lot of things here.
T: Of all your essays, which one do you think is the best?
S: I think the persuasive essay I wrote is the best.
T: What makes you think so? Maybe you can tell me how you wrote it.
S: Well... I think the topic I chose was quite engaging. I enjoyed the writing process throughout. And it feels good being able to see the progress I've made.
T: Yes, that's the benefit of this kind of project. I can see some improvement in your use of transitions. Your ideas are nicely connected and organized now.
S: Thanks. What else should I include?
T: Well, did you work on the self-assessment form and the editing checklist?
S: Yes, I did. I completed them and included them with all of my drafts right here.
T: Perfect! I'll be able to finish grading all of your work by the end of next week.

T=teacher, S=student

(2) Journals

- **Purpose**: To provide students with an opportunity to share privately in writing their reaction, questions, and concerns about school experiences with the teacher without any threat of reprisal or evaluation.

- **Rationale**: The notion of these strategies is a partial refinement of journal writing. Their major characteristic is the importance given to communications between the student and the teacher. They provide the teacher with the opportunity not only to learn what students are thinking and doing but also to share thoughts and suggestions with them.
  Often journals were used to encourage diarylike entries of what took place in the way of progress on a project; sometimes they were used to give students the opportunity to respond freely to what took place at school or home, or to respond to a book or some other forms of literature.
  While the teacher might not respond to every entry, the intent of this activity is to have students write to the teacher and to have the teacher write a genuine response to the student. The teacher does not evaluate the student's comments as either right or wrong. What is important to note is the teacher's respect for the privacy of the journal as well as the nonjudgmental and nonprescriptive nature of the teacher's reaction. Discussions to be made are left up to the student.

(3) Self-and Peer-Assessment

Class Participation

Please fill out this questionnaire by checking the appropriate box.

Yes, Definitely [A] Sometimes [B] Not Yet [C]

a. I come to class on time.	[A]	[B]	[C]
b. I ask the teacher questions.	[A]	[B]	[C]
c. I ask my classmates questions.	[A]	[B]	[C]
d. I answer questions that the teacher asks.	[A]	[B]	[C]
e. I take equal turns in all three roles.	[A]	[B]	[C]
f. I cooperate with my group members.	[A]	[B]	[C]
g. I use the new vocabulary.	[A]	[B]	[C]
h. I complete all of the peer-reviews.	[A]	[B]	[C]

comments: ______________________________

8 Scoring Method – Holistic vs. Analytic

Data Analysis

Read the English test task specifications in <A> and the teacher's reflective journal in <B>, and follow the directions.

A

Test Task Specifications	
Category	Description
Purpose	To determine students' current levels and place them into the most appropriate speaking courses
Time allocation	2 minutes (1 minute for preparation and 1 minute for speaking)
Task type	Picture-cued tasks
Scoring method	Analytic a. Criteria: Content, Fluency, Accuracy, Pronunciation b. Each criterion is worth 5points and the score for this task is added up to 20.
Scoring procedure	a. Two examiners: a primary examiner who conducts the test and a secondary examiner who observes the test b. If there is a difference of more than 2points in total, the examiners discuss rating disagreements based on the recorded test to arrive at a rating that they agree upon.

B

I understand that some students have potential strengths in learning languages, and in order to check my students' aptitude in English, I conducted a speaking test with picture-cued tasks. For each task, students looked at pictures and prepared for 1 minute and then described them for 1 minute. I found that 1 minute was not enough for my students to prepare their answers, so I felt that I needed to change the time allocation for the task. In addition, although my rating and the other examiner's rating seemed consistent, I realized that my approach, providing a global rating with overall impressions using a single general scale, was not very effective because the scores didn't give much helpful information to students. … There was one student's test yielding very different scores, so we (primary and secondary examiners) had a discussion about the recorded test and found that I gave the wrong score by mistake. It was good that we recorded the test even though both of us were present during the test.

Q1 Identify TWO categories that the teacher did NOT follow in the test task specifications from <A>.

Q2 Support your answers with evidence from <B>.

>> Possible Answers p.287

Possible Answers

p.260

Q1 According to the data, this test demonstrates high reliability and authenticity, whereas it has low validity and lacks washback.

Q2 This test ensures fair scoring and covers topics relevant to student's real lives. However, it includes task that students have not practiced in class, and no comments or feedback are provided to guide their further study.

---

p.265

Q1 split–half

---

p.267

Q1 Steps 4 and 5 have a problem in the process of test development.

Q2 To increase internal consistency, in Step 4, the teacher should remove items with zero or negative item discrimination, rather than those with high discrimination values. In Step 5, to improve construct validity, he should ask colleagues to review the test with reference to the test specifications.

---

p.269

Q1 concurrent validity

---

p.275

Q1 Items 1 and 3 in ⟨B⟩ are appropriately revised based on guideline ② and ③ respectively.

Q2 Item 1 simplifies the original complex stem into a simple and straightforward(direct) sentence. Additionally, Item 3 in ⟨B⟩ now presents a clear, single problem on an 'indirect question' by standardizing the tense in the options into the past perfect 'had gone'.

p.284

Q1 The teacher in 〈B〉 does not follow two test task specifications from 〈A〉: Purpose and Scoring method.

Q2 Specifically, she conducts a test to assess students' aptitude in English rather than to place students into a level-appropriate speaking course. Additionally, instead of using an analytic scoring method, the teacher applies a holistic scoring method with a single, general scale.

NEW

Build Up

박현수 영어교육론 Ⅱ

Worksheets for Pre-service Teachers
Authentic Data for Classroom Teaching

초판인쇄 | 2025. 1. 15. **초판발행** | 2025. 1. 20. **편저자** | 박현수
발행인 | 박 용 **발행처** | (주)박문각출판 **표지디자인** | 박문각 디자인팀
등록 | 2015년 4월 29일 제2019-000137호
주소 | 06654 서울시 서초구 효령로 283 서경빌딩 **팩스** | (02)584-2927
전화 | 교재주문·학습문의 (02)6466-7202

정가 29,000원
ISBN 979-11-7262-502-3

NEW

Build Up

다음 카페 유희태 전공영어
cafe.daum.net/YHT2S2R

네이버 블로그 유희태 전공영어
blog.naver.com/kmo7740

NEW 교원임용시험 전공영어 대비 [제1판]

Build Up

박문각 임용 동영상강의 www.pmg.co.kr

박현수 영어교육론 

Worksheets for Pre-service Teachers
Authentic Data for Classroom Teaching

2026년 대비 기출문제 풀이연습 및 실전문제 풀이전략

NEW

Build Up

Ⅱ

NEW 교원임용시험 전공영어 대비 [제1판]

Build Up

박문각 임용 동영상강의 www.pmg.co.kr

박현수 영어교육론 II

Worksheets for Pre-service Teachers
Authentic Data for Classroom Teaching

2026년 대비 기출문제 풀이연습 및 실전문제 풀이전략

Contents

01

선택형 기출문항 서답형 접근

01 선택형 기출문항 서답형 접근

모범답안 p. 40

Item 1 Coursebook Evaluation 2011 15번

Below is part of the coursebook evaluation by two teachers. They are supposed to use the same coursebook next semester. So, they want to prepare extra teaching materials for only those categories that they both marked as "poor."

Categories of Evaluation	Teacher A			Teacher B		
Language Content	3	2	1	3	2	1
(1) Are vocabulary exercises presented which exploit words that frequently occur next to each other?			✓			✓
(2) Are new grammar items introduced in context?			✓			✓
(3) Is appropriate attention given to pronunciation?	✓				✓	
(4) Are there enough models of discourse in which language is used for effective communication?		✓				✓
(5) Is there any attempt to match language styles to social situations?			✓			✓
(6) Is more than one variety of English used to meet the demand for international English?			✓	✓		

3=Excellent, 2=Good, 1=Poor

Direction

Based on the evaluation results in the box, identify three categories of language content which both of teachers mark as "poor" and then suggest extra teaching materials to complement the identified categories respectively.

Keyword list

language styles, speech styles, world Englishes, formality, mnemonic devices, collocations, authentic story, grammar in context

Item 2 Teachers' Perspectives on English Classes 2011 16번

Teacher A: My students tend to transfer the forms and meanings of their native language to English both productively and receptively. I believe that where the two languages differ, negative transfer will result. That is, the students make errors due to L1 interference. So, I decide on what to teach in my English class after identifying the similarities and differences of grammatical points between their native language and English. Also, I prepare teaching materials based on the scientific description of English, carefully compared with a parallel description of their native language.

Teacher B: I think rote learning of isolated units of grammar is not very helpful for communicative language use. So, I usually work with units of language above the sentence level when collecting the grammar structures to be taught in class. For instance, I provide student-centered learning materials in which my students can learn to comprehend and produce grammatical points in context. I am sure it will be helpful for them to develop their ability to use the forms appropriately for particular situations.

Direction

Referring to the above, identify the type of language analysis underlying Teacher A's or Teacher B's teaching perspectives and choose one that is more suitable for a communication-oriented classroom and support your choice with evidence from the passages.

Keyword list

interference, communicative language use, sentence level, student-centered learning, contrastive analysis hypothesis, discourse analysis, focus on form approach, intralingual error, formal instruction, controlled practice, contexualized language use

Item 3 Reading Lesson 2011 17번

Below is an excerpt of a reading lesson based on a three-part framework. The reading passage, about 300 words long, is about a boy's adventure. The ending of the story is intentionally omitted by the teacher so that students can learn how to construct a cohesive and coherent text.

Lesson Procedure

Pre-reading Activity

- Have Ss watch a 2-minute English video clip related to the reading passage and then answer questions about the clip.
- Give Ss half a minute to find previously learned discourse markers (e.g., *however*, *therefore*, *as a result*, etc.) in the passage while reading quickly through it.

Reading Activity

- Have Ss first read the story by themselves, complete the story in pairs by predicting the ending based on the storyline, and then write it down in about 50 words. While they carry out the task on their own, T circulates, offering feedback, suggestions, or language help Ss may need to accomplish the task.

Post-reading Activity

- Have each pair make a presentation about their version of the ending of the story in English.
- Have Ss vote for the most interesting ending.

T=teacher, Ss=students

Direction

Referring to the lesson procedure above, identify two ways Ms. Park supports students who might suffer from writing task difficulty. All data should drawn from the passages.

Keyword list

cohesive, coherent text, discourse marker, language help, cooperative learning skill, facilitator, resource, background knowledge, prediction, scanning strategy, schemata

Item 4 Grammar Instruction 2011 18번

Activity A

Change the sentences as in the example, and check your answers with your partner. Then explain to your partner the grammatical rule(s) you applied.

(1) I have been to New York several times.
⇒ I went to New York last month.
(2) She has read the book before.
⇒ ________________ a month ago.
(3) We have known about the problem for ages.
⇒ ________________ yesterday.

Activity B

In pairs, read the following conversation extracts, focusing on the parts in italics. What is the difference between what Person A and Person B say? When would you use one form or the other? Share your thoughts with your partner.

(1) A: I*'ve won* a prize in the English-speaking competition.
B: Yeah? I *won* a prize in the poetry competition *last year.*
(2) A: I*'ve seen* Romeo and Juliet *twice.*
B: Me, too. I *saw* it *last Tuesday* and again *on the weekend.*
(3) A: A strange thing *happened* to me *yesterday.* I couldn't remember my cell phone number.
B: Really? That *has happened* to me *several times,* too.

Direction

Of Activities A and B choose the one that combines formal instruction on the target forms and their communicative use and support your choice with concrete evidence from the data.

Keyword list

formal instruction, target form, communicative use, implicit knowledge, discourse level, deductive, inductive, meaning-focused input, consciousness-raising, input enhancement

Item 5 English Only Classroom 2011 19번

Mr. Hwang's Teaching Log

I wanted to increase the amount of English in the classroom. To do this, I first investigated how much I used Korean during my teaching. I listened to three tapes recorded at different times over a two-week period just to determine the proportion of English to Korean I was using. It was about 50% English, 50% Korean. I then listened to the tapes again to find out the purposes for which I was using Korean. I found I was using Korean for two main purposes: classroom management and giving feedback. I drew up a plan to reduce the amount of Korean I was using for these two purposes. I first made a list of English expressions commonly used for classroom management and feedback, and familiarized myself with them. I wrote out the expressions on cards, and put them in a conspicuous place on my table. This served to help me remember the expressions I wanted to use. I then continued recording my lessons and after a few weeks checked my tapes. My use of English had increased considerably.

Direction

Considering information in the box, identify what Mr. Hwang does to increase the amount of English in the classroom and support your idea with details from the passage.

Keyword list

English only classroom, classroom management, teacher talk, student talk, critical self-examination, professional development, teacher-initiated classroom management, reflective teaching, affective dimension, action research

Item 6 Classroom Discourse (1) 2011 20번

(Before the teacher starts his lesson in a middle school English class, he asks students questions to warm up, starting with Mina.)

T: What did you do last weekend, Mina?
S: I visit my uncle in the hospital.
T: You visited your uncle in the hospital?
S: Yes, I visit him.
T: I see. Did you do anything else?
S: Yeah. Um, I see a movie.
T: You saw a movie?
S: Yes.
T: Great. What movie did you see?
S: I see the movie *Avatar*.

T=teacher, S=student

Direction

Referring to the classroom talk in the box, identify two reasons Mina repeats past-tense errors and then, in terms of behaviorist and innatist point of view respectively, suggest how to teach past-tense rules for Mina to use them correctly.

Keyword list

output hypothesis, pushed output, behaviorist, repetition and drill, focus-on-form approach, focused intervention, function word, content word, comprehensible input, affective filter

Item 7 Classroom Discourse (2) 2011 28번

(*In a class, a teacher and students are talking about what makes them unhappy.*)

S1 : When it rain I am unhappy.
T : Why does rain make you unhappy?
S1 : When I walk to school, I wet.
T : Oh, I see. Do you live close to school?
S1 : Yeah. 10 minute.

(S2 *raises a hand.*)

S2 : When mosquitoes ... eat me.
T : Oh, mosquitoes bite me. Bite me!
S2 : Oh, OK. When mosquitoes bite me. They bite me everyday's evening.

(S3 *interrupts the conversation.*)

S3 : Yeah, me, too. Everyday's evening, mosquitoes bite me, too.
T : That's terrible. I think mosquitoes make many people unhappy.

T=teacher, S=student

Direction

Referring to the classroom talk in the box, explain the type of questions Ms. Park uses and write the role of the identified question type within the classroom discourse.

Keyword list

display question, referential question, uptake, corrective feedback, interlanguage, clarification request, meaning negotiation, interlingual transfer, reformulate, negative evidence

Item 8 Pronunciation Work (1) 2011 29번

Student A's Worksheet

Directions: Read sentences 1-4 to your partner, and then circle the words you hear in sentences 5-8 as they are read by your partner.

1. He gave me a hug.
2. Hand me the pin.
3. This room is full of cats.
4. The men will come soon.
5. I'd like to see the chimp / champ.
6. That's my luck / lock.
7. They spun / spin around.
8. I fell over a rock / rack.

Student B's Worksheet

Directions: Circle the words in sentences 1-4 as they are read by your partner, and then read sentences 5-8 to your partner.

1. He gave me a hug / hog.
2. Hand me the pen / pin.
3. This room is full of cots / cats.
4. The man / men will come soon.
5. I'd like to see the champ.
6. That's my lock.
7. They spun around.
8. I fell over a rock.

Direction

Referring to the above, identify the purpose of the pronunciation activity and write its main characteristic compared to traditional ways of teaching pronunciation.

Keyword list

phonemic difference, segmentals, suprasegmentals, accuracy, fluency, register, speech styles, formality, minimal pairs, meaningful minimal pairs

Item 9 English Only Language Classroom 2012 15번

Teacher A is talking about his beliefs and teaching practices in English classes and his student, Student A, is reflecting on her experience.

Teacher A: I think it's important to expose students to as much English as possible. And it's also important to create situations where they use English. And so I design classroom activities to have students work with understandable English both receptively and productively. I require students to use English in class. I don't allow them to talk to other students in Korean or to look words up in a dictionary. I believe interactive activities maximize student-student talk time. During these activities, I prefer to let students sort out their own problems when they don't understand each other. I rarely interrupt or stop to correct their grammar.

Student A: I really enjoy learning English, but I sometimes feel frustrated in class. I don't always understand what the teacher is saying and sometimes I wish I could get help in Korean, but the teacher is so strict about using English in his class. He doesn't even let us use a dictionary. Because of that, I often feel nervous and anxious. I do like the activities where we talk to other students though. But even then, I get embarrassed especially when he doesn't give us time to prepare. I want to recall some expressions that I know. And he doesn't really help us when we're having problems talking. I don't even know if what I'm saying is correct. I just wish he'd give us more help instead of just letting us work on our own.

Direction

(1) Identify three teaching principles Teacher A thinks important in her English classes and address the actual problems her students are experiencing during the class.

(2) Suggest how teachers should decide on the medium of communication in the classroom to prevent the side effect caused by English Only principle.

Keyword list

English-only class(principle), comprehensible input, natural communication, anxiety(facilitative & debilitative), affective filter, scaffolding, form-focused instruction

Item 10 Classroom Feedback 2012 17번

In the middle of a class, the teacher provides feedback when talking to Minho and Sujin.

(1) T: Minho, I hear you went to Jeju last month. Did you buy anything?
S: Yes. Uh, I have brother. I bought chocolate for brother.
T: You bought chocolate for your brother.
S: Right. Chocolate for brother. I bought small pretty doll, too. It's for sister.
T: I'm sure your sister liked it.

(2) T: Sujin, why don't you read page 24?
S: I have no book today. Minho borrowed book yesterday. He lost book.
T: Pardon? I'm confused. Lost whose book?
S: U-uh, umm, my book. He lost my book.
T: Sorry to hear that.

T=teacher, S=student

Direction

Based on classroom data presented in the above, choose the teacher who provides feedback leading to self-repair, citing the concrete feedback utterance. And then support your choice with evidence.

Keyword list

positive evidence, negative evidence, zone of proximal development, self-repair, pushed output, explicit focus, implicit focus, reformulation, explicit correction, recast, clarification request, elicitation, metalinguistic feedback, repetition

Item 11 Textbook Evaluation (1) 2012 18번

Materials evaluation is conducted on a candidate textbook by a high school teacher.

Rating Scale

Evaluation Criteria	1	2	3	4	5
Content and Presentation					
Do the activities exploit language in a communicative or 'real-world' way?		✓			
Do the activities support level-differentiated learning?				✓	
Do the materials provide opportunities for self-study?		✓			
Are communicative functions recycled in subsequent units?		✓			
Is vocabulary selected according to how often it is used in everyday English conversation?	✓				
Are grammar items presented progressively in terms of learnability?				✓	
Teacher's Manual and Supplementary Materials					
Are there suggestions on how to supplement the textbook, or to present lessons in different ways?					✓
Does the manual provide materials for on-going evaluation and ready-made achievement tests?			✓		

1=Totally lacking, 2=Weak, 3=Adequate, 4=Good, 5=Excellent

Direction

Referring to the results of the candidate textbook, identify the strongest and the weakest point it shows and then briefly write the benefit and drawback which the candidate textbook provides for students.

Keyword list

level-differentiated learning, spiral learning, learnability(teachability), on-going evaluation, ready-made achievement test, self-directed study, materials adaptation, multiple proficiency group, spoken language corpora

Item 12 Classroom Testing: Reading test 2012 19번

English teachers are looking for a standardized test. They will use the test results to award scholarships to the top 10%. With this in mind, they are looking over the test manual of a standardized test. The following is an excerpt from the manual:

Reading Section: This section measures the students' ability to understand written English. It is not linked to any particular textbook or specific course of study. The reading section assesses the comprehension of main ideas and factual information, and the ability to infer. This section consists of (1) traditional multiple-choice questions, (2) true/false questions, and (3) questions that require students to click on a word or phrase to answer.

Students will receive a total score for the reading section and a percentile rank.

Direction

Addressing English teachers' testing purpose described in the above, identify the testing type they seek for and support your choice with evidence from the passage.

Keyword list

standardized test, norm-referenced, criterion-referenced, proficiency test, objective test, summative(formative) feedback, constructed-response items

Item 13 Classroom Testing: Oral test 2012 22번

The teacher has been working with first year high school students and decides to test their speaking ability using an oral task. The students who get over 10 out of 20 will pass the conversation course.

Procedure

1) The students are divided into five groups and each group writes a script for an English drama.
2) Each group hands in a copy of the script and rehearses.
3) On the evaluation day, each group takes turns performing in front of the class.
4) The teacher observes the performance and scores each student according to the following criteria:

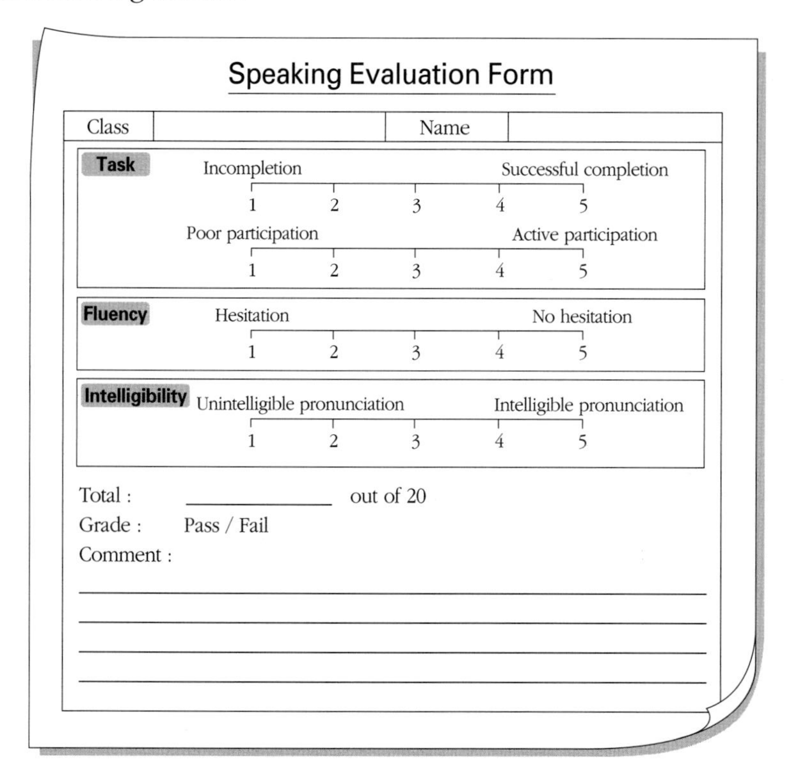

Speaking Evaluation Form

Class		Name	

Task
Incompletion — Successful completion: 1 2 3 4 5
Poor participation — Active participation: 1 2 3 4 5

Fluency
Hesitation — No hesitation: 1 2 3 4 5

Intelligibility
Unintelligible pronunciation — Intelligible pronunciation: 1 2 3 4 5

Total : ________ out of 20
Grade : Pass / Fail
Comment :

5) The teacher reports the grades as 'PASS' or 'FAIL' and gives comments to each student.

Direction

Referring to the testing procedure, identify the testing type and the scoring method the teacher chooses to evaluate students' speaking ability. Then, support each of your choices with details from all the data.

Keyword list

integrative test, criterion-referenced, norm-referenced, analytical scoring, holistic scoring, intelligibility, narrative feedback, performance-based testing

Item 14 Focus on Form Approach: Consciousness-raising techniques 2012 23번

Teaching Procedure

Step 1: The teacher asks students where they went last summer and what they took on their journey. Then she writes down the following sentences on the board and explains the difference in form and meaning between the two sentences using the terms "past tense" and "past participle (pp)".

I took a light jacket.

I should have taken a warm jacket.

Step 2: The teacher hands out a story from a magazine that includes the target structure "should+have+pp". She asks students to read the story carefully and look for the examples of "should+have+pp" in the given text.

Kate travelled across the Australian desert. She made no preparations. She didn't take a map, and she didn't take a cell phone. Soon after she set off, she got lost and got trapped in a flash flood. Later, looking back on it, she said, "I should have taken a map. I should have taken a cell phone...."

Step 3: The teacher asks students to think about their own previous journey and complete the worksheet below.

Worksheet

I ___________ on my journey.	I should have _________ on my journey.
I took a light jacket on my journey.	*I should have taken a warm jacket on my journey.*

Step 4: The teacher asks students to write a story using the sentences they have produced in the worksheet above, and to share their writings with the partners.

Direction

Referring to the teaching procedure above, identify the type of a grammar-based activity used in Step 2 and, also, explain how students can personalize the target structure in Steps 3 and 4.

Keyword list

metalinguistic term, inductive/deductive approach, focus on forms/focus on form approach, input flooding, noticing, personalization, rule discovery/rule presentation, proceduralize, consciousenss-raising techniques, proceduralize

Item 15 Pronunciation Work (2) 2012 24번

An English teacher developed the following procedure for teaching pronunciation. (Prominent syllables are marked by large-size capital letters.)

Step 1

a. The teacher writes the following three versions of the sentence *I'm listening* on the board.

– I'm **LIS**tening. – **I'M** listening. – I **AM** listening!

b. Students practice producing all three versions.

Teacher asks:	Student should respond:
What are you doing?	I'm **LIS**tening.
Who's listening?	**I'M** listening.
Why aren't you listening?	I **AM** listening!

Step 2

With an explanation on how to chunk, the teacher asks students to listen and circle the prominent words.

A: I'm starved. / Let's go grab a bite to eat.
B: Good idea. / Where do you want to go?
A: Well, / there's a nice restaurant. / It's a

Step 3

a. Students write down words for the items that they want to bring for a picnic.

apple, pasta, napkin, pear, pepper, popcorn, pizza, spoon, soup…

b. The teacher asks students to play a game called 'The perfect picnic' with the whole class, using the words that they chose.

Example: Student A says, "We're having a picnic, and I'm bringing pears." Student B says, "We're having a picnic. A is bringing pears, and I'm bringing popcorn." Student C says,...

Direction

Referring to the procedure for teaching pronunciation in the above, explain how this procedure facilitates students' movement from controlled to automatic proceeding of a target phonological feature.

Keyword list

suprasegmentals, segmentals, meaningful/communicative/mechanical drill, controlled/automatic processing, prominent word, chunk, sentence stress

Item 16 Writing Instruction: Dicto-comp 2012 25번

This is a procedure for teaching writing used by a middle school English teacher.

1) The teacher shows pictures of pets to students and asks what kinds of pets they like.
2) The teacher gives each of the students a short story of a dog and a set of four sequential pictures showing its storyline, telling them that they are going to read and write the story as accurately as possible. The story contains a number of regular past tense verbs.
3) Students read the story silently for 3 minutes and return the story to the teacher but keep the pictures.
4) After putting some key words from the story on the board, the teacher reads the whole story aloud.
5) With the aid of the pictures and key words, students write the story as closely as they can remember.
6) The teacher collects students' writings and later corrects them by crossing out incorrect regular past tense forms, providing corresponding correct forms above them.
7) In the next class, students receive their writings and look over their errors and the teacher's corrections.

Direction

Referring to the procedure for teaching writing in the box, identify the writing approach the teacher reflects and write two ways to lessen students' cognitive processing load placed on retelling the story in writing.

Keyword list

product-oriented/process-oriented approach, dicto-comp, cognitive load

Item 17 Classroom Activities: Audio-motor unit & Communicative activity 2012 28번

Two middle school English teachers instruct their classes.

Teacher A: "Today I'm going to show you how to set a table. Before I do, I'll pass out spoons, forks, plates, and knives.... Now watch what I do and follow along. I'm putting a plate on the table.... Now put a plate on the table. On the table. OK?... Good job! Now I'm putting the fork on the left side of the plate. [*Teacher continues with other utensils.*] Well done! Now, what I'd like you to do is practice setting a table in pairs. One partner tells the other what to do and that partner follows the commands..."

Teacher B: "Everybody, today we have a mystery to solve. I have six picture clues. You will each be given just one picture. Then find a partner and exchange information in your own words. After that, find another partner and do the same until you have sufficient clues or the alloted time runs out. After gathering information, you will form groups of four and come up with a solution to the mystery. There are many possible solutions. You'll have 15 minutes. Finally, one member from your group will report your group's solution back to the class."

Direction

Explain the main difference of the instruction model Teacher A and Teacher B show respectively in their classes.

Keyword list

audio-motor unit, task-based instruction, problem-solving, decision-making, information gap, information exchange, command-based technique, predetermined items, realia, accuracy-based/fluency-based activity

Item 18 Grammar Instruction 2013 15번

Activity A

1. Complete the table below with the things you have to do this week, using "be going to." Leave two spaces empty.

	Mon.	Tues.	Wed.
Afternoon			
Evening			

2. Talk to several other students and arrange a time to see a movie with them. You might need to change your schedule.

Activity B

In pairs, do the following tasks in English:

1. Talk about the differences between adjectives ending in *-ed* and *-ing*.

> We felt <u>moved</u> by his story.
> *We felt <u>moving</u> by his story.
> It was a really <u>exhausting</u> day.
> *It was a really <u>exhausted</u> day.

2. Indicate whether the sentences below are grammatical or ungrammatical, focusing on the underlined words.

> 1. They seemed <u>pleasing</u> with the outcome.
> 2. I saw the most <u>amazed</u> film yesterday.
> 3. He felt <u>disappointed</u> about the test results.
> 4. The most <u>annoyed</u> thing was her rude attitude.
> 5. The incident could be <u>embarrassing</u> for him.

3. Write a rule that can explain the differences between the two types of adjectives.

Direction

Compare two grammar-based activities and choose more suitable one for the communicative setting.

Keyword list

discovery learning, inductive approach, metalinguistic terms, automatize

Item 19 Syllabus 2013 18번

Ms. Park's Notes

In my English lesson, I want to emphasize performing certain functions while students participate in communicative interactions. In addition, I always try to require students to use skills aligned with topics and arrange related activities.

Syllabus 1

Topics	Functions	Skills and activities
Friends	Asking about and giving personal information	Listening & Speaking: listen and talk about friends Reading & Writing: read and write about friendship
School	Expressing likes and dislikes; asking about and describing school subjects	Listening & Speaking: listen and talk about school subjects Reading & Writing: read and write about school life

Syllabus 2

Situations	Grammar	Vocabulary
In the classroom	*Be*: present affirmative *Be*: present interrogative *Be*: negative interrogative	People around you: *friend, stranger, classmate, teacher, student*
At a restaurant	Simple present *Be*: past Regualr simple past	Food: *menu, fish, meat, fruit, vegetable*

Direction

Referring to Ms. Park's Notes, identify the syllabus Ms. Park could prefer and explain why.

Keyword list

structural syllabus, functional syllabus, process-oriented syllabus, product-oriented syllabus, prefabricated phrase

Item 20 Textbook Evaluation (2) 2013 20번

Ms. Park's Teaching Principles

For successful language learning, I think that topics and strategy training are the most important. That is, the interesting topics can motivate students, who actively participate in classroom activities. Also, through strategy training they can raise their awareness on their own learning, resulting in being autonomous learners

Below are the results of a high school textbook evaluation.

Prerequisites		Textbook A		Textbook B	
Do the aims of the textbook correspond with the aims of the teaching program and the needs of the learners?		Yes		Yes	
Is a teachers' guide available?		Yes		Yes	
Initial Status		Accepted		Accepted	
Criteria	WT* (1-3)	SC* (1-5)	WT x SC	SC (1-5)	WT x SC
Are design and layout attractive to learners?	2	5	10	3	6
Does the textbook include appropriate materials for pronunciation work?	1	5	5	2	2
Does the textbook contain enough skill-integrated activities?	2	3	6	3	6
Are topics interesting for learners?	3	2	6	3	9
Does the textbook include materials for strategy training?	3	2	6	5	15
Total		17	33	16	38
Final Status		Rejected		Selected	

* WT=weight (1=not very important; 2=important; 3=very important)
* SC=score (1=very poor; ... 5=excellent)

Direction

Choose the textbook which is more suitable for Ms. Park's class and support your choice based on the evaluation results.

Keyword list

skill integration, strategy training, needs analysis

Item 21 Reading Lesson 2013 22번

Below is an excerpt of a reading lesson. The teacher selected two different reading texts from a magazine. The texts shared a common topic on nature conservation. Each text had 10 sentences and was about 100 words long. She combined the two original texts and scrambled the sentences.

Lesson Procedure

Step 1

- Show Ss several pictures about environmental pollution, and then have them talk about why it happens and what they can do to prevent it.
- Have Ss read the newly-formed text quickly, for about 30 seconds, to find out what the text is about, without focusing on every word.

Step 2

- Have Ss read the text individually, but now more carefully.
- Explain that the text is a combination of two shorter ones.
- In groups of three, have Ss divide the text into two separate ones that make sense.
- Have a member of each group give a presentation about how and why they divided the text the way they did.

Step 3

- Show Ss the original versions of the two texts, and have Ss compare them with their own.
- Have Ss vote for the most accurately restored versions.

Ss=students

Direction

Write two lesson objectives which correspond with the lesson procedure presented in the above.

Keyword list

skimmimg, coherence, cohesion, scrambled sentences, discourse competence, passive vocabulary, active vocabulary, noticing the gap

Item 22 Coursework Evaluation 2013 23번

A high school English teacher conducted a survey with 50 high school English teachers in her school district as part of action research. The teachers were asked to indicate how well the statements in the survey described their teaching practice. Below are the results.

How Do You Teach English Writing?

Statements	No. of respondents per category*			
	1	2	3	4
1. I emphasize students' final writing products.	30	10	8	2
2. I involve students in the process of planning, drafting, revising, and editing.	1	4	35	10
3. I focus mostly on grammar and mechanics when giving feedback.	22	14	9	5
4. I focus mostly on content and organization when giving feedback.	5	8	25	12
5. I involve students in group writing tasks more than individual writing tasks.	34	3	6	7
6. I have students keep a journal and write as often as possible in English at home.	32	5	7	6
7. I meet with individual students to help with work in progress.	5	6	18	21

*1=not at all, 2=not really, 3=well, 4=very well

Direction

Referring to the survey in the above, provide two suggestions so that teachers can organize improved writing lessons next semester.

Keyword list

action research, product-oriented approach, process-oriented approach, conferencing, collaborative writing, revision, journal, mechanics, editing

Item 23 Giving Feedback 2013 24번

Ms. Park's Teaching Principles

When giving feedback on students' written products, I always focus on content and organization by priority. Also, I try to look for strengths as well as weakness. First, I let students know what strengths are. Then, I give some tips on what they need to improve to be good writers.

The following excerpts are two students'writing samples with feedback from their teachers:

Sample 1

Do you remember your middle school's life? Well, compared to high schools, middle schools end up more earlier. also, middle school students don't worry about their future as much as high schoolers. However, there is a big similarity between middle school and high school, which is both students have to study a lot, and the fact that most of them go to academy.

Teacher comments:

Nice work! You started with an attractive question, which is a good organizational skill for the introduction of an essay. When you rewrite, please try to add your own story about your school life to make the essay more appealing.

Sample 2

All Koreans enters (Agr) school, and learns (Agr) many things. They entered (Tns) elementary school, Middle school, High school. Total, there is (Agr) twelve grade (Agr). In elementary school, Koreans learned (Tns) six year (Agr). In middle school, they learned (Tns) three year (Agr) and same in high school.

Agr = Agreement, Tns = Verb tense

Direction

Of two feedback samples choose the one which better reflects Ms. Park's teaching principles. Also, support your choice with evidence from the data.

Keyword list

error correction code, narrative feedback, written comments, revision

Item 24 Multiple Choice Item Test 2013 25번

A

The following are guidelines for constructing multiple-choice items to assess knowledge of word meanings:

1. Make sure there is only one correct answer for each item.
2. Make sure the distractors are the same grammatical class as the key.
3. Do not provide inadvertent clues to the key which allow students to answer an item correctly without knowledge of word meanings.
4. Make sure the key cannot be selected based on students' world knowledge.

B

Below are some examples of multiple-choice items that are intended to measure students' knowledge of word meanings.

Choose the one that best fits in each blank.

a. I want to be a poet. I have had an ________ in writing poems, since I was a child.
① interest ② doubt ③ concern ④ worry

b. I was hungry, so I went home ________ to eat dinner.
① run ② rate ③ quickly ④ rapid

c. I usually go to the dentist to have my teeth ________ once a year.
① examined ② checked ③ seen ④ fixed

d. Inventors are always coming up with new ideas because they are very ________.
① creative ② sad ③ lazy ④ guilty

e. When tourists from Seoul go to Jeju on vacation, they travel ________.
① north ② west ③ east ④ south

Direction

Among testing items in <B> identify the one which follows all guidelines for constructing multiple-choice items in <A> and explain why.

Keyword list

distractor, key answer, stem, options, unintended clue, lexical categories, background knowledge

Item 25 Item Facility and Item Discrimination 2013 27번

Below are the results from a 10-item test that Mr. Park gave to his 11 students to compare their English abilities. Based on the test results, Mr. Park divided the students into three groups–upper, middle, and lower. He wanted to determine the effectiveness of the test by examining item facility (IF) and item discrimination (ID). To calculate IF, Mr. Park divided the number of students who correctly answered a particular item by the total number of students who took the test. ID indicates the degree to which an item separates the students who performed well from those who did poorly on the test as a whole. Mr. Park used the following formula to calculate the ID for each item: $ID = IF_{upper} - IF_{lower}$.

Test Results

Groups	Students	Items										Total
		1	2	3	4	5	6	7	8	9	10	
Upper	A	1	1	1	1	1	1	1	1	1	1	10
	B	1	0	1	1	1	1	1	1	1	1	9
	C	1	0	1	0	1	1	1	1	1	1	8
	D	1	1	0	1	1	1	1	0	1	1	8
Middle	E	0	1	0	1	1	1	1	1	0	0	6
	F	1	0	1	1	1	0	1	0	1	0	6
	G	1	1	0	0	1	0	1	0	1	1	6
Lower	H	1	1	0	0	1	0	1	0	0	0	4
	I	0	0	0	0	1	1	0	0	1	1	4
	J	0	1	1	0	0	0	0	0	1	1	4
	K	1	0	0	1	1	1	0	0	0	0	4
Total		8	6	5	6	10	7	8	4	8	7	

1=a correct response, 0=an incorrect response

Direction

Based on the test results, identify the item which should be changed or revised. Also, write the reason.

Keyword list

item facility (IF), item discrimination (ID), criterion-referenced, norm-referenced

선택형 기출문항 서답형 접근 답안

Item 1

본문 p. 04

According to the results of the coursebook evaluation, two teachers rated the vocabulary exercises, grammatical items, and language styles as "poor." Therefore, they need to prepare additional teaching materials on collocation activities, sets of formal and informal speech, and target grammatical forms used in authentic contexts.

Item 2

본문 p. 06

For English classes, Teacher A chooses a contrastive analysis approach, while Teacher B selects a discourse analysis approach. For a communication-oriented classroom, the latter (discourse analysis) is more suitable than the former. Discourse analysis enables students to use language appropriately in specific situations by understanding and applying grammatical points in context.

Item 3

본문 p. 07

Ms. Park helps students successfully complete the writing task in two ways. First, she arranges pair work in which students collaboratively write the ending of the story. Additionally, as she walks around the classroom, she provides students with feedback, suggestions, and language assistance as needed, which helps reduce the task's difficulty.

Item 4

본문 p. 08

Activity B combines formal instruction on the target forms—the past tense and present perfect—with their communicative use. In this activity, students learn when and how to use forms like "won" and "saw" or "have won" and "have seen" by noticing these target forms, which are presented in italics within short conversation extracts.

Item 5

본문 p. 09

Mr. Hwang conducts action research (critical self-examination or classroom investigation) to increase the use of English in the classroom. First, he examines the ratio of English to Korean by reviewing recordings of his lessons over a two-week period. Following this critical self-examination, he familiarizes himself with key expressions for classroom management and feedback, which helps him reduce his use of Korean even further.

Item 6

본문 p. 10

Mina makes repeated errors for two main reasons: first, the teacher provides implicit feedback that focuses only on meaning. Second, she has not fully acquired past-tense rules. For the acquisition of past tense, innatists suggest that she should be exposed to more comprehensible input containing past-tense forms in a low affective filter environment. In contrast, behaviorists argue that she needs more repetition and drills of past-tense forms.

Item 7

본문 p. 11

Ms. Park uses referential questions in the example above, aiming to elicit genuine responses from students about what makes them unhappy. Through these questions, she encourages students' authentic, communicative language use within classroom discourse.

Item 8

본문 p. 12

The given activity places greater emphasis on phonological accuracy, focusing on phonemic differences in vowel sounds such as "hog/hug," "pen/pin," and "man/men." Unlike traditional minimal pair exercises, it distinguishes target sounds within meaningful contexts or sentences, rather than in isolated word pairs.

Item 9

본문 p. 13

(1) Teacher A follows three key teaching principles: maximizing interaction with others, speaking only English in the classroom, and avoiding interruptions to correct students' grammar. However, according to Student A, these principles seem to raise students' affective filter during class, as they are not allowed to use Korean, receive no rehearsal time, and lack support when they struggle to communicate.

(2) When students are forced to speak only English, they often lapse into silence, which is contrary to the teacher's intentions in an interaction-based classroom. Therefore, teachers need to decide on the medium of communication in the classroom, taking into account various factors, including learners' proficiency levels, learning styles, and learning goals.

Item 10

본문 p. 14

In (2), Ms. Park (the teacher) provides feedback that prompts the student's self-repair by saying, "Lost whose book?" By explicitly indicating where the student made an error, she facilitates a successful uptake, resulting in the student's response, "my book."

Item 11

본문 p. 15

The candidate textbook includes sufficient supplementary materials for adaptation. However, it does not recycle communicative functions in subsequent units. This availability of supplementary materials allows the teacher to manage lessons in varied ways, which can be highly motivating for students. However, the lack of recycling communicative functions means that students have few opportunities to practice and reinforce the learned functions in future lessons.

or

The candidate textbook includes sufficient supplementary materials for adaptation. However, it does not provide vocabulary selected based on data from spoken language corpora. The availability of supplementary materials allows the teacher to manage lessons in varied ways, which can be highly motivating for students. However, the lack of corpus-based vocabulary selection means that students have few opportunities to learn and use colloquial words or expressions.

Item 12

본문 p. 17

English teachers want to award scholarships to the top 10% of students based on test results. Accordingly, to facilitate comparisons between individuals, they should implement norm-referenced testing, which provides students with a total test score and a percentile rank.

Item 13

본문 p. 18

The teacher chooses criterion-referenced testing because it measures students' performance against a specific criterion (scoring over 10 out of 20) and provides students with a "Pass" or "Fail" grade along with feedback. Additionally, the teacher uses analytical rating scales to assess students' performance across three main components: "task completion," "fluency," and "intelligibility."

Item 14

본문 p. 20

The grammar-based activity used in Step 2 is called input flooding, as the teacher uses material that contains numerous instances of the target structure, "should+have+past participle." In Step 3, students personalize the target structure by connecting it to their own experiences, and in Step 4, they write their own story with a focus on meaning.

Item 15

본문 p. 22

In Steps 1 and 2, students learn about sentence stress by practicing three different stress patterns of "I'm listening," depending on the context, and then circling the prominent word after listening to a short dialogue. In Steps 3 and 4, they practice using sentence stress naturally by taking turns saying the items they want to bring to a picnic.

Item 16

본문 p. 24

In the given writing lesson, the teacher takes a product-oriented approach. To reduce students' cognitive load for the writing task, she provides key words and pictures that illustrate the storyline.

Item 17

본문 p. 25

Teacher A chooses an audio-motor unit approach, while Teacher B selects task-based instruction. In the former, the teacher demonstrates appropriate responses to commands using realia and asks students to follow them. In contrast, the latter encourages students to communicate actively to exchange information, leading to successful task completion.

Item 18

본문 p. 26

Activity A has students use the target form "be going to" through communicative practice. In contrast, Activity B encourages students to learn the target forms—adjectives ending in "-ed" and "-ing"—through a discovery activity. Therefore, Activity A is more suitable for a communicative setting.

Item 19

본문 p. 28

Ms. Park might prefer Syllabus 1 over Syllabus 2 because it emphasizes performing functions in communicative interactions. For example, it enables students to talk and write about friends and school life, topics that are closely related to their real lives.

Item 20

본문 p. 30

Textbook B is more suitable for Ms. Park's class because it scores higher than Textbook A on the criteria with the highest weight: "topic" and "strategy training."

or

Textbook B is more suitable for Ms. Park's class because it scores higher than Textbook A in terms of "topic" and "strategy training," the criteria with the highest weight.

Item 21

본문 p. 32

1. Students will be able to unscramble the text and separate it into two distinct texts.
2. Students will be able to explain how coherent texts are constructed.

Item 22

본문 p. 33

Two suggestions are as follows: First, teachers should utilize collaborative writing tasks more frequently than usual. Second, they should encourage writing habits through homework assignments.

or

Two suggestions are as follows: First, teachers should utilize collaborative writing tasks more frequently than usual. Second, they should encourage students to keep journals to develop their writing habits.

Item 23

본문 p. 34

Sample 1 reflects Ms. Park's approach, as she prioritizes organization and content when giving feedback. For example, in Sample 1, she highlights the student's strong organizational skills as a positive aspect. Additionally, in terms of content, she advises the student to add a personal story about her school life.

Item 24

본문 p. 36

"D" is a good test item for the following reasons. First, it has only one correct answer: "creative." Additionally, all options belong to the same grammatical class. Furthermore, it does not provide any unintended clues to the correct answer. Lastly, answering correctly does not require students' general knowledge.

Item 25

본문 p. 38

Item 2 should be revised because it does not effectively distinguish between upper-level and lower-level students.

or

Item 2 should be revised because it has zero item discrimination between upper-level and lower-level students.

Memo

02

2024학년도 기출 동형 평가

02 2024학년도 기출 동형 평가

01. **Read the passages in <A> and <B>, and follow the directions.** [4 points]

A

Research suggests that L2 learners use various reading strategies to improve their comprehension. These strategies can be categorized into two types: local or micro-strategies and global or macro-strategies. Below are specific examples:

Micro-strategies & Macro-strategies

(1) Looking up the meaning of unknown words in a dictionary.
(2) Scanning for specific information or keywords.
(3) Recognizing grammar patterns to make sense of sentences.
(4) Skimming a text to grasp the general idea.
(5) Focusing on word formation and word family to understand the text.
(6) Summarizing the text to understand the main points.

B

To enhance his students' reading comprehension, Mr. Jung, a middle school English teacher, assigned an article about the effects of technology on society. He asked his students, Minji and Dongho, to read selected passages and then describe their thoughts and strategies used while reading. Below are the two passages Mr. Jung used and the reflections from Minji and Dongho.

Passage 1

Many people believe that technology has made life easier, but at what cost? Our privacy is often compromised. For instance, the convenience of smartphones and social media comes with the risk of personal information. On the positive side, technology provids access to online courses and resources, and allows students from remote areas to receive quality education.

This sounds serious. I think it's saying technology can be both good and bad.

Minji

Passage 2

Statistics show that 80% of teenagers check their phones over 100 times a day. Mobile phone addiction can lead to several significant problems. Physically, the constant use of phones can cause eye strain, headaches, and sleep disturbances due to prolonged exposure to blue light. The repetitive motion of texting and scrolling can also result in repetitive strain injuries such as "text neck" and carpal tunnel syndrome.

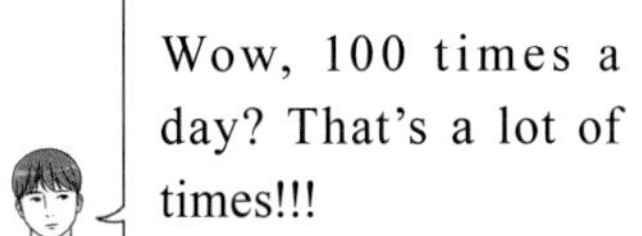

Wow, 100 times a day? That's a lot of times!!!

Dongho

Identify the ONE specific reading strategy in <A> that Minji and Dongho applied to their reading process in <B>, respectively. Then explain your answers with evidence from <A> and <B>.

>> 채점기준 p.64
>> 학생 첨삭 p.70

02. Read the passages in <A> and <B>, and follow the directions. [4 points]

A

Ms. Park, an English teacher at a middle school, conducted a survey among 40 local English teachers to identify the teaching strategies they find most effective for enhancing language skills. The purpose was to gather insights from experienced educators that Ms. Park could incorporate into her own teaching practices. The survey results are tabulated as follows:

No.	Teaching Strategies	Vote Counts
1	Conducting interactive Role-plays	12
2	Employing games for vocabulary learning	8
3	Integrating multimedia elements into lessons	5
4	Facilitating literary analysis through guided questions	10
5	Organizing peer review sessions for writing assignments	5
Total Counts		40

B

Following the survey, Ms. Park designed several activities that incorporated the most popular strategies.

Activity 1

- Work in pairs. Each student in a pair receives a role card that details their character's background and objectives.

Tourist: Your card explains that you're visiting from another country and have lost your wallet and passport.

Police Officer: Your card outlines your duty to assist the tourist by providing guidance, ensuring they know where to go for a replacement passport, and helping them feel secure.

- Pairs perform their roles, engaging in a dialogue where the tourist explains their predicament and the police officer provides assistance.
- Allow each pair approximately 5-7 minutes to interact.

Activity 2

- The teacher (or a student) thinks of a word and draws a line for each letter of the word on the board.
- Students take turns guessing letters.
- If the guessed letter is in the word, the teacher writes the letter in the correct spaces on the board.
- If the guessed letter is not in the word, the teacher begins drawing the image of a hangman (start with the gallows, then the head, body, arms, and legs).
- The game ends when either the word is fully guessed (students win) or the hangman is completely drawn (teacher wins).

Activity 3

- Create a worksheet with a series of questions that guide students through a critical analysis of "Alice in Wonderland". These questions should encourage students to think about narrative technique, character interactions, and thematic elements.

> 1) What is happening in this scene? Who are the main characters involved?
> 2) How does Carroll use language to create a sense of wonder and confusion?
> 3) What do you think the Mad Hatter represents in this story?
> 4) Which part of the story did you find most surprising or confusing, and why?

Based on <A>, for each of the two most popular teaching strategies, identify the ONE activity in <B> that the principle has been applied to, respectively. Then explain your answers with evidence from <A> and <B>.

>> 채점기준 p.64
>> 학생 첨삭 p.73

03. Read the conversation in <A> and the draft of the syllabus in <B>, and follow the directions. [4 points]

A

T1 : Hi, Mr. Lee. We need to set up our three-week English Literature course for next semester quickly. What kind of topics do you think we should teach?

T2 : I think we should focus on literature from different eras per unit, including old works and more recent ones.

T1 : That's a good idea. From recent literary works to old ones!! The class will be enriched. So, what kinds of writing genres do you want to include?

T2 : How about poems and plays? I want to include different types of writing every unit, like poems, plays or short stories..

T1 : Agreed. Besides, I think it would be good to have activities where students can discuss literary works, and maybe write something on their own.

T2 : That sounds great! One more thing, I want students to analyze story characters.

T1 : Definitely. Finally, what do you want students to learn through this coursework?

T2 : I want students to understand literary works in different eras. I hope they will understand what a story is about and what the people in the story are like. At the end, they should be able to compare literary works from different eras which they have learned during a three-week coursework.

T1 : Sounds good. So, can you write our plan and show it to me later? I'm excited to see it.

T=teacher

B

This is the draft of course plan Mr. Lee(T2) wrote.

Components	Unit 1	Unit 2	Unit 3
Topics	Modern Literature -works by Wolf and Eliot	Renaissance Literature -Shakespeare's Romeo and Juliet	Medieval Literature -Chaucer's The Canterbury Tales
Writing Genre	Poems	Plays	Report
Activities	Read aloud	Character Analysis	Group Discussion
Achievement	Understanding Main Ideas	Describing Characters	Comparing literary works from different eras

Based on <A>, choose the TWO components in <B> that do NOT correspond to the teachers' ideas about their course plan. Then explain your answers with evidence from <A> and <B>.

>> 채점기준 p.65
>> 학생 첨삭 p.76

04. Read the passages in <A> and <B>, and follow the directions. [4 points]

A

Below are the posts made by two English teachers on an online teacher community where teachers can share their ideas and provide each other with help regarding the use of digital technology.

Teacher 1's Post

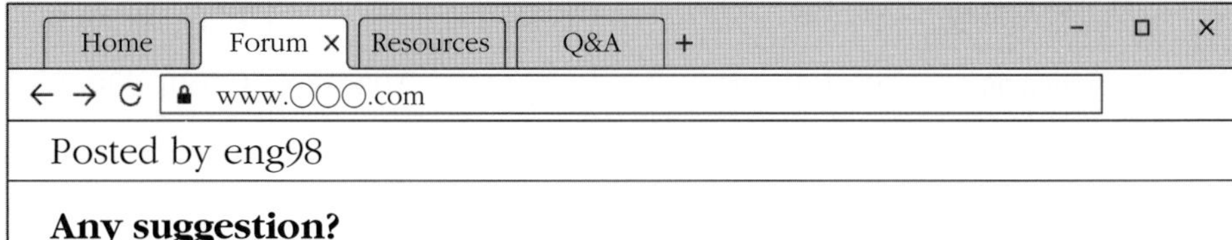

Any suggestion?

I am managing a level-differentiated English language class. Although there are many difficulties, the greatest challenge is that my low-level students are struggling with basic vocabulary, grammar, and overall language comprehension. In class, students frequently encounter new words or grammatical structures they do not understand, which hinders their reading comprehension and writing skills. Nevertheless, they are eager to learn. Therefore, I think it would be beneficial for them to receive additional support that can be accessed independently at home. By incorporating a suitable digital tool, I hope to provide them with an engaging and effective way to improve their language skills. Can you recommend a technological tool that would be appropriate for my low-level students?

Comment Share

Teacher 2's Post

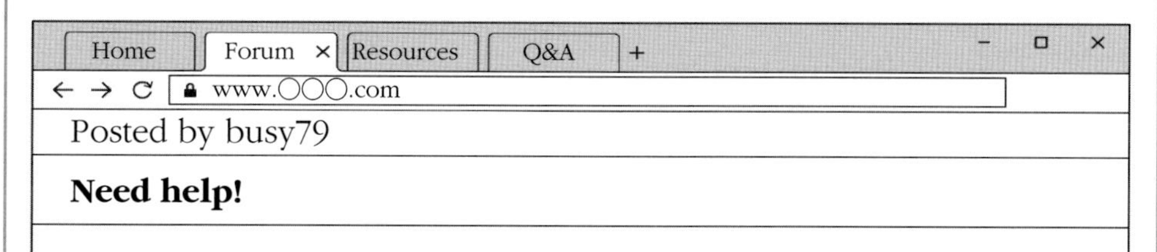

In observing my class, I've noted a significant challenge: students are struggling with a disparity between their oral and written English skills. For example, students who are proficient in written English often struggle with pronunciation and oral fluency. They say they do not recognize where they mispronounce. Inaccurate pronunciation impacts students' confidence, making them hesitant to participate in spoken activities. While our class exercises focus on both spoken and written English, there is a clear need for more specialized pronunciation practice.

Comment Share

B

Tool 1

This is a cloud-based quiz platform. Teachers can create quizzes to help learners to practice what they have learned. Various question formats are available including true or false, matching, multiple choice, etc. It generates a report of student performance after the quizzes are completed.

Tool 2

This is an online platform that is user-friendly and can be accessed from home, allowing students to practice vocabulary, grammar, and language skills for remedial education. By providing valuable resources tailored to each student's proficiency level, this tool can help bridge their learning gaps and enhance their proficiency in English.

Tool 3

Students can use advanced speech recognition technology, which provides instant feedback on pronunciation, helping them refine their speaking abilities. By using this app, they can also bridge the gap between oral and written language. They can read a text on the screen and then record their voice, with the tool highlighting any mispronunciations on the screen.

Tool 4

When teachers use this virtual reality simulation app, they can invite their students into the virtual space they have created. Students can communicate with others in English in simulated real-life situations taking place in airports, markets, and cinemas. Here students can create an avatar and converse with each other.

Tool 5

Using this app, teachers can create a mind map for teaching English vocabulary. It shows groupings or relationships between words visually. Moreover, there is a link to an online dictionary. QR codes can also be created to share the mind map with students.

Based on <A>, for each teacher, respectively, suggest the ONE most appropriate tool in <B> that satisfies their needs. Then explain your answers with evidence from <B>. Do NOT copy more than FOUR consecutive words from the passages.

>> 채점기준 p.66
>> 학생 첨삭 p.79

05. **Read the passages in <A> and <B>, and follow the directions.** [4 points]

A

An English proficiency test was administered to 3rd graders (n=300) of a middle school. In order to check how well the test components contribute to the construct that's being measured, Ms. Kim, who is an English teacher, did the following with the test results:

1. She divided the questions into even and odd numbers.
2. She scored each half of the test for each student.
3. She found the correlation coefficient for the two halves to learn how strong a relationship between two halves there was.

Figure 1. Score of each student

Student	Score	Even questions	Odd questions
1	42	22	20
2	66	36	30
3	88	46	42
4	90	50	40
5	60	38	22
6	100	50	50
7	45	23	22
8	68	38	30
9	80	46	34
10	85	45	40

(ellipsis)

Figure 2. Correlation graph (r=0.87)

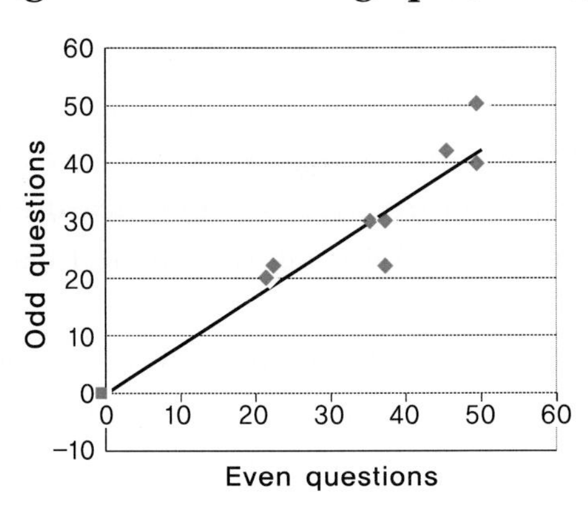

B

The trainer asked six teachers to interpret the results. The following are their interpretations.

- Teacher 1: The resulting correlation coefficient was 0.87, indicating a strong positive relationship between the two halves of the test. This suggests the test has good internal consistency.
- Teacher 2: The correlation coefficient of 0.87 between the even and odd numbered questions indicates a high level of reliability in the test.
- Teacher 3: The high correlation coefficient (r=0.87) means that the test is difficult for all students. Therefore, it indicates low item facility.
- Teacher 4: The test items are reliable indicators of the students' English proficiency. Consequently, the test can be considered a reliable tool for assessing the English proficiency of 3rd graders.
- Teacher 5: The test is measuring different constructs. A high correlation between even and odd questions indicates that the test has low construct validity.
- Teacher 6: The strong correlation (r=0.87) between the scores on even and odd questions indicates that this test has the split-half reliability.

Identify the TWO teachers in <B> whose interpretation is NOT correct. Then support your answers with evidence from <A> and <B>.

>> 채점기준 p.66
>> 학생 첨삭 p.81

06. Read the passages in <A> and <B>, and follow the directions. [4 points]

A

Mr. Kim, a middle school English teacher, attended a materials development workshop last week. There he learned that a variety of factors impact a learner's task performance which he could manipulate to adjust the level of task difficulty. One is language of input that learners have to process, such as the range and complexity of vocabulary and grammar. Another factor has to do with the processing demands of a task, which refer to the amount of mental effort required in working out answers. Besides these two factors, the conditions under which a task is performed also play an important role. Below are the notes he took during the workshop.

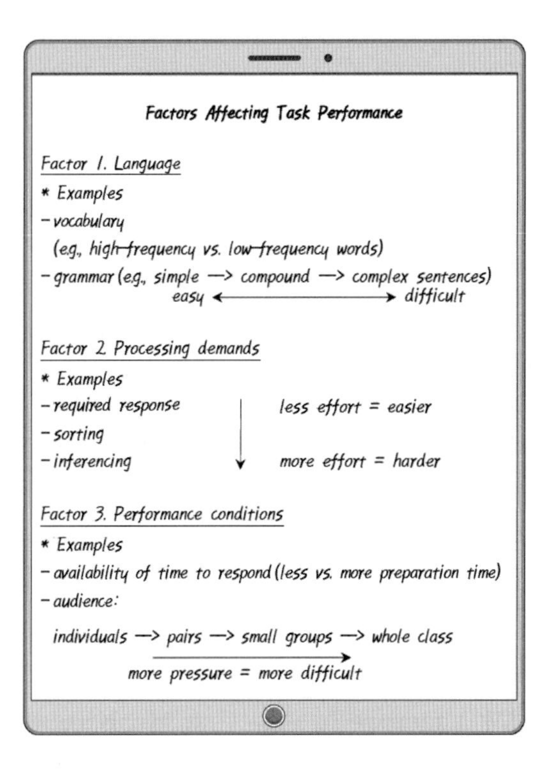

B

Based on what he learned at the workshop, Mr. Kim adapted one of the tasks from the textbook as shown below.

The original task

1. Write a paragraph about your favorite holiday. Describe what you do, who you spend it with, and why it is your favorite.

Student Written Product:

My favorite holiday is Christmas. On Christmas day, I wake up early to open presents with my family. We spend the morning together, eating a special breakfast of pancakes and hot chocolate. Later, we visit my grandparents and have a big lunch with all of my cousins. I love Christmas because I get to spend time with my family, and the festive decorations make everything feel magical.

The adapted task

1. Write a few sentences about a holiday you like. Write what you do on that day, who you are with, and why you like it.

Student Written Product:

(1) I like Christmas.
(2) On that day, I open presents with my family and eat pancakes for breakfast.
(3) We visit my grandparents for lunch and see my cousins.
(4) I like Christmas because I spend time with my family and everything looks pretty with decorations.

Identify the TWO factors in <A> that Mr. Kim addressed to adjust the difficulty of the original task in <B>. Then explain how each factor was addressed in the adapted task, respectively, with evidence from <A> and <B>.

>> 채점기준 p.67
>> 학생 첨삭 p.84

07. **Read the passages in <A> and <B>, and follow the directions.** [4 points]

A

This semester, Ms. Kang, a high school English teacher, has been assigned to teach a new elective course called the 'Culture of English Speaking Countries.' The goal of the course is to help students develop intercultural competence. She consulted multiple resources including the national curriculum, books, and her colleagues from other schools who have taught similar courses in order to achieve the course goal. Based on her research, she has come up with the teaching plan presented below.

A Teaching Plan for 'Culture of English Speaking Countries'

1. Teaching Contents

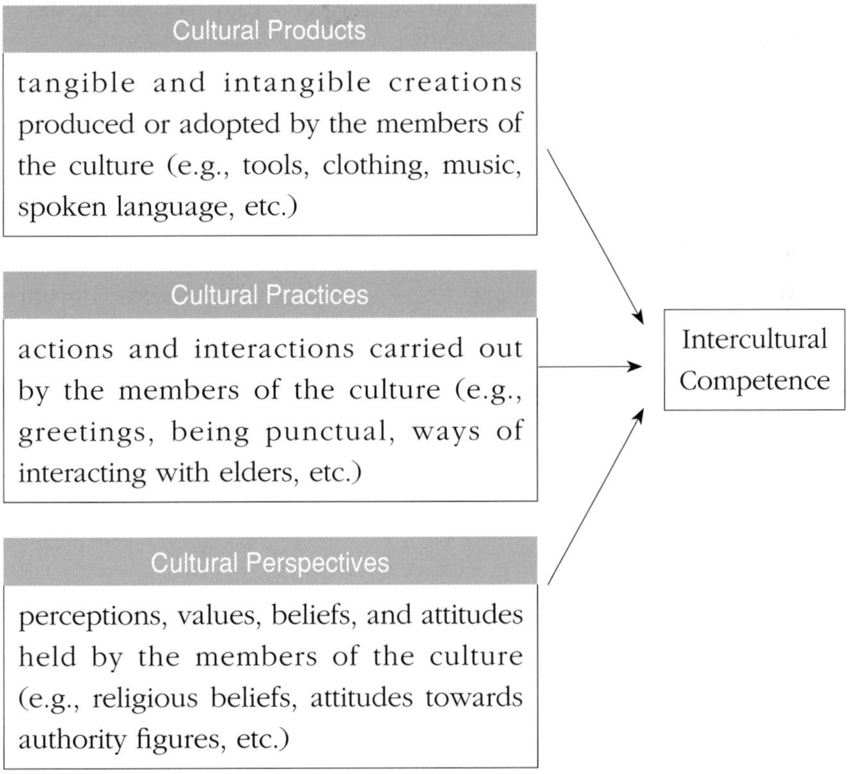

Cultural Products
tangible and intangible creations produced or adopted by the members of the culture (e.g., tools, clothing, music, spoken language, etc.)

Cultural Practices
actions and interactions carried out by the members of the culture (e.g., greetings, being punctual, ways of interacting with elders, etc.)

Cultural Perspectives
perceptions, values, beliefs, and attitudes held by the members of the culture (e.g., religious beliefs, attitudes towards authority figures, etc.)

→ Intercultural Competence

2. Teaching Principles
   1) Integrate language skills and culture.
   2) Utilize different types of audiovisual aids.
   3) Avoid reinforcing associations between nationalities(countries) and cultures.
   4) Involve students in discovering English culture, instead of transmitting information.
   5) Assess students' achievements based on their performances at the end of the lesson.

B

Below is one of the lesson sequences that Ms. Kang developed to implement her teaching plan.

1. Preparation: Assemble a selection of pictures and videos illustrating greetings and dining etiquette in English-speaking countries.
2. In Class:
   1) Write the word 'Greetings and Dining Etiquette' on the board. Ask students to share greetings and dining etiquette they are familiar with in their own culture.
   2) Show pictures and videos of different way of greeting and dining etiquette on the screen.
   3) Introduce each practice one by one and briefly explain its significance.

Greetings: Show a video of people greeting each other with handshakes or hugs and explain the context in which each greeting is used.

Dining Etiquette: Show a picture of a typical American dining setting and discuss the use of utensils and tipping culture.

4) Play a video of two people discussing various cultural practices in English-speaking countries. After watching, check students' comprehension by asking specific questions about the video.

Questions could include: "How do people typically greet each other in the video?" "What is a common practice during a Thanksgiving dinner?"

5) Hand out a worksheet with pictures and descriptions of various cultural actions. Have students match the pictures to the correct descriptions and classify them into categories (e.g., Greetings, Dining Etiquette).
6) Check the answers together as a class.
7) Have each group give a short presentation in English about what they learned today.
8) Assess the presentations using a scoring rubric that includes criteria such as content accuracy, presentation skills, and language use.

Based on <A>, identify the ONE teaching content that Ms. Kang incorporates and the ONE teaching principle that she does NOT conform to in her lesson sequence in <B>. Then explain your answers with evidence from <A> and <B>.

>> 채점기준 p.68
>> 학생 첨삭 p.87

08. Read the teacher's beliefs in <A> and the part of the lesson plan in <B>, and follow the directions. [4 points]

A

I believe that lesson goals should be framed from the students' perspective, focusing on what they can achieve through the lesson. Furthermore, I usually ask my students to vocalize these goals together. I also place importance on teachers trying to motivate their students. So, I seek out some interesting video clips online that can keep my students engaged. Crucially, I prefer incidental vocabulary learning and try to expose students with target words during the listening and reading. Lastly, I believe it's essential to conclude the lesson by summarizing the main points, and especially at the final stage, I like to ask referential questions that are more related to the students' life.

B

Stages	Teaching & Learning Activities
Introduction	• T and Ss exchange greetings. • T presents today's lesson objective on screen and reads it together with Ss: "We will be able to describe different dream jobs and understand related vocabulary."
Development #1	• T plays a video clip that shows various people talking about their dream jobs and what they entail (e.g., doctor, teacher, artist, engineer). • T checks Ss' understanding of the video clip. • T provides reading passages that include the following target words related to jobs. *doctor, teacher, artist, engineer, lawyer, chef, firefighter, pilot, writer, scientist* • T explicitly teaches the vocabulary words by writing them on the board and providing definitions and example sentences for each word. • T asks Ss to use the vocabulary words in their own sentences to demonstrate understanding.

Development #2	• T presents the target rules: "In English, it is more typical, more frequent, so unmarked, for the person who experiences emotional feelings to appear in the subject position of the sentence." • T distributes the following handout. In the following sentences, the arrows indicate who experiences the feelings described by the verbs 'inspire' and 'worry.' (1) <u>The teacher</u> loves the students. ↪ (unmarked, more typical) (2) The teacher frightens <u>the students</u>. (marked, less typical) ↩ Sentence (1) is more typical, so unmarked, because the subject, *the teacher*, experiences the feeling of love. Sentence (2) is marked because the object, *the students*, experiences the feeling of being frightened. Now, let's work on the following sentences and determine whether they are unmarked or marked: a. The scientist envied his colleague. (ⓐ) b. The scientist impressed his colleague. (ⓑ)
Consolidation	• T assigns homework without reviewing the lesson content: "Write a short essay on your dream job and explain why you chose it." • T asks some questions that relate to Ss' own lives: "What is your dream job and why?" "How do you plan to achieve your dream job?" • T bids farewell to Ss.

T=teacher, Ss=students

Fill in the blanks (ⓐ) and (ⓑ) with "unmarked" or "marked." Then choose the TWO stages in <B> that do NOT correspond to the teacher's beliefs in <A>, and explain your answers with evidence from <A> and <B>.

>> 채점기준 p.69
>> 학생 첨삭 p.89

2024학년도 기출 동형 평가 채점기준

1.

하위내용영역	배점	예상정답률
영어교육론 A형 서술형	4점	65%

모범답안

Minji and Dongho use different strategies in their reading process. Minji applies strategy (4), while Dongho uses strategy (2). Minji skims the text to find the general idea that the technology can be both good and bad. On the other hand, Dongho scans for the specific information "100 times a day" from the passage in <B>.

채점기준

Minji and Dongho use different strategies in their reading process. Minji applies strategy (4)(1pt), while Dongho uses strategy (2)(1pt). Minji skims the text to find the general idea that the technology can be both good and bad(1pt). On the other hand, Dongho scans for the specific information, '100 times a day'(1pt) from the passage in <B>.

* 각 학생의 strategy를 잘못 찾았으면 evidence가 정답과 일치하더라도 0점을 준다.
* 각 학생에 해당하는 evidence를 〈A〉와 〈B〉에서 모두 옳게 찾았으면 1점을 준다.

2.

하위내용영역	배점	예상정답률
영어교육론 A형 서술형	4점	60%

모범답안

Principle No. 1 is applied in Activity 1, whereas Principle No. 4 is utilized in Activity 3. Activity 1 requires interactive role-play where one student, acting as a tourist, explains their problem situation, and the other student, acting as a police officer, provides assistance. Additionally, Activity 3 requires students to facilitate a literary analysis of "Alice in Wonderland" based on guided questions about narrative technique, character interactions, and thematic elements.

채점기준

Principle No. 1 is applied in Activity 1(1pt), whereas Principle No. 4 is utilized in Activity 3(1pt). Activity 1 requires interactive role-play(0.5pt) where one student, acting as a tourist, explains their problem situation, and the other student, acting as a police officer, provides assistance(0.5pt). Additionally, Activity 3 requires students to facilitate a literary analysis(0.5pt) of "Alice in Wonderland" based on guided questions about narrative technique, character interactions, and thematic elements(0.5pt).

* 〈A〉와 〈B〉에서 찾을 수 있는 evidence를 모두 올바르게 작성했으면 1점을 준다. 단, 내용을 누락했을 경우 부분점수는 없다.

3.

하위내용영역	배점	예상정답률
영어교육론 A형 서술형	4점	60%

모범답안

Writing Genre and Activities in <B> do not align with the teachers' ideas. In the syllabus, the writing Genre for Unit 3 is 'Report', not short stories as preferred by two teachers. Additionally, the activity for Unit 1 is 'Read Aloud', instead of personalized writing.

채점기준

Writing Genre(1pt) and Activities(1pt) in <B> do not align with the teachers' ideas. In the syllabus, the writing Genre for Unit 3 is 'Report', not short stories as preferred by two teachers(1pt). Additionally, the activity for Unit 1 is 'Read Aloud', instead of personalized writing(1pt).

* 〈A〉와 〈B〉에서 찾을 수 있는 evidence를 모두 올바르게 작성했을 경우 감점하지 않는다. 단, 내용을 누락했을 경우 부분점수는 없다.

4.

하위내용영역	배점	예상정답률
영어교육론 A형 서술형	4점	70%

모범답안

Tool 2 is best for Teacher 1 whereas Tool 3 is ideal for Teacher 2. Tool 1 allows low-level students to practice language skills, grammar and vocabulary for remedial study at home, using various level-appropriate resources. On the other hand, Tool 3 not only helps students bridge the gap between oral and written language but also improves their speaking abilities by providing immediate feedback on mispronunciations using advanced speech recognition technology.

채점기준

Tool 2 is best for Teacher 1(1pt) whereas Tool 3 is ideal for Teacher 2(1pt). Tool 1 allows low-level students to practice overall language skills vocabulary, and grammar for remedial study at home, using various level-appropriate resources(1pt). On the other hand, Tool 3 not only helps students bridge the gap between oral and written language but also improves their speaking abilities by providing immediate feedback on mispronunciations(1pt) using advanced speech recognition technology.

* 〈B〉 안에서 〈A〉에 해당하는 정보를 찾아 썼으면 점수를 부여한다.
* Tool 3의 정보 'immediate feedback' 대신 'highlighting any mispronunication'을 사용했으면 점수를 부여한다.
* 〈B〉의 정보를 paraphrasing 하지 않고, 연속된 4자 이상을 가져다 썼을 경우 0.5점씩 감점한다.

5.

하위내용영역	배점	예상정답률
영어교육론 A형 서술형	4점	45%

모범답안

Teacher 3 and Teacher 5 misinterpret the correlation analysis results between test items. The high correlation coefficient(r=0.87) indicates there is strong a relationship between even and odd numbered questions, not the difficulty of the test. Additionally, a high correlation between two halves of a test indicates high reliability(or the same underlying construct) not the measurement of different constructs. Thus, this test has high construct validity.

채점기준

Teacher 3(0.5pt) and Teacher 5 misinterpret(0.5pt) the correlation analysis results between test items. The correlation coefficient indicates there is a strong relationship between scores on even and odd numbered questions(1pt), not the difficulty of the test(0.5pt). Additionally, a high correlation(r=0.87) between two halves of a test indicates high reliability(or the same underlying construct)(0.5pt) not the measurement of different constructs(0.5pt). Thus this test has high construct validity(0.5pt).

* 반분 신뢰도 측면에서 각 Teacher 3과 5의 오류를 살펴보도록 한다.

6.

하위내용영역	배점	예상정답률
영어교육론 A형 서술형	4점	55%

모범답안

Mr. Kim adjusts the task difficulty based on Language and Processing demands. In the adapted task, he simplifies the vocabulary used for giving directions by changing more difficult words like 'favorite' and 'describe' to easier ones such as 'like' and 'write'. Additionally, he modifies the response requirements from writing a paragraph, which demands more effort, to writing just a few sentences, thereby requiring less effort.

채점기준

Mr. Kim adjusts the task difficulty based on Language(1pt) and Processing demands(1pt). In the adapted task, he simplifies the vocabulary used for giving directions by changing more difficult words like 'favorite' and describe' to easier ones such as 'like' and 'write'(1pt). Additionally, he modifies the response requirements from writing a paragraph(1pt), which demands more effort, to writing just a few sentences, thereby requiring less effort.

* 〈A〉와 〈B〉에서 찾을 수 있는 evidence를 모두 올바르게 작성했으면 1점을 준다. 단, 내용을 누락했을 경우 부분점수는 없다.
* 'favorite'과 'like' 또는 'describe'와 'write' 각 한 가지만 제시해도 점수를 부여한다.

7.

하위내용영역	배점	예상정답률
영어교육론 A형 서술형	4점	75%

모범답안

Ms. Kang incorporates Cultural Practices as teaching content in her lesson. She addresses greetings such as handshakes or hugs and dining etiquette like a Thanksgiving dinner as actions carried out by the members in English-speaking countries. However, she does not conform to Principle 4) by introducing each practice one by one and explaining its significance, rather than involving students in discovering English culture.

채점기준

Ms. Kang incorporates Cultural Practices(1pt) as teaching content in her lesson. She addresses greetings such as handshakes or hugs and dining etiquette like a Thanksgiving dinner(0.5pt) as actions carried out by the members in English-speaking countries(0.5pt). However, she does not conform to Principle 4)(1pt) by introducing each practice one by one and explaining its significance(0.5pt), rather than involving students in discovering English culture(0.5pt).

8.

하위내용영역	배점	예상정답률
영어교육론 A형 서술형	4점	55%

모범답안

ⓐ unmarked ⓑ marked

Development #1 and Consolidation do not align with the teacher's beliefs as described in <A>. Firstly, the teacher explicitly instructs the target words by providing definitions, example sentences, and having students use the words in their own sentences, rather than promoting incidental vocabulary learning through listening and reading skills. Additionally, in the Consolidation phase, the teacher does not summarize the main points of the lesson but merely assigns homework.

채점기준

ⓐ unmarked ⓑ marked (각 1pt)

Development #1 and Consolidation do not align with the teacher's beliefs as described in <A>. Firstly, the teacher explicitly instructs the target words by providing definitions, and example sentences, and having students use the words in their own sentences(0.5pt), rather than promoting incidental vocabulary learning through listening and reading skills (0.5pt). Additionally, in the Consolidation phase, the teacher does not summarize the main points of the lesson(0.5pt) but merely assigns homework(0.5pt).

* Development #1와 Consolidation에 해당하는 evidence를 〈A〉와 〈B〉에서 모두 올바르게 찾아 썼으면 각 1점을 준다.

2024학년도 기출 동형 평가 학생 첨삭

01 (4pts)

Case 1 (4pts)

Minji applied the strategy Type 2 (1) in that she makes predictions about the content will be something negative about using social media based on the phrasal cue, “a waste of time”. Dongho applied the strategy Type 1 (3) in that he skips the unknown word, “sneaky” because he doesn’t think he needs to know its meaning at the moment.

(1pts) 〈A〉 정보 (0.5pt) 〈B〉 정보 (0.5pt) (1pts) 〈A〉 정보 (0.5pt) 〈B〉 정보 (0.5pt)

Summative Feedback

전반적으로 directions에서 요구하는 key phrase 중심으로 필요 정보를 명확하게 제시하고 있다.

Revised Version

Minji applied Strategy Type 2 (1), predicting that the content would be negative about using social media based on the phrasal cue “a waste of time.” Dongho used Strategy Type 1 (3) by skipping the unknown word “sneaky” because he didn’t think he needed to know its meaning at the moment.

Case 2 (3pts)

~~The Type 1 in <A> is focus on form strategy. Because using context to infer the meaning of words is an example of focus on form strategy. The Type 2 in <A> is focus on forms strategy. Because focus on form uses content.~~ And Minji is making prediction about the audio segment, so Minji is using Type 2-(1). And Dongho is determining to skip unknown word (new word). So, Donho is using Type 1-(3).

Type 1의 전략들을 focus on form strategy로 보는 근거는 무엇인가? “맥락 안에서 단어를 유추”하는 것을 focus on form strategy라고 하는가?

focus on forms strategy라는 근거는 무엇인가?

〈A〉 정보 (0.5pt)

〈B〉 정보이나, 보다 구체적으로 prediction에 대한 근거를 명시해야 한다. (-0.5pt)

(1pts)

〈A〉 정보 (0.5pt)

〈B〉 정보 없음 (-0.5pt)

(1pts)

Summative Feedback

- 불필요한 정보뿐만 아니라 잘못된 정보로 답안을 채울 경우, 0점 처리가 될 수 있으므로 directions을 준수해 답안을 작성하도록 한다. 특히, 자신의 추측이나 관련 없는 배경지식으로 답안을 채우는 일이 없도록 각별히 유념한다.
- <A>와 <B>에서 각각 답에 대한 근거를 찾도록 했으나, <B>의 정보가 모호하게 제시되거나 누락된 경우는 감점 처리된다.

Case 3 (3.5pts)

Minji used a listening strategy in type 2 to make predictions about the content by predicting negative mood of the content based on the phrase "a waste of time". And Dongho used a listening strategy in type 1 to skip unknown words by ignoring the difficult word, "sneaky".

identify로 명시되고, 해당 전략 등에 번호가 있을 경우, 명확하게 번호를 같이 언급해주도록 한다. (1pts)

(0.5pt)

(0.5pt)

(1pts)

〈B〉에 나와 있는 정보만 제시한 것으로 간주 (0.5pt)

Summative Feedback

'a listening strategy in type 2 to make predictions about the content'를 identify에 해당하는 정보로 간주해 1점을 제시했으나, text상에서 얻을 수 있는 정보는 사실상 'type 2에 있는 listening strategy를 사용하고 있다'가 전부이기 때문에 type 2에 있는 어떤 전략인지 모호하게 생각될 수 있다. 목적으로 해당 전략을 설명하고 있는 'make predictions'을 제공하고 있으나, 이것은 앞에서 언급하고 있는 'listening strategy'와 동격으로 보기는 어렵기 때문이다. 또한, 해당 전략에 대한 근거로 <A>에서 찾아 쓸 수 있는 정보가 make predictions이므로 identify에 해당하는 부분은 기호로 언급해주고, evidence로 설명을 이어나가며 답안을 작성하는 것이 보다 감점에 방어를 할 수 있다.

Type 1과 2에는 각각 여러 유형의 strategy가 있으나 명확히 밝히고 있지 않아 identify에 대한 답변이 없는 것으로 간주 -2pts

〈A〉 정보 0.5pt

〈B〉 정보 0.5pt

〈A〉 정보 0.5pt

〈B〉 정보 0.5pt

Case 4 2pts

Minji applied 'Type 1' listening strategy and Dongho applied 'Type 2' listening strategy. Firstly, Minji made a prediction about the content based on the phrasal 'a waste of time', predicting 'he's going to say something negative about using social media'. Secondly, Dongho determined to skip the unknown word 'sneaky', thinking that he doesn't need to know its meaning at the moment.

잘못된 전략 선택: a waste of time에 대한 뜻을 유추하고 있는 건가? -1pts

앞의 전략의 규명과 불일치, 부적절한 동사 'infer' 사용 -1pts

1pts

〈B〉 정보만 제시 0.5pt

Case 5 1.5pts

First, Minji's listening strategy is using context to infer the meaning of words because she infers 'a waste of time' has negative meaning about using social media from the context. Second, Dongho's listening strategy is determining to skip unknown words because he thinks he doesn't need to know the meaning of the word 'sneaky'.

#02 4pts

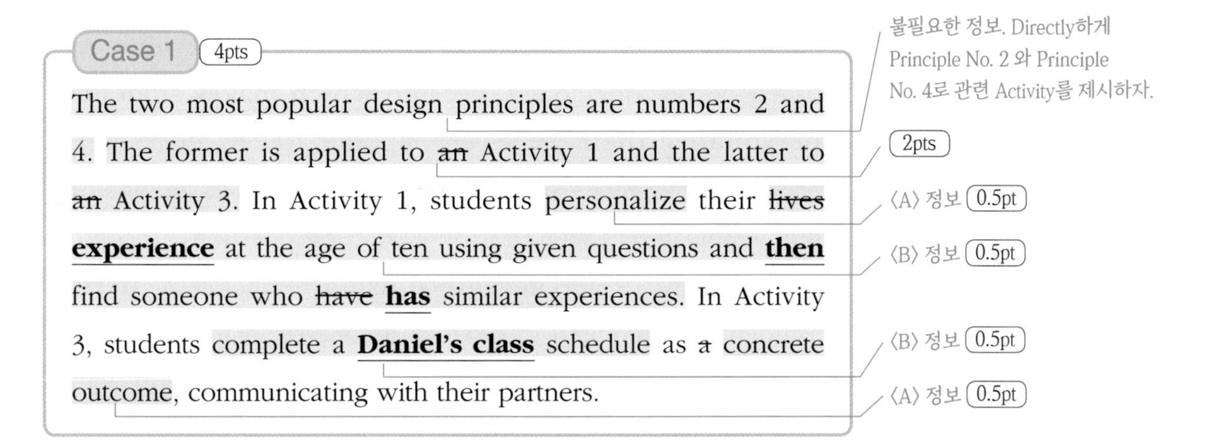

Case 1 4pts

The two most popular design principles are numbers 2 and 4. The former is applied to ~~an~~ Activity 1 and the latter to ~~an~~ Activity 3. In Activity 1, students personalize their ~~lives~~ **experience** at the age of ten using given questions and **then** find someone who ~~have~~ **has** similar experiences. In Activity 3, students complete a **Daniel's class** schedule as ~~a~~ concrete outcome, communicating with their partners.

Summative Feedback

- directions에서 요구하고 있는 정보를 <A>와 <B>에서 각각 찾아 제시하고 있다. 다만, 보다 정확한 표현과 구체적 정보를 제시하면 효과적일 것으로 보인다.
- 일부 문법적 오류(an, have 등)가 보이니 답안을 작성한 뒤, grammatical error에 대한 proofreading을 하도록 하자.

Revised Version

Principle No. 2 is applied to Activity 1, and Principle No. 4 is utilized in Activity 3. In Activity 1, students personalize their experiences at the age of ten using given questions and then find someone who has similar experiences. In Activity 3, students complete Daniel's class schedule as a concrete outcome, communicating with their partners.

Case 2 (3.5pts)

불필요한 언급이므로 답안 작성 시 칸이 부족할 경우 빼도록 하자. - Directions 준수

1pts

〈A〉 정보, but 해당 원리를 잘 반영할 수 있는 word choice (personalized)를 하자. 0.5pt

너무 막연한 정보 -0.5pt

1pts

〈A〉 정보 0.5pt

〈B〉 정보 0.5pt

The two most popular design principles were principle number #2 and principle number #4. First, [activity 1] was designed based on the principle 2, ~~because~~ **which makes students personalize their** ~~are given opportunities to share their personal expressions and opinions~~ **experiences at the age of ten.** ~~within group members~~ by ~~answering questions~~. Second, [activity 3] was ~~made~~ **developed using** ~~p~~**P**rinciple 4. **Here**, ~~S~~**s**tudents are required to produce **a** concrete outcome, which is Daniel's class schedule ~~here~~, by sharing information with their partners.

Summative Feedback

- Directions을 준수해 각각 필요한 정보를 먼저 규명한 뒤, outline을 잡아 답안을 작성하는 연습을 하도록 하자.
- 답안을 작성한 뒤, grammatical error에 대한 proofreading을 하도록 하자.

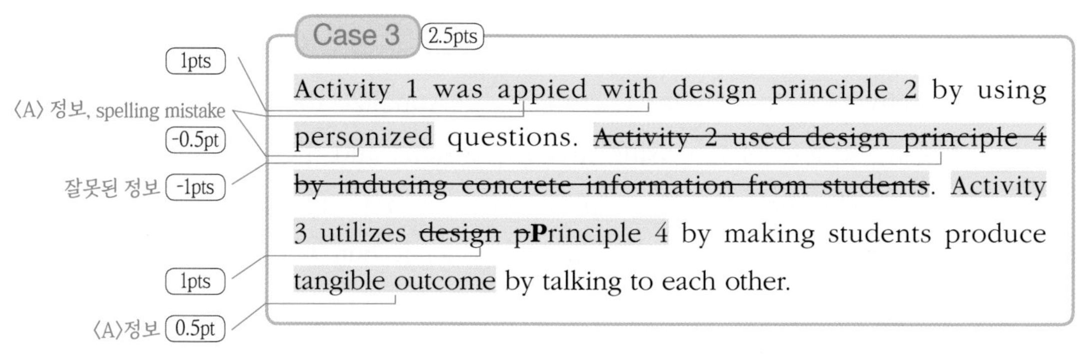

Case 3 (2.5pts)

1pts

〈A〉 정보, spelling mistake -0.5pt

잘못된 정보 -1pts

1pts

〈A〉정보 0.5pt

Activity 1 was appied with design principle 2 by using personized questions. ~~Activity 2 used design principle 4 by inducing concrete information from students~~. Activity 3 utilizes ~~design~~ ~~p~~**P**rinciple 4 by making students produce tangible outcome by talking to each other.

Summative Feedback

- 불필요하고 잘못된 정보를 답안으로 작성할 경우, 올바른 정보가 포함돼 있더라도 감점될 가능성이 높다. 따라서 directions와 각 정보에 대한 data 분석을 철저히 한 뒤, 답안으로 옮기는 연습을 하도록 하자.
- Case 3의 경우, identify에 해당하는 정보를 각각 <A>와 <B>에서 명확하게 찾아내는 연습이 절대적으로 필요하다.

Case 4-(1) 0pt

In the Activity 1 of <B> has applied the principles 2 and 4 of <A>. By thinking about students' own life in Activity 1 process, they can immerse into the personalized activity. Also, when they talk about their own thoughts and experience following the suggested questions, they can have purpose and result of the communication.

잘못된 'identify'- Directions 준수

Identify가 잘못됐으므로 그 뒤 evidence나 설명이 맞았더라도 0점 처리된다.

Summative Feedback

- "Based on <A>, for **each** of the two most popular design principles, identify **the ONE activity** in <B> that **the principle has been applied to, respectively**."의 의미가 무엇인가? 밑줄 친 부분을 유의하면서 directions에서 요구하는 정보를 어떻게 나열해야 할 것인지 파악해보자.
- Rewriting 하도록 하자.

Case 4-(2) 0pt

The two most popular design principles are experiential principle and Task-based principle. Experiential principle has been applied to activity 1 because in this activity, students talk about their experiences through personalized questions. Task-based principle has been applied to activity 2 because students produce concrete outcomes such as a map and flag by asking questions and answering each other.

주어진 Data에 없는 정보는 임의적으로 답안에 포함시키지 말자. 오답으로 파악돼 감점된다. 각각 주어진 principle을 명명하라고 할 경우 해당 principle의 명칭이 언급될 수 있지만 주어진 문항의 Directions은 Activity를 규명하는 것이다.

의미적으로 맞았다고 해도 experience principle이 어떤 것인지 규명하지 않았으므로 감점 처리된다.

inidentified

Summative Feedback

- 문제에서 언급하지 않는 것은 명명할 필요가 없다. Principle 2와 Principle 4가 각각 'experiential principle'과 'task-based principle'로 파악된다고 해도 directions은 각각의 principle이 적용된 활동을 찾으라는 것이다. 따라서 Activity가 중심이고 Activity에 적용된 principle에 대한 matching과 해당 근거를 <A>와 <B>에서 각각 찾도록 해야 한다.
- Rewriting 하도록 하자.

#03 4pts

Case 1 4pts

2pts
〈A〉 정보 0.5pt
〈B〉 정보 0.5pt
〈A〉 정보 0.5pt
〈B〉 정보 0.5pt

Two components are 'skills' and 'vocabulary'. In the aspect of skills, teachers want to include both receptive and productive skills, but the syllabus in <B> includes only receptive skills, such as 'listening' and 'reading'. In 'vocabulary', They want to emphasize the multi-word units but it focuses on only single words such as 'employer', 'sales', and 'appointment'.

Summative Feedback

전반적으로 directions에서 요구한 정보를 균형감 있게 잘 구성하고 있다. Evidence와 해당 근거에 대한 예시를 작성할 경우 동일하게 정보를 구성하는 것이 보다 효과적일 것이다. 가령, multi-word units like collocations and idioms는 single words such as 'employer', 'sales', and 'appointment'와 대구를 이룰 수 있다.

Revised Version

주어진 답안에 대한 구문 및 뉘앙스적인 측면에서 명확한 의미를 살릴 수 있는 version을 제공하니 참고만 해보자.

Two key components are 'skills' and 'vocabulary'. In terms of skills, teachers aim to include both receptive and productive skills, but the syllabus at <B> includes only receptive skills, such as listening and reading. Regarding vocabulary, while there is a desire to emphasize multi-word units like collocations and idioms, the focus remains solely on single words, such as 'employer', 'sales', and 'appointment'.

Case 2 3pts

Skills and Vocabulary are not correspond to the teacher's ideas because there are not speaking and writing skills in the component of skills and there are lack of multi word units in vocabulary.

2pts
0.5pt
0.5pt

Summative Feedback

Directions에서 <A>와 <B>에서 evidence를 찾으라고 했으므로 각각 <A>와 <B>에서 정보를 찾도록 해야 한다.

Case 3 2pts

Including productive skills and teaching multi-word units are not in the teachers' syllabus. In the syllabus, there are only listening and reading skills which are both receptive skills rather than productive. Also there are only single words in the syllabus rather than multi-word units.

답안의 첫 문장이 이렇게 시작되기 위해서는 directions에서 주어진 첫 질문이 Identify the main differences between teachers' ideas and the completed syllabus 여야 한다.

0.5pt

not including productive skills의 의미를 명확히 제시할 필요가 있다.

0.5pt

1pts

Summative Feedback

- Directions의 모든 질문은 하나의 text를 구성하기 위한 것이므로 서로 밀접한 연관이 있지만 주어진 답안에서는 'choose' 없이 evidence만으로 답을 구성하고 있다. 따라서 실전에서는 identify를 하지 않거나 잘못한 경우, evidence를 바르게 작성했더라도 모두 0점 처리될 가능성이 있으니 주의가 필요하다.
- 주어진 답안 자체도 word choice에 부적절해 의미가 모호하게 전달된다.

Revised Version

다음 version(original answer를 유지)을 읽고 차이점을 찾아보자.

The teachers' syllabus does not include productive skills or the teaching of multi-word units. It only features listening and reading skills, which are both receptive, and focuses solely on single words rather than multi-word units.

〈A〉의 교사 대화에서 언급된 내용인 productive skills와 multi-word units가 어디에서 빠졌다는 것인가? Syllabus 또는 〈B〉에 대한 언급이 반드시 필요하다.

0.5pt

0.5pt

Case 4 1pts

~~Based on <A>,~~ Teacher 2 **failed** ~~missed~~ to ~~involve~~ **include** productive skills and ~~some~~ multi-word units ~~for the activities~~ **in the completed syllabus in <B>**, which two teachers **had previously** ~~already~~ agreed ~~to do~~ **upon**. ~~First~~ Firstly, ~~on~~ in <B>, ~~there are~~ only receptive skills activities, such as listening and reading, **are present**. **Additionally**~~Also~~, there are no mentions ~~about~~ of collocation**s** or other multi-word units ~~for~~ **in** the vocabulary components ~~on~~ **of** <B>.

Summative Feedback

'Choose' 없이 전체적으로 내용을 모호하게 설명하고 있다. 특히, 교사들의 대화에서 언급한 내용과 실제 대화 후 작성된 syllabus와의 차이점을 명시하지 않았다.

Case 5 0pt

First, there is no productive skills in <B>. In <B> Ss can only learn receptive skills such as Listening and Reading. Second, there is no multi-word units in <B>. In <B> Ss can learn collocation and idioms however there is no fixed expression in <B>.

Summative Feedback

- 'Choose' 없이 내용을 설명하고 있고, <A>와 <B>의 정보도 혼재돼 있다. 가령, there is no productive skills in <B>가 틀린 말은 아니지만 data에서 가져올 수 있는 정보는 'There is receptive skills only such as Listening and Reading in <B>'가 맞으며, productive skills은 교사들의 대화에서 나온 것으로 언급해야 할 것이다.
- 주어진 data에서 학생들의 언급이 없음에도 불구하고 행위의 주체를 Ss로 명명해 내용에 대한 불명확함과 모호함을 가중시켰다.

#04 (4pts)

Case 1 (4pts)

Tool 2 is for the teacher 2 and Tool 4 is for the teacher 1. The teacher 1 requires a tool to provide audience who will read students writing and various multimodal resources to express their thinking more creatively. Tool 4 provides online platform in which other students can reply to the written work and exchange reply with the writer, and they can attach photos or videos. The teacher 2 requires enough opportunities for students to communicate with other people outside the classroom. Tool 2 provides virtual reality in simulated real-life circumstances to communicate with other people in English through an avatar.

(1pts)

(1pts)

정보 및 구문이 너무 장황하고 길어서 정보와 구문을 함축적이고 명료하게 정리할 필요가 있다. (1pts)

(1pts)

Summative Feedback

Directions에 따른 정보가 다 있으나, 요구하지 않은 정보까지 자세히 제공함으로써 답안이 장황하고 길어졌다. 따라서 directions을 철저히 분석하고 필요한 정보만 명확히 골라 제시하는 연습을 하자. 가령, “Suggest **the ONE most appropriate tool** in <B> that satisfies their needs. Then explain your answers with **evidence from <B>**.” 밑줄 친 부분에 근거해서 다시 답안을 분석해보자. 필요한 답안은 각 교사에게 맞는 TOOL을 고르는 것이며, 각각의 Tool이 어떻게 교사의 needs에 맞는지 <B>에서 찾아 쓰는 것이다. 따라서 각 교사의 needs를 답안에 작성할 필요는 없고, 교사의 needs에 맞는 문구를 각 tool의 설명에서 찾아 evidence로 제시하면 되는 것이다.

Revised Version

For Teacher 1, Tool 4 is most appropriate because it offers an online platform where students can express their thoughts creatively by attaching photos or videos to their written work, providing an audience that can reply to their writings(posts). For Teacher 2, Tool 2 is the best fit as it provides a virtual reality in simulated real-life situation so that students can communicate with others through avatars in English.

Case 2 (2.5pts)

The suggestion for Teacher 1 is Tool 4. Teacher 1's students have a problem in writing because of only one reader. If they use this Tool, they could give a feedback each other and then have an interest in writing. For teacher 2, the suggestion is tool 2. Using this tool, students can communicate with others in English in free for developing their interpersonal skills.

1pts
〈B〉 정보의 내용을 좀 더 명확하게 제시할 필요가 있다. 0.5pt
1pts
〈B〉의 정보인가?

Case 3 (2pts)

For the teacher 1, the Tool 4 is adaptive because the teacher think their students need audience who read their writing and multimodal sources. And, the Tool 2 is good for the teacher 2 because the teacher said that their students want to communicate with others in English outside of the class, and an avatar in the Tool 2 can help less anxious.

1pts
〈B〉에서 나온 정보인가?
1pts
〈B〉에서 나온 정보인가?

#05 (4pts)

Case 1 (4pts)

Teacher 5 and teacher 6 interpretations are not correct. First, teacher 5 mentioned that item 1 should be deleted in order to increase the internal consistency. However, since item 1 is over 0.3 which is considered satisfactory discrimination, it doesn't have to be deleted. **Instead**, ~~Only~~ item 3, which is rated minus 0.21 should be deleted. Second, teacher 6 compared this test and the ERAT ~~and illustrates it is~~ **citing as** the evidence of predictive validity. However, it should be concurrent validity because this test is being compared ~~to the test that is validated~~. **with another validated test(ERAT)**.

(1pts) (1.5pts) (0.5pt) (1pts)

Summative Feedback

Directions에서 요구한 정보를 충실하고 정확하게 답안으로 작성하고 있다.

Revised Version

맥락의 흐름과 word choice만 참고해보자.

Teachers 5 and 6 have offered incorrect interpretations. First, Teacher 5 suggested that deleting item 1 would increase internal consistency. However, since item 1 has a discrimination index of over 0.3, which is considered satisfactory, it does not need to be deleted. Instead, item 3, which has a discrimination index of -0.21, should be removed. Second, Teacher 6 compared this test with the ERAT, citing it as evidence of predictive validity. However, the correct term is concurrent validity, since this test is being compared with another validated test.

Case 2 (3.5pts)

(0.5pt)
부족한 증거: 동일한 수치이므로 item 1과 item 3의 구분이 어렵다.
(1pts)
satisfactory discrimination value 0.3의 구체적 수치 언급이 필요하다. (-0.5pt)
(0.5pt)
(1.5pt)

First, teacher 5's interpretation is not correct, **because** ~~in that this test indicates satisfactory internal consistency because Cronbach's alpha is 0.86. Also~~, only item 3 should be deleted because its item discrimination **score of** ~~is~~ '-0.21' **falls below the satisfactory threshold of** ~~which indicates non-satisfactory discrimination~~ **0.3**. Second, the interpretation of teacher 6 is incorrect in that the correlation between this test and ERAT, which **have been** ~~was already~~ validated **previously**, displays the evidence of concurrent validity, not a predictive validity.

Summative Feedback

Identified factor에 대한 명확한 evidence를 찾는 연습이 필요하다. 이를 위해서 data에 대한 분석과 필요 구문에 대한 underline을 통해 숙지하면서 필요한 정보를 얻도록 하자.

Revised Version

보다 논리적인 정보 구성과 정확한 표현에 초점을 두자.

First, Teacher 5's interpretation is incorrect because only item 3 should be deleted, not the other item 1. Item 3's discrimination value '-0.21' falls down the satisfactory threshold of 0.3. Second, Teacher 6's interpretation is also incorrect. The correlation between this test and the ERAT, which has been validated previously, demonstrates evidence of concurrent validity, not predictive validity.

Case 3 (2.5pts)

The interpretation of teacher 5 and 6 for each is incorrect. Whereas item 3 must be deleted in order to increase internal consistency, as Teacher 5 said, item 1 should not be deleted since its item facility and item discrimination is perfectly fine. And by contrast to teacher 6's interpretation what can be displayed from the analysis is not predictive validity. It is concurrent validity.

(1pts)

근거 부족: item 1과 3의 차이에 대한 언급(satisfactory discrimination value 0.3)이 필요하다. (1pts)

<A>의 정보로 validated test에 대한 언급이 없으므로 어떻게 predictive validity가 아니라 concurrent validity가 되는지에 대한 설명을 할 수 없다. (0.5pt)

Summative Feedback

Data analysis에 대한 정확한 분석이 요구되므로 directions을 토대로 각 주어진 data에 대한 개별 중요 요소를 점검하는 연습을 하면서 필요한 정보를 모으도록 하자. 이때 중요한 정보에 해당하면 표시를 하고 directions와 함께 관련지어 최종적으로 답안을 작성해 나가도록 하자.

#06 4pts

Case 1-(1) 4pts

규명해야 할 항목이 'word level'일 경우, 가급적 구체적으로 명시하자. 1pts

어떤 task를 언급하는가? original task or adjusted task? 답안만 봐서는 명확히 구분이 되지 않는다.

0.5pt

0.5pt

1pts

0.5pt

0.5pt

Factor 1, especially grammar, was addressed to the task by ~~substituting~~ **simplifying** complex sentences into simple**r** ~~sentences~~ **ones**. ~~In detail~~ **Specifically**, the teacher deleted sentences with a relative pronoun and **a** If-clause, ~~and used~~ **replaced them** with a preposition and splitted sentences ~~instead~~. And Factor 3 was applied to the task by allowing students to introduce their opinions to their partners, not the whole class. Conducting speaking activities ~~with~~ **in** pairs can reduce students' pressure.

Summative Feedback

- Directions에 맞춰 필요한 정보를 전반적으로 다 제공한 답안이다. 다만, 답안의 명확성을 위해 실제 언급할 필요가 있는 중요 항목은 지칭어가 아닌 명칭으로 정확히 제시하자. (→sore objectivity를 높임)
- Original task의 난이도 조정을 위한 두 항목으로 language와 performance conditions를 문두에 언급하면 답안을 명확히 보여줄 수 있다. 또한, 막연한 'task'은 두 개의 task 중 무엇을 의미하는지 파악하기 어려운 점을 유의해 감점 요소를 줄여 나가도록 하자.

Revised Version

명확성과 논리적 전개에 따른 필요 구문에 대한 차이를 파악해 보도록 하자.

Language, particularly grammar, was addressed in the task by simplifying complex sentences into simpler ones. Specifically, the teacher eliminated sentences containing relative pronouns and if-clauses, replacing them with prepositions and splitting the sentences. Additionally, Performance conditions was applied to the task by allowing students to share their opinions with their partners rather than with the whole class. Conducting speaking activities in pairs can reduce the students' pressure.

Case 1-(2) 4pts

The two factors in <A> that Mr. Kim addressed to adjust the difficulty of the original task in <B> are factor 1 and factor 3. First, factor 1 is adapted since Mr. Kim simplified complex sentences, for example, using prepositional phrase and not using if-clause. Next, factor 3 is adapted since Mr. Kim modified the question to introduce in pairs instead of introducing to while class to reduce pressure and difficulty.

가급적 해당 요소를 쓰자. 2pts

1pts

부정확한 정보를 제공함으로써 자칫 감점이 될 수 있다. Mr. Kim modified the task~(not question)

1pts

Revised Version

The two factors in <A> that Mr. Kim addressed to adjust the difficulty of the original task in <B> are Language and Performance Conditions. First, the language was adapted; Mr. Kim simplified complex sentences by using prepositional phrases and avoiding if-clauses. Next, the performance conditions were adapted; Mr. Kim modified the task so that students would introduce their work in pairs rather than to the whole class, reducing pressure and difficulty.

Case 2 3pts

1pts

language에 따른 과업의 난이도가 어떻게 조정되었는지에 대한 구체적 설명이 없다. 평가자에 따라 감점으로 이어질 수 있다. 0.5pt

1pts

0.5pt

Mr. Kim uses Language Factor when he gives a passage. He made some sentences simple for students' better understanding such as changing conditionals to short sentences. And he uses Performance conditions factor by changing the audience from the whole class to a partner at the end of the task.

Summative Feedback

Directions에 따른 정보를 사용할 경우, 해당 정보를 가장 잘 설명할 수 있는 word choice를 하도록 하자. (simplify 등)

Revised Version

Mr. Kim employs the Language Factor when he provides a passage by simplifying some sentences to enhance students' understanding, such as converting conditionals into shorter sentences. Additionally, he uses the Performance Conditions Factor by changing the audience from the whole class to a partner at the end of the task.

Case 3 1pts

의미적으로 이해되지만 directions에서 two factors를 'identify'하도록 했으므로 ⟨A⟩에 나와 있는 항목을 정확하게 찾아 규명해야 한다.

0.5pt

0.5pt

Mr. Kim adjusts the task difficulty by syntactic modification and changing task performance. First, he changes language of input in a easier way, like "You may get lost", not "If you get lost". Also, he modifies the task to introduce to partner, not to the whole class.

Summative Feedback

- 답안에 language와 performance에 대한 용어가 있으나, directions의 'identify' 측면에서 답안을 작성한 것이 아니므로 점수 부여가 어렵다.
- Directions을 준수한 답안 쓰기 연습이 절대적으로 필요하다.

07 (4pts)

Case 1 (3.5pts)

Ms. Kang incorporates 'cultural products' ~~as~~ **into** a teaching content, but she does not conform to teaching principle (3) in her lesson sequence. First, in the former, she introduces pictures of British and American houses which are tangible creations. Second, in the latter, she makes students classify the houses into two groups, houses in the UK and houses in the US, so she does not follow teaching principle (3).

(1pts)
(1pts)
(1pts)
〈A〉에 해당하는 정보가 결여됐다. (0.5pt)

Revised Version

Ms. Kang incorporates 'cultural products' into her teaching content, but she does not adhere to teaching principle (3) in her lesson sequence. Initially, she introduces pictures of British and American houses, which are tangible creations, as part of the lesson. Subsequently, she asks students to classify the houses into two groups: those in the UK and those in the US. This classification reinforces the association between nationalities and specific cultural traits, which contradicts Principle (3).

Case 2 (2pts)

(1pts) (1pts)

The teaching content is cultural products because the students talked about British and American dwellings. And teacher does not avoid reinforcing associations between nationalities and cultures, because she makes students classify the house styles between UK and US.

Summative Feedback

- Data analysis를 할 경우, <A>와 <B>를 분석하고 관련된 활동을 언급할 때 각각 해당하는 정보가 무엇인지 밑줄을 그어 명확히 파악해 답안을 작성하는 연습을 하도록 하자.
- 가령, cultural product로 teaching content를 제시했다면 <A>의 tangible and intangible creation에 대한 부분을 <B>에서 찾도록 한다. 실제 <B> 안에서 cultural product로 제시하는 것이 US와 UK의 실물에 해당하는 houses를 비교하는 것이므로 tangible creation 측면의 활동이 이뤄지고 있는 것이다.

Case 3 (0pt)

Ms. Kang **uses various audiovisual aids, including** ~~some~~ pictures of houses and a video of two people talking in ~~English~~, **English**. However, ~~which is the fact that Ms. Kang utilize different types of audiovisual aids.~~ ~~Ms. Kang~~ **she** requires her students to classify the houses into two groups, Houses in the UK and in the ~~US~~, **US. This approach** ~~which~~ is not conform to the principle ~~that~~ **avoiding** reinforcing associations between nationalities and cultures ~~is avoided~~.

Summative Feedback

- Directions을 명확하게 준수할 것! Teaching content에 대한 내용을 <A>에서 찾아 명시해야 한다.
- 해당 요소가 명시되지 않는 상태에서 evidence에 대한 설명이 있다고 해도 채점자에 따라 0점으로 처리될 수 있으니 각별히 조심하자.

#08 4pts

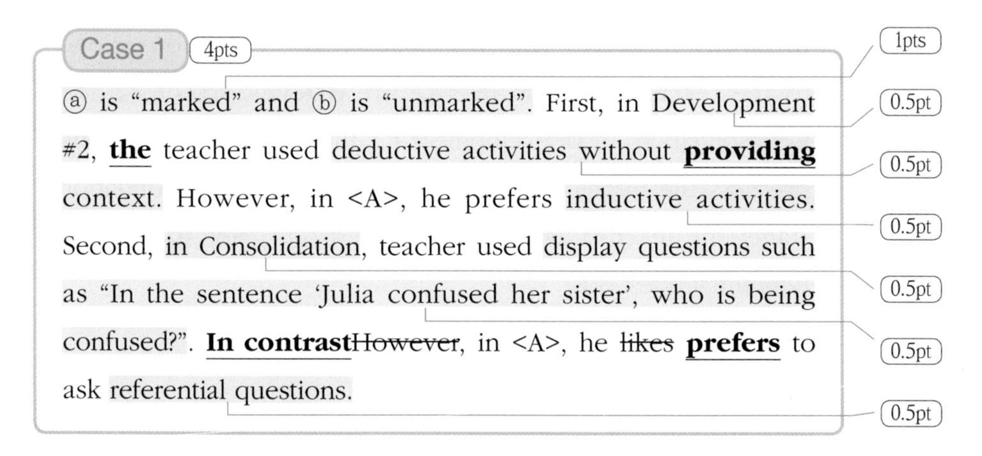

Case 1 4pts

ⓐ is "marked" and ⓑ is "unmarked". First, in Development #2, **the** teacher used deductive activities without **providing** context. However, in <A>, he prefers inductive activities. Second, in Consolidation, teacher used display questions such as "In the sentence 'Julia confused her sister', who is being confused?". **In contrast**~~However~~, in <A>, he ~~likes~~ **prefers** to ask referential questions.

Summative Feedback

- 전반적으로 directions에 대한 정확한 분석을 통해 <A>와 <B>에서 필요한 정보를 찾아 각각 대구를 이룰 수 있도록 답안을 작성했다.
- 다만, 명확한 의미를 제공하기 위해 문맥간의 접속사나 행위 동사 사용에 대한 정확성을 키운다면 명확한 답안 작성이 될 것이다.

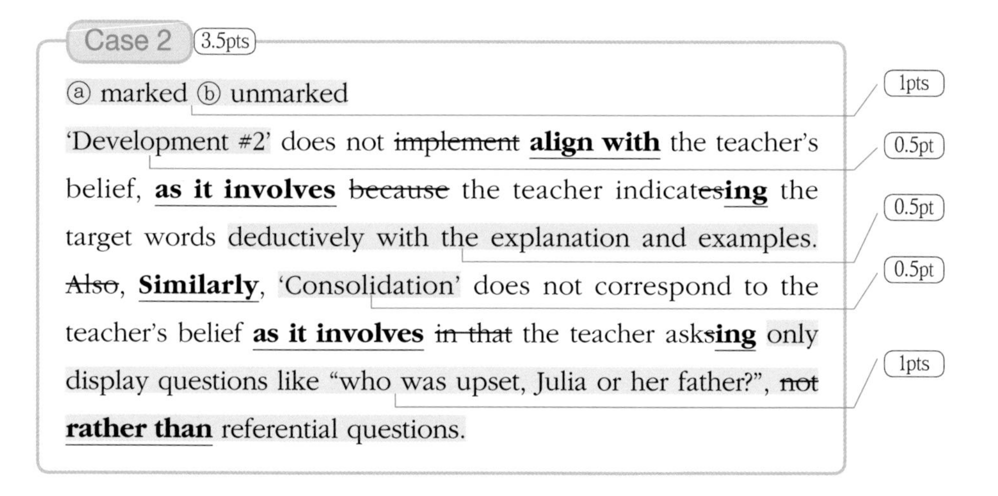

Case 2 3.5pts

ⓐ marked ⓑ unmarked

'Development #2' does not ~~implement~~ **align with** the teacher's belief, **as it involves** ~~because~~ the teacher indicat~~es~~**ing** the target words deductively with the explanation and examples. ~~Also~~, **Similarly**, 'Consolidation' does not correspond to the teacher's belief **as it involves** ~~in that~~ the teacher ask~~s~~**ing** only display questions like "who was upset, Julia or her father?", ~~not~~ **rather than** referential questions.

Case 3 2pts

-1pts

1pts

0.5pt

display question에 따른 <B>의 예문이 누락됐다. 0.5pt

The blank ⓐ should be filled with "unmarked" and the blank ⓑ "marked". The two stages that do not correspond to the teacher's beliefs in <A> are ~~d~~**D**evelopment #2 and **C**~~c~~onsolidation. In **D**~~d~~evelopment #2, the teacher **immediately** presents the target rules ~~immediately~~. In **the** **C**~~c~~onsolidation stage, the teacher asks 'display questions', ~~not~~ **instead of** referential questions.

Summative Feedback

- Data analysis에 보다 집중적인 연습이 필요하다. 주어진 directions에 따르면 <A>와 <B>에서 모두 evidence를 찾도록 했으나 위의 답안에서는 <A> 또는 <B>의 정보만을 제시하고 있다.
- <B>에서 display questions이라는 말은 없으므로, 답안에 display questions을 제시해주기 위해 반드시 example을 함께 제공해야 한다.

03

2022년 개정 교육과정의 주요 쟁점과 중·고교 수업 방향

03 2022년 개정 교육과정의 주요 쟁점과 중·고교 수업 방향

1 주요 쟁점

(1) 핵심 역량 중심 교육

학생의 창의성, 비판적 사고, 의사소통 능력 등을 강화하는 방향으로 개정됐고, 단순 암기식 교육에서 벗어나 실제 문제 해결 능력을 길러 주는 교육을 강조한다.

In the Classroom

1. Middle School English Class

- Theme: Environmental Protection Campaign Project
- Class Objectives
  - Understand the importance of environmental protection and express it in English.
  - Develop creative thinking and collaboration skills.
  - Enhance English communication abilities.

Lesson Procedure

Introduction

- Watch a video in English about environmental protection and summarize key words and phrases.
- Have a brief discussion with students about the necessity of environmental protection.

Main Activities

① Group Work: Divide students into groups of 4-5 and have them plan an environmental protection campaign.
- Assign Roles: Each student takes on a role such as presenter, researcher, or poster creator.
- Research: Use internet and library resources to gather information about environmental issues.

- Create Posters and Presentation Materials: Based on the gathered information, make English posters and presentation materials.
- Presentation Preparation: Each group practices presenting their campaign in English.

② Presentation and Feedback
- Each group presents their campaign in English.
- After the presentations, other groups and the teacher provide feedback.
- Students revise and improve their presentations based on the feedback.

Conclusion
- Display the posters and presentation materials in the classroom for students to view.
- Have students write down small actions they can take for environmental protection in English.

2. High School English Class
- Theme: English Debate on Global Issues
- Class Objectives
  - Improve reading and listening skills about global issues in English.
  - Develop critical thinking and logical communication abilities.
  - Enhance English debating skills.

Lesson Procedure

Introduction
- Provide recent news articles or videos in English on global issues (e.g., climate change, human rights).
- Summarize key words and phrases and have a brief discussion about the issue with students.

Main Activities

① Individual Activity: Students read the provided materials and submit a summary of the main points.

② Question Making: Each student creates debate questions based on the reading.

③ Group Activity: Divide students into groups of 3-4 and prepare for the debate.

- Assign Roles: Each student takes on a role such as proponent, opponent, or neutral party.
- Debate Preparation: Research and build arguments according to their roles.
- Conduct Debate: Each group debates the given global issue in English.
- Teacher Feedback: The teacher observes the debates and provides feedback.

Conclusion

- Summarize the debate content and write the main points and conclusions in English.
- Gather all students to share the results of their debates and provide comprehensive feedback.
- Students write an essay based on what they learned from the class.

➡ These examples aim to help students use English in real-life contexts and develop key competencies.

(2) 교육 내용의 적정화

과도한 학습 부담을 줄이기 위해 학습 내용을 축소하고 필수 내용을 중심으로 재구성했다. 또한, 학습량을 줄여 학생들이 자기 주도적 학습 시간을 확보할 수 있도록 했다.

Teacher Meeting Discussion on Curriculum Streamlining for Next Semester

- Participants
  - Ms. Kim, Head of English Department for 3rd grade of a middle school
  - Mr. Lee, New English Teacher
- Meeting Agenda

Step 1. Introduction and Purpose
Step 2. Overview of 2022 Curriculum Revision
Step 3. Discussion on Streamlining Curriculum
Step 4. Planning Next Semester's Lessons
Step 5. Conclusion and Next Steps

Ms. Kim: Good afternoon, Mr. Lee. Thank you for joining this meeting. Today, we will discuss the direction of our English classes for the next semester in light of the 2022 curriculum revision.

Mr. Lee: Good afternoon, Ms. Kim. I'm glad to be here and eager to contribute. What specific changes are we focusing on?

Ms. Kim: One of the key changes is the streamlining of educational content. The goal is to reduce the learning burden on students by focusing on essential knowledge and skills. Let's start by reviewing the main points of the curriculum revision.

Step 1. Introduction and Purpose

Ms. Kim: As you know, the 2022 curriculum aims to create a more balanced and student-centered learning environment. This includes reducing excessive content and emphasizing core competencies like creativity, critical thinking, and communication. Our task is to align our lesson plans with these objectives.

Mr. Lee : That sounds great. How do we ensure that we are covering all essential content without overwhelming the students?

Step 2. Overview of 2022 Curriculum Revision

Ms. Kim: The revision highlights a few strategies:
- Focus on essential learning outcomes.
- Integrate cross-curricular themes.
- Encourage student-led learning activities.
- Utilize formative assessments to guide instruction.

Mr. Lee : Understood. So, we need to identify what is essential and find ways to make lessons more engaging and manageable.

Step 3. Discussion on Streamlining Curriculum

Ms. Kim: Correct. Let's discuss how we can streamline our curriculum. For example, we can:
- Combine units that have overlapping content.
- Use project-based learning to cover multiple objectives.
- Implement more interactive and collaborative activities to enhance engagement.

Mr. Lee : I think integrating project-based learning is a fantastic idea. It allows students to apply what they've learned in a meaningful way. We could start with a project on environmental issues, which ties into both language skills and global awareness.

Ms. Kim: That's a good suggestion. It aligns well with the new curriculum's emphasis on real-world application. We can design a project where students research, present, and discuss environmental issues in English. This would cover reading, writing, speaking, and listening skills.

Step 4. Planning Next Semester's Lessons

Mr. Lee : How should we plan the lessons? Should we draft a detailed plan for each week or keep it flexible?

Ms. Kim: A flexible framework would be best. We should outline key projects and activities for the semester and allow for adjustments based on students' progress and interests. We can break down the semester into monthly themes, each culminating in a project or presentation.

Mr. Lee : That makes sense. For the first month, we could focus on building foundational skills and introduce the environmental project. In subsequent months, we could explore other themes like technology and cultural diversity.

Ms. Kim: Exactly. Let's also incorporate regular formative assessments to monitor students' understanding and provide timely feedback. This will help us adjust our teaching strategies as needed.

Step 5. Conclusion and Next Steps

Ms. Kim: To summarize, we will streamline our curriculum by focusing on essential content, integrating cross-curricular projects, and maintaining flexibility in our lesson plans. Let's start drafting the monthly themes and key projects. We will meet again next week to review our plans.

Mr. Lee : Sounds like a solid plan. I'll begin working on some project ideas and share them with you before our next meeting.

Ms. Kim: Great. Thank you, Mr. Lee. I look forward to collaborating with you to create an engaging and effective learning experience for our students.

Mr. Lee : Thank you, Ms. Kim. See you next week.

➡ This structured meeting ensures that the teachers align their efforts with the revised curriculum while fostering a collaborative and adaptable teaching environment.

(3) 맞춤형 교육 강화

다양한 학습자들의 특성을 고려한 맞춤형 교육 방안을 마련했고, 학생 개개인의 학습 속도와 스타일에 맞춘 교육을 제공한다.

In the Classroom

Personalized Education Examples for Middle and High School Classes

1. Middle School Example: Personalized Reading Program

- Objective: Enhance individual reading skills and foster a love for reading.
- Class Activities
  - Initial Assessment: Conduct a reading level assessment for each student.
  - Customized Reading Lists: Create personalized reading lists based on students' reading levels and interests.
  - Reading Journals: Students keep a reading journal to summarize and reflect on their readings.
  - One-on-One Conferences: Schedule regular one-on-one meetings with students to discuss their progress and adjust their reading lists as needed.
  - Peer Sharing: Organize small group discussions where students share their favorite books and insights with classmates.
- Outcome: Students improve their reading skills at their own pace and develop a deeper interest in reading.

2. High School Example: Personalized Project-based Learning in Science

- Objective: Develop critical thinking and problem-solving skills through personalized projects.
- Class Activities
  - Interest Survey: Conduct a survey to identify students' interests in various scientific topics.
  - Project Proposal: Each student proposes a project based on their interests and prior knowledge.
  - Mentorship: Assign a mentor (teacher or advanced student) to guide each project.
  - Research and Development: Students conduct research, design experiments, and develop their projects with periodic check-ins for feedback.
  - Presentation and Reflection: Students present their projects to the class and write a reflection on their learning process and outcomes.
- Outcome: Students engage deeply with scientific inquiry and apply their learning to real-world problems, tailored to their interests and abilities.

(4) 디지털 및 정보화 교육 강화

디지털 시대에 맞는 정보 활용 능력 및 디지털 리터러시 교육을 강화하고 온라인 학습 자원과 플랫폼을 적극적으로 활용해 학생들의 학습 경험을 확대한다.

Minji and Youngho's Thoughts on the Differences in English Classes After the 2022 Curriculum Revision

Minji:
After experiencing the new English classes focused on digital and information literacy, I noticed a significant change compared to our previous classes. Before, we mostly relied on textbooks and traditional exercises. Now, we use various digital tools and online resources. For example, we watch educational videos, participate in virtual discussions, and use interactive apps to practice vocabulary and grammar. This approach makes learning more engaging and relevant to our daily lives. I feel more confident using English in digital contexts.

Youngho:
I agree with Minji. The integration of digital tools has transformed our English lessons. Previously, our classes were more teacher-centered, with a lot of lecturing and written assignments. Now, we have more interactive activities like online quizzes, digital storytelling, and collaborative projects using platforms like Google Docs and Padlet. This not only makes the lessons more fun but also helps us develop important skills like digital communication and online collaboration. I think this approach better prepares us for the future.

(5) 평가 방식의 다양화

학습자의 다양한 역량을 평가할 수 있는 여러 가지 평가 방법을 도입하고, 서술형과 수행평가 등 다양한 평가 방식을 통해 학생들의 전반적인 역량을 파악한다.

Diverse Assessment Methods for a Semester-Long English Course

1. Formative Assessments
   - Quizzes and Short Tests: Regular short quizzes to check understanding of vocabulary, grammar, and reading comprehension.
   - Exit Tickets: Quick reflections or summaries at the end of each class to gauge student understanding.
   - Peer Reviews: Students review each other's work to provide feedback and improve their own understanding.

2. Summative Assessments

   Midterm and Final Exams: Comprehensive tests covering all material taught during the semester, including multiple-choice, short answer, and essay questions.

3. Performance-based Assessments
   - Presentations: Students prepare and deliver presentations on various topics, demonstrating their speaking and research skills.
   - Projects: Group or individual projects that involve research, writing, and presentation, such as creating a digital story or a research poster.
   - Role-Playing: Simulated real-life scenarios where students must use English to navigate and solve problems.

4. Portfolios

   Learning Portfolios: Students collect their work throughout the semester, including essays, projects, and reflections. This portfolio demonstrates their progress and areas of improvement.

5. Self and Peer Assessments
   - Self Assessment: Students evaluate their own work and progress using rubrics or checklists.
   - Peer Assessment: Students assess their classmates' contributions in group projects or their performance in presentations.

6. Digital Assessments
- Online Quizzes and Assignments: Use platforms like Google Forms, Quizlet, or Kahoot for interactive and immediate feedback.
- Multimedia Projects: Assessments involving the creation of videos, podcasts, or blogs.

7. Oral Assessments
- Interviews and Conversations: One-on-one or small group interviews to assess speaking and listening skills.
- Debates: Structured debates on various topics to evaluate students' ability to articulate and defend their viewpoints.

➡ By incorporating these diverse assessment methods, teachers can provide a comprehensive evaluation of students' English skills, catering to different learning styles and strengths.

2 중·고교 수업 방향

(1) 프로젝트 기반 학습

협업과 문제 해결 능력을 기르는 수업 방식으로서, 학생들이 실제 문제를 해결하는 프로젝트를 통해 학습 내용을 직접 적용하고 체험할 수 있다.

(2) 융합 교육

STEAM(Science, Technology, Engineering, Arts, Mathematics) 교육 등 여러 교과를 통합해 문제를 해결할 수 있는 융합적 사고 능력을 배양한다.

(3) 학생 주도 학습

학생들이 주도적으로 학습 목표를 설정하고 학습 과정을 계획하며 진행한다. 이때, 교사는 학습 코치로서 학생들의 학습을 지원한다.

In the Classroom

Example of an English Class Based on STEAM Education (3rd Grade of a middle school)

1. Lesson Theme: "The Science of Climate Change and Its Impact on Society"

Objectives
- Integrate English language skills with scientific knowledge.
- Foster critical thinking, creativity, and problem-solving abilities.
- Encourage collaboration and communication through project-based learning.

2. Lesson Plan

① Introduction (10 minutes)
- Begin with a short video about climate change to grab students' attention.
- Discuss the main points of the video and introduce key vocabulary (e.g., greenhouse gases, global warming, carbon footprint).

② Reading and Comprehension (20 minutes)
- Provide students with an article about the science behind climate change and its effects on the environment and society.
- Assign students to read the article in pairs and answer comprehension questions.

③ Group Discussion (15 minutes)

Organize students into small groups to discuss the following questions:

– How does climate change affect our planet?

– What are some examples of its impact on different regions of the world?

– What actions can individuals and communities take to combat climate change?

④ STEAM Project (45 minutes)

- Science : Research the scientific causes and effects of climate change.
- Technology : Use digital tools (e.g., Google Slides, Canva) to create a presentation.
- Engineering : Design a simple prototype or model that demonstrates an innovative solution to reduce carbon emissions (e.g., a miniature wind turbine, a solar-powered gadget).
- Art : Create visually appealing infographics or posters to illustrate the project findings and solutions.
- Mathematics : Analyze data and statistics related to climate change (e.g., carbon dioxide levels, temperature changes) and include them in the presentation.

Steps for the Project:

- Research: Each group researches a specific aspect of climate change using provided resources.
- Design and Create: Groups design their prototype or model and create supporting visuals.
- Presentation Preparation: Groups prepare a presentation to share their findings and solutions with the class.

⑤ Presentation and Peer Review (30 minutes)

- Each group presents their project to the class.
- After each presentation, classmates provide constructive feedback and ask questions.

⑥ Reflection and Discussion (10 minutes)

- Students reflect on what they learned about climate change and how they used STEAM disciplines in their project.
- Discuss how integrating different subjects can help solve real-world problems.

⑦ Homework Assignment

Write a reflective essay on the importance of addressing climate change and how individuals can contribute to sustainability efforts.

3. Outcomes

- Students will improve their English reading, writing, speaking, and listening skills through integrated STEAM activities.
- They will gain a deeper understanding of climate change and its global impact.
- Students will develop teamwork, creativity, and problem-solving skills by working on interdisciplinary projects.
- This lesson not only reinforces English language skills but also demonstrates how STEAM education can be applied to address important global issues.

(4) 플립 러닝(Flipped Learning)

사전에 온라인 강의나 자료로 기본 내용을 학습하고 수업 시간에는 심화 학습이나 토론, 실습을 진행한다. 이는 학생들의 자기 주도적 학습 능력을 강화하고 수업 시간을 효율적으로 활용하는 데 용이하다.

T1 : There's no doubt that young children beginning school need the basics of reading, writing, and math.
T2 : I agree. But the big problem is determining the best way for them to get it. I think the classic mode of a teacher at the chalkboard, and books and homework is outdated.
T1 : True. That's why I have been looking at some teaching literature based on the ideas, Honathan Bergman and Aaron Sams came up with.
T2 : What do they suggest?
T1 : Well, they have reconsidered the role of the traditional classroom and home. So home becomes a classroom, and vice versa in this way of learning. Students view lecture materials, usually in the form of videos, as homework before class.
T2 : That's interesting. What's the focus in class?
T1 : That's the best part. Class time is reserved for activities such as interactive discussions or collaborative work supervised by the teacher.
T2 : I like it. But how does it benefit the students?

T1 : They can study the lectures at home at their own pace, or re-watch the videos, if needed, or even skip parts they already understand.
T2 : Right, And then, in class the teacher is present when they apply new knowledge. What about traditional homework?
T1 : That can be done in class, too. So, the teacher can gain insights into whatever concepts, if any, students are struggling with and adjust the class accordingly.
T2 : What does the literature say about its effectiveness?
T1 : Amazingly, according to one study, 71% of teachers who have tried this approach in their classes noticed improved grades, and 80% reported improved student attitudes, as well.
T2 : That's fantastic. Let me read that when you're done. I want to look further into this.

(5) 디지털 도구 활용

온라인 플랫폼과 교육용 소프트웨어 등 디지털 도구를 활용한 수업으로, 실시간 피드백 및 데이터 기반 학습 관리 등을 통해 맞춤형 교육을 제공한다. 이러한 방향은 학생들이 21세기 사회에서 필요로 하는 다양한 역량을 길러주기 위한 것으로, 개정 교육과정의 취지를 반영해 보다 유연하고 창의적인 교육 환경을 조성하려는 목표를 가지고 있다.

문형별(기입 및 서술 유형) Worksheet

기입형

Read the conversation in <A> and comments in <B>. Fill in the blanks with appropriate terms of TWO words. [2 points]

A

T1 : Ms. Choi, how was your speaking class? Did your students actively participate?

T2 : Yes, they seem to really enjoy speaking activities! How about your students?

T1 : They like speaking activities the most, but they make some errors that seem to have become ingrained.

T2 : Oh yeah? So, how do you usually handle these errors when they occur?

T1 : I normally make note of the crucial errors that have become permanently ingrained during the activity and later explain them to the whole class. I want students to maintain the communicative flow without interruptions.

T2 : That's right! I thought the same. However, I do notice some minor slips that have become ingrained when my students speak during the activity.

T1 : Can you give me some examples of these errors?

T2 : Some students tend to omit the '-s' in the third person singular form of verbs. For instance, they say "as she say," "what he mention," "what Minji experience," and so on.

T1 : Even advanced students make such mistakes while speaking!

T2 : Yes, that's true. I used to think these were simple mistakes, but I realized they were actually ingrained errors in their language use.

T1 : Yeah, these errors would continuously occur if not addressed.

T2 : Exactly. The incorrect form seems to have been permanently incorporated into their speaking competence. So, starting from the next speaking activity, I will make sure to remind my students not to omit the third person singular '-s'. For those who continue to make mistakes, I will explicitly correct these errors to prevent this learning phenomenon.

T1 : That's a great idea. With your help, they'll be able to correct these errors quickly since they are intelligent students.

T2 : I'm glad you think so.

B

The two teachers, Ms. Choi and Mr. Kim discuss the classroom issue, ingrained language errors in their students' speaking performances. They recognize that these incorrect language forms become ingrained and habitual, making them difficult to correct over time. To solve this issue, the teachers plan to take the following steps:

- Identify ________________: Both teachers recognize the importance of identifying errors that have become ingrained in their students' language use. Mr. Kim, for instance, notes that his students often omit the third person singular '-s' in verbs.
- Maintain Communicative Flow: Ms. Choi emphasizes the need to maintain the flow of communication during speaking activities. She prefers to note crucial errors and address them after the activity rather than interrupting the students.
- ____________________ and Reminders: Mr. Kim decides to take a more proactive approach by explicitly reminding his students to use the correct forms and correcting errors as they occur. He aims to prevent further fossilization by consistently addressing these mistakes.
- Reinforcement and Continuous Practice: Both teachers agree on the importance of continuous reinforcement and practice to help students overcome permanently internalized errors. By regularly addressing these issues and providing corrective feedback, they hope to gradually eliminate the ingrained mistakes.

Through these strategies, the teachers aim to improve their students' language accuracy and prevent the persistence of ingrained errors in their speaking performance.

1. Matching Work & Evidence

Read the passages and follow the directions. [4 points]

A

After reading an article about the importance of action research, two English teachers, Ms. Park and Ms. Song, conducted action research on their recent English speaking and writing lessons. The following are classroom principles that Ms. Park and Ms. Song want to achieve through action research.

1. Offer timely and constructive feedback on students' speaking and writing performances. Highlight their strengths and provide specific suggestions for improvement to help them develop their productive skills.
2. Design activities that mimic real-life scenarios, allowing students to practice their productive skills in contexts that are meaningful and relevant to them. This can increase their motivation and engagement.
3. Encourage students to work in pairs or small groups to complete tasks. Collaborative learning helps students practice language in a social context, which can enhance their speaking and writing skills.
4. Integrate technology and multimedia tools to create interactive and engaging activities. Tools like language learning apps, video recordings, and online discussion forums can provide additional practice and exposure.
5. Ensure that students have regular opportunities to practice their speaking and writing skills. Incorporate revision sessions where students can reflect on their progress, revisit previous errors, and make improvements.

B

Ms. Park's lesson

I integrated technology into my lessons by using language learning apps like Duolingo and Quizlet to provide interactive exercises for students. I also incorporated video recordings of English conversations and speeches from platforms like TED Talks and YouTube, as well as facilitating online discussion forums through Google Classroom, which allows students to engage in dynamic discussions and practice their speaking and writing skills in a modern and interactive way. As a result, students showed increased motivation and engagement, with noticeable improvements in their ability to use language in various contexts due to the diverse and multimedia-rich learning experiences.

Ms. Song's lesson

To help students improve their productive skills, I scheduled weekly practice sessions where students work on speaking and writing tasks, followed by revision periods where they review their work and receive feedback. Specifically I used error logs to track common mistakes and organizes peer review activities to encourage students to reflect on their progress and make necessary corrections. Consequently, students demonstrate steady progress and increased accuracy in their language use, as they are continuously reinforcing their learning and addressing errors, leading to greater confidence and proficiency in their speaking and writing abilities.

Considering the information in <A> and <B>, identify the classroom principle that Ms. Park and Ms. Song each choose, respectively. Then, explain how each teacher applies these principles to their lessons based on the evidence from <B>.

2. Identify & Evidence

Read the classroom conversation and follow the directions. [4 points]

During the lunch break Minsoo and Junghee talk about their learning preferences.

Junghee : Hey, Minsoo, how do you usually study for exams?

Minsoo : I usually study by reading the textbook and taking detailed notes. I find that writing things down helps me remember them better. What about you?

Junghee : Usually I use a lot of diagrams, charts, and videos to understand the concepts. I feel like I can remember things better when I see them in this way.

Minsoo : That's interesting. I've tried using diagrams and videos, but I find them a bit distracting. I need the structure of written notes to stay focused. I love it. What's the biggest advantage for you?

Junghee : The biggest advantage is that I can grasp complex ideas quickly when they're presented in visual format. It makes studying more engaging for me. But the downside is that it can be time-consuming to find or create the right formats.

Minsoo : I get that. For me, the advantage of taking notes is that it forces me to process the information as I write it down, which helps with retention. However, it can be really time-consuming, especially with dense material.

Junghee : Yeah, every learning style has its pros and cons. I sometimes feel like I miss out on detailed explanations because I focus more on visuals.

Minsoo : True, and sometimes I get overwhelmed with too many notes but tried to focus on details when I'm reviewing.

Junghee : Maybe we could combine our methods a bit. Like, you could try adding some diagrams or flow charts to your notes, and I could try summarizing my visuals with some written explanations.
Minsoo : That's a great idea! We could even study together and share our notes. It might help us cover all bases and understand the material better.
Junghee : Absolutely! Let's give it a try for the next exam. It could be a good way to balance our learning styles.
Minsoo : Sounds like a plan. Here's to better studying!

Based on the conversation, identify the learning preference that Minsoo and Junghee each have, and support your answer with evidence from the conversation. Do not copy more than FOUR consecutive words from the passage.

3. 영어학과 통합 문항

Read Ms. Park's lesson plan and follow the directions. [4 points]

Ms. Park's Lesson Plan

1. Objective

Students will be able to distinguish between stative and dynamic verbs and use them correctly in sentences.

2. Lesson Outline

Step 1. Introduction (10 minutes)

Greeting and Warm-up:

- Greet the students and ask them how they are feeling today.
- Briefly discuss what they know about verbs.

Objective Presentation:

Explain the lesson objective: understanding the difference between stative and dynamic verbs.

Step 2. Explanation and Examples (15 minutes)

Definition and Explanation:

- Define stative verbs (verbs that describe a state or condition).
- Define dynamic verbs (verbs that describe an action or process).
- Explain that some verbs can be both stative and dynamic depending on the context.

Examples:

Write examples on the board and explain the context

① "I know the answer." ② "She is running in the park." ③ "I have a car."
④ "I'm having lunch."

Step 3. Grammar-based Activities (25 minutes)

Activity Procedure

① Explain Imperative and Progressive Sentences
- Imperative: Commands or requests (e.g., "Run fast!").
- Progressive: Actions happening now (e.g., "She is running.").

② Pair Work Using Groups A and B
- Group A: learn, explain, barks, run
- Group B: know, taste, like, own

③ Task Instructions
- Make imperative and progressive sentences using verbs from Group A.
- Make imperative and progressive sentences using verbs from Group B.

④ Example Sentences and Expected Errors

*Know how to swim.

*The chef is tasting the soup.

*He is liking a new video game.

⑤ Discussion and Reevaluation
- Check and discuss why verbs from Group B cannot regularly occur with the imperative and progressive forms, unlike verbs from Group A.
- Reevaluate the rule distinguishing dynamic and stative verbs.

Step 4. Practice and Production (10 minutes)

Sentence Creation:

Ask students to create their own sentences using verbs in both their stative and dynamic senses.

Example prompts:

"Write a sentence with 'have' in a stative sense and another in a dynamic sense."

Step 5. Peer Review
- Students exchange their sentences with a partner and check each other's work.
- Provide feedback and correct any errors.

Step 6. Wrap-Up (5 minutes)
- Review the main points of the lesson: the difference between stative and dynamic verbs and how to use them correctly.
- Assign a short writing task where students must use at least five verbs in both their stative and dynamic senses.

Example:
"Write a paragraph describing your weekend plans and another about your general likes and dislikes."

According to Ms. Park's lesson plan, distinguish whether the underlined verbs in Step 2 are used in a stative or dynamic sense. Also, identify the name of Activity from Step 3 and explain your answer with evidence from the data.

Possible Answers

기입형

fossilized errors, explicit correction

서술형

1. **Matching Work & Evidence**

   Ms. Park applies Principle 4 by using apps like Duolingo and Quizlet for interactive exercises and incorporating TED Talks and YouTube videos in her lessons, along with online discussion forums through Google Classroom. Ms. Song, on the other hand, follows Principle 5 by scheduling weekly practice and revision sessions, tracking mistakes with error logs, and organizing peer review activities.

2. **Identify & Evidence**

   Junghee is a visual learner, while Minsoo has an analytic learning style. Specifically, Junghee prefers using diagrams, charts, and videos to understand concepts. On the other hand, Minsoo prefers reading the textbook and taking detailed notes. He likes to write things down and organize his notes to stay focused.

3. **영어학 통합 문형**

   In Step 2, the underlined verb 'is running' implies a dynamic verb sense, while 'have' belongs to a stative verb sense. Ms. Park employs a garden path activity in Step 3 by providing the general rule (partial information) about how to form the imperative and the progressive. She then leads students to overgeneralized errors (expected errors, or incorrect use of stative verbs) and finally has them reevaluate the usage of stative and dynamic verbs.

NEW

Build Up

박현수 영어교육론 Ⅱ

Worksheets for Pre-service Teachers

Authentic Data for Classroom Teaching

2026년 대비 기출문제 풀이연습 및 실전문제 풀이전략

초판인쇄 | 2025. 1. 15. **초판발행** | 2025. 1. 20. **편저자** | 박현수

발행인 | 박 용 **발행처** | (주)박문각출판 **표지디자인** | 박문각 디자인팀

등록 | 2015년 4월 29일 제2019-000137호

주소 | 06654 서울시 서초구 효령로 283 서경빌딩 **팩스** | (02)584-2927

전화 | 교재주문·학습문의 (02)6466-7202

저자와의 협의하에 인지생략

ISBN 979-11-7262-502-3

New Build Up

박현수 영어교육론 시리즈

- Ⅰ Theoretical Background for Classroom Teaching
  Classroom Teaching and Learning
- Ⅱ Authentic Data for Classroom Teaching
- Ⅲ 2011~2023학년도 기출문항 분석
- Ⅳ Topic별 문항 정리-임용시험 최적화 훈련

2024 고객선호브랜드지수 1위
교육(교육서비스)부문 1위

2023 고객선호브랜드지수 1위
교육(교육서비스)부문 1위

2022 한국 브랜드 만족지수 1위
교육(교육서비스)부문 1위

2021 조선일보 국가브랜드 대상
에듀테크 부문 수상

2021 대한민국 소비자 선호도 1위
교육부문 1위

2020 한국 산업의 1등
브랜드 대상 수상

2019 한국 우수브랜드
평가대상 수상

2018 대한민국 교육산업 대상
교육서비스 부문 수상

브랜드스탁 BSTI
브랜드 가치평가 1위

박현수 영어교육론 II

ISBN 979-11-7262-502-3 (13740)

www.pmg.co.kr 학원 문의 02) 816-2030 동영상강의 문의 02) 6466-7201

박현수 영어교육론 Ⅱ

Worksheets for Pre-service Teachers
Authentic Data for Classroom Teaching